THE ORIGIN OF THE BIBLE:
A GUIDE FOR THE PERPLEXED

T&T Clark *Guides for the Perplexed*

T&T Clark's Guides for the Perplexed are clear, concise and accessible introductions to thinkers, writers and subjects that students and readers can find especially challenging. Concentrating specifically on what it is that makes the subject difficult to grasp, these books explain and explore key themes and ideas, guiding the reader towards a thorough understanding of demanding material.

***Guides for the Perplexed* available from Continuum:**

New Testament and Jewish Law: A Guide for the Perplexed,
    James G. Crossley
Paul: A Guide for the Perplexed, Timothy G. Gombis

THE ORIGIN OF THE BIBLE:
A GUIDE FOR THE PERPLEXED

LEE MARTIN McDONALD

t&t clark

Published by T&T Clark International
A Continuum imprint
The Tower Building, 11 York Road, London SE1 7NX
80 Maiden Lane, Suite 704, New York, NY 10038

www.continuumbooks.com

British Library Cataloguing-in-Publication Data
A catalogue record for this book is available from the British Library.

ISBN: HB: 978-0-567-17802-2
       PB: 978-0-567-13932-0

Typeset by Newgen Imaging Systems Pvt Ltd, Chennai, India
Printed and bound in the United States of America

With love and appreciation for
Karl Martin McDonald
A delightful son who makes his father proud!

CONTENTS

CHAPTER ONE

INTRODUCTION AND PRELIMINARY OBSERVATIONS

WHY THE FORMATION OF THE BIBLE MATTERS

The Bible significantly influences the faith of Jews and Christians, giving to them their understanding of God, the will of God, their own identity as the people of God, and their mission in the world. While both Jews and Christians accept the sacredness of the books of the Old Testament as their sacred literature, Christians accept several other sacred books as well. It matters which books are received into the biblical canon and it is also important for people of faith to know the text of those books, namely which words in those books are inspired by God. Many other religious books were produced in antiquity and Jews and Christians selected those books that added to their understanding of God and gave clarity to their own identity and mission in the world. Unfortunately, how the Jewish and Christian sacred writings came together to form their Bibles is more complex, less obvious, and often an untold story. This small volume aims at shedding some light on some of the most important aspects of how we got our Bible.

We begin with a brief clarification of what is in the Bible. The Jewish Bible includes 24 books (or 22 books, depending on how the same books are combined and counted) and generally they are called the Hebrew Bible (HB) or the Tanakh and even Miqra. The Tanakh is something of an acronym that is taken from the three parts of the Jewish Bible, namely Law, Prophets, and Writings. In Hebrew those categories are *Torah*, *Nebiim*, and *Ketubim*, hence TNK or TaNaKh (*Tanakh*). Some biblical scholars use First Testament instead of Old Testament since the latter sometimes carries with it an unintended notion that the "Old" Testament is outdated and of less consequence. That, of course, was never the intention of those who first selected this term, but today some have found it offensive and as a result a few biblical scholars have spoken of a "First" Testament and a "Second" Testament instead of Old and New Testament. Christians accept the same books as their Old Testament but count them differently (39 books) and they place them in a different sequence. For example, in the HB, 1 and 2 Samuel, 1 and 2 Kings and 1 and 2 Chronicles are each counted as one book and the twelve Minor Prophets are counted as one book and often referred to simply as the "Twelve." These are all counted individually in the Christian Bibles. The Protestant, Catholic, and Orthodox churches all have the same New Testament, but differ in the books they include in their Old Testaments. They all contain the same books that are in the Protestant Old Testament, but the Catholics and Orthodox include other books also that Protestants often call "Apocrypha" but Catholics call "Deutero-canonical" books.

Eventually, Jews and Christians concluded that more writings were necessary to clarify their faith and mission. For Jews, these additional writings included oral traditions from the first two centuries of the Common Era (CE)[1] and their interpretation. The Jewish oral traditions that began in the time of Jesus and continued roughly to the early part of the third century CE focused on keeping the Law as it applied to daily living and religious conduct. This material is commonly known as the Mishnah.[2]

Similarly, early on Christians recognized the value of many Christian compositions that told the story of Jesus (the Gospels) and the implications of his story for Christian living and Christian faith (some of the Letters of Paul). Before the Christians separated from the Jews roughly between 62 and 135 CE, they had already acknowledged as Scripture those books that many Jews had widely accepted as Scripture. By the end of the second century Christians *began* to refer to Christian writings as Scripture and some began to refer to an "Old Testament" and a "New Testament". We will discuss these terms more below. Christians saw considerable value in reading these other books as well as their inherited Jewish Scriptures.

Why did the Jewish and Christian communities see the need to add additional books to their sacred collections? Also, why did they select the books that were eventually included in their Bibles? Why also were some popular books among those that were eventually excluded such as *1 Enoch, Wisdom of Solomon, Psalms of Solomon, Testaments of the Patriarchs, Shepherd of Hermas, the Didache, Epistle of Barnabas,* and *1 Clement* and others. Some excluded books are not significantly different theologically from books that were included in the Bible, for example, Wisdom of Jesus ben Sirach (Ecclesiasticus), Didache, 1 Clement, and others. Early Christians included some of these books in their Old Testament and some Jews continued to read them for centuries, especially the *Wisdom of Jesus Ben Sirach,* and the *Wisdom of Solomon.* Likewise, many other *Christian* writings that initially circulated in some churches as inspired writings (e.g., *Didache, Letters of Ignatius, Epistle of Barnabas, Shepherd of Hermas*) were eventually excluded from the Scriptures. These books were believed to be of divine origin and to convey the will of God and were placed in sacred collections in various Christian communities.

These so-called noncanonical writings informed the faith of the early Christians adding to their identity and providing the basis for their conduct and mission. Since the process of limiting sacred writings to the current biblical literature took several centuries, and since Christians have not agreed on the complete scope of their Bible, we must ask which if any group is right. What criteria were used in the selection process, and why were some books initially welcomed but later rejected? Should those books be added again to the current Bibles? On the other hand, should we continue to include books that no longer appear as relevant or meaningful to contemporary religious communities, for example, "slaves obey your masters" (Eph. 6.5), and similar such sayings?

Because of the considerable attention given to canonical inquiry in recent years, we are more able to understand some of the processes that were involved in the stabilization of the books of the Bible and also answer a few of the complex questions surrounding its formation. Does this mean that Christians will eventually agree on all matters of canon formation once they have a better understanding of the historical context of the Bible? Probably not because many ambiguities still remain, but through a careful examination of the various issues related to the origins of the Bible we now have a greater understanding of why we agree or disagree with others on many related questions. Of more value, we now can see why some of the choices were made. That produces greater understanding with those with whom we disagree.

Today Christians and Jews are asking how decisions about the scope of the Bible were made and whether its books were appropriately selected. Because the biblical books are determinative for the faith, conduct, and mission of religious communities that approve them, the origin and development of the Bible will never be irrelevant. If one's faith is rooted in the trustworthiness of the biblical books, then these questions have considerable consequence and importance today.

It is appropriate to make this information available to a wider audience than the academic community and it can stimulate helpful discussions in both churches and synagogues. I have been happily surprised in recent years to see the considerable interest in churches and student groups in the formation of the Bible. I have received many invitations not only to address these questions in academic communities, but also in a growing number of churches and pastoral conferences. Not infrequently, I hear colleagues in pastoral ministry say that they have never shared such questions with their congregations or even had such discussions fearing that the questions were too complex or too divisive for the church. I believe, however, that the church should be capable of discussing all matters that influence our faith and conduct, even if some of the lessons that we learn from careful biblical inquiry are sometimes unsettling and challenging. Such opportunities provide important steps of spiritual and educational growth.

It is far too easy to hide behind our traditional dogmas and fail to encourage members of our congregations to ask legitimate questions about the origin and development of their Bible and their faith. It is next to impossible to suppress curious minds, however, and when we allow questions we are able to hold on to some of the brightest and most promising members of our communities of faith. Unfortunately, inquisitive persons whose questions are not allowed or discouraged often depart for places they can be shared. Hopefully, this volume will not only be a contribution toward an informed church laity, but also offer evidence to those outside of the church or the synagogue that it is appropriate to raise questions that enable us to examine our faith and the significant issues that impact it.

SOME IMPORTANT QUESTIONS

Years ago when I was a pastor in Nebraska, I was teaching a Bible study one evening when a perceptive young layperson raised several questions about the origins of the Bible and the books that were *not* accepted into the Christian Bible. He had taken a religion course at a local university and was told quite correctly that there were many other ancient books that had been candidates for inclusion in Bible, but for various reasons they were rejected by both Jews and Christians. He wanted some clarification on this topic, and also about when and why the churches selected the books that they did.

After offering some initial and unsatisfactory responses to his questions based on what I had been taught earlier in the seminary, I concluded that I needed to postpone my full response until I could look into the matter more carefully. As I was attempting to answer his questions, I found myself thinking of several exceptions to the responses I gave him! At the time, I was simply not equipped to answer his valid questions, though I was quite familiar with the traditional responses. Since I already knew many exceptions to those earlier views of how the Bible came to be, I deferred my responses for a week or so and began to study the matter in more detail than I had in my earlier seminary days.

As I began to examine his and other questions more carefully by looking into the early Jewish and Christian traditions, I found better and more informed answers than those that I gave in my initial response to the university student. His questions led me to an investigation of the historical context of the formation of the Bible. After some 30 years of reading and writing on the questions, I found that questions related to the origin and development of the Bible were essentially either dated or inadequately answered. It is important for readers to know that attempts to answer them do not undermine the faith that many of us have embraced and tried to live. Faith does not depend on such inquiries, but knowing of the origins of the Bible can enhance our understanding of faith. The conspiracy theorists claiming that the church is trying to hide valuable information from the public are, of course, misguided or confused. Biblical scholars regularly, and rightly, challenge these popular notions and demand better evidence for these popular media assertions.

New positions on the origin and development of the Bible also require convincing evidence. While it is true that few advances are made without someone challenging previously held positions, there should always be good evidence for changing well-established positions. Biblical scholars often disagree on matters of interpretation of the available evidence, but that disagreement always promotes more careful attention to the details of the biblical and historical data that is available to all scholars. When new positions are advanced, the evidence is generally compelling and not simply the result of some popular presentations or sound bites in the news. Biblical faith has been around a long time and simplistic popular criticisms are not likely to change one's commitment to that faith.

Questions about the biblical books often lead scholars to ask other important questions, namely, should we now be open to including other ancient books in it? Likewise, should some books that no longer seem as relevant to the church be dropped or replaced by other books? Should *newer* books that appear to be relevant to the church's needs today be included? Finally, what about some biblical texts that appear to pose an embarrassment to modern churches today? I am thinking here in particular of those texts that deal with slavery (Eph. 6.5–9; Col. 3.22–4.1; and 1 Cor. 7.21–24), women's submission to their husbands (Eph. 5.22–33; 1 Tim. 2.11–15), or matters relating to the purification of men's and women's bodily discharges, as well as biblical commands that deal with the beginning and ending of a woman's menstrual cycle, or purifications following the birth of a child (Lev. 12.1–8; 15.1–33)? Are such passages still relevant to believing communities of faith today? Can they be reinterpreted to make them more relevant? Also, does one have to expand the biblical canon in order to appreciate the noncanonical writings?

Scholars are sometimes asked theoretical questions about the discovery of lost ancient books? If found, should they be included in the Bible? Some biblical scholars think that such books would be worthy of study, but since they had no influence in the history of the church and had no influence on the churches' decisions or theology they should not be added to the Bible. Others suggest that if an apostle wrote it, the book would be quite relevant to Christian faith today and worthy of inclusion. Paul claimed to have written letters that we do not have today (see 1 Cor. 5.9 and Col. 4.16), so, if we should happen to discover them, what should we do with them?

To carry this argument a bit further, early Christians undoubtedly acknowledged Jesus as the Lord of the church and the central authority figure of early Christianity. What if someone found an authentic saying of Jesus tucked away in a recently discovered ancient manuscript? Since what Jesus said was authoritative for the early Christians, what would we do if someone discovered an authentic saying of Jesus in an ancient manuscript? What would we do with it? As biblical scholars know, this is not a remote possibility. For many decades now, they have been aware of several sayings of Jesus that are not in the Bible, but have survived in ancient biblical manuscripts and written church traditions. These so-called unwritten sayings of Jesus that are more than 200 in number are generally referred to as the *agrapha* (sing. form = *agraphon*) and many scholars concede that at least some of them are authentic! So, if Jesus said these things, how can we dismiss them? Should they be included in the Bible?

Is the Bible still open for inclusion of other writings or is it closed? Is there a biblical or theological argument that says that the Christian Bible is or should be closed to any further additions? Historically, the Bible has been closed for Jews and Christians for more than a thousand years now, but is there a biblical or theological argument to support a *closed* biblical canon? Does not God speak today to those who faithfully follow him? Theologians occasionally address this question, but churches by and large seldom do. The Mormon Church, on the other hand, makes use of this argument for including the *Book of Mormon, Pearl of Great Price,* and *Doctrine and Covenants* to their sacred collections. Are they right? I have addressed this matter elsewhere, but for now I will say that the early churches largely adopted the criterion of orthodoxy to determine which books to include in their Scriptures. It is not clear to me that the Mormons' claims for these additional books would survive the ancient test of orthodoxy, but that is another matter that will not be pursued here. It is nonetheless difficult to argue biblically or theologically for a closed collection of Scriptures.

Christian scholars today often debate these and other issues, but they have not yet agreed on how to resolve them. No doubt the beginning of any attempt to resolve such questions must begin with an historical inquiry into the origin of the Bible and what the early Christians meant when they spoke of "scripture," "inspiration," "canon," "noncanonical," "apocryphal," "pseudepigraphal," and other such terms. For the most part, these are anachronistic terms that were *later* introduced into discussions of ancient Jewish and Christian religious texts.

By examining the limited evidence that remains, we can discover why some books were included in the biblical canon and why others were rejected, but some questions still remain about other books. A majority of ancient churches eventually concluded that some books simply did not reflect the understanding of the faith that had historically been faithfully passed on to them in their churches. Some books seemed like obvious candidates for inclusion, for example, the books of the Law, or Pentateuch, and the Gospels. Some of the Prophets and some of the Pauline letters were also more obvious candidates for inclusion, but others books raised more questions. For example, Esther never mentions the name of God so why should it be included? Ezekiel seems to hold views in opposition to the Law. Also, Song of Songs is actually a love story between a man and woman and says little if anything of theological significance. Only by spiritualizing its text has it been made relevant to contemporary Jewish and Christian audiences. Ecclesiastes also often has a depressing attitude about life ("all is vanity under the sun") and is rather pessimistic about God's interest in human affairs. The book says little about God's mission for his people or what we might call a prophetic call to godly living.

Why were these books included but others with a more positive message about God and the will of God, for example, the Wisdom of Solomon and the Wisdom of Jesus ben Sirach, excluded by the Jews and many Christians? In terms of Christian writings, it is not clear why the *Didache* and *1 Clement* were excluded but 2 Peter and Jude were included. Also, the *Shepherd of Hermas,* an apocalyptic book that was very popular among Christians for the first two centuries, in fact more copies of it are preserved in antiquity than for any other books of the New Testament except Matthew and John. Why? Initially it was more popular among Christians than the Revelation of John in the New Testament? *1 Clement* was likely written *before* several of the New Testament books and it is every bit as orthodox in its teachings as books that were eventually included in the New Testament. Why was it eventually excluded from the Christian Scriptures when it was included in several important early Christian biblical manuscripts? We can make informed guesses about the inclusion or exclusion of some ancient religious texts, but in many cases we simply do not know the answer.

Questions about the formation of the Bible have been raised from time to time since the years of the Reformation in the sixteenth century. Until the recent discoveries of several ancient Jewish and Christian writings, they received little attention, but with the discovery of the famous Dead Sea Scrolls and several other collections of ancient Jewish and Christian religious texts, these questions have come to the front of theological discussions and have been the inspiration for many fictional books and movies and have moved into the public arena. There is little question that the media hype surrounding *The Da Vinci Code* or *Holy Blood and Holy Grail* and other popular fictions contributed to current popular interest in the origins of the Bible. Some of the recent focus has been on "what the church does not want you to know," as if there was some sort of conspiracy in the church to hide the truth of the origin of its Bible. As a result, biblical scholars have taken to the printed page and the airwaves to clarify much of the confusion.

Although interest in these "canon" questions has been around for centuries, today such interest has moved into the mainstream of scholarly and church attention. Many academic institutions and even churches have sponsored conferences on questions related to the origin and final shape of the Bible. Some theological seminaries are now offering complete courses on excluded books. Conservative, moderate, and liberal scholars alike are finding mines of valuable information for understanding the context of Jewish and Christian origins in this previously ignored literature. Interestingly, academic societies have also been focusing considerable attention on these ancient sources. For several years now the Society of Biblical Literature, the largest international gathering of biblical scholars, has several sections focusing exclusively on ancient excluded books.

SOME IMPORTANT DISTINCTIONS: SCRIPTURE AND CANON

As we begin this brief study of the origin and development of the Bible, there are some important distinctions between the notion of Scripture and canon that call for clarification. These distinctions often are the source of considerable debate among biblical scholars. After a brief discussion of these terms we will also look at the terms "Old Testament" and "New Testament."

The origin and notion of scripture

The acknowledgment of sacred biblical books is rooted in an ancient belief that a "heavenly book" contains divine knowledge, wisdom, decrees from God, and a book of life. This notion likely goes back to ancient Mesopotamia and Egypt where the heavenly book not only indicated the future plans of God, but also the destinies of human beings. This belief is also reflected in Ps. 139.15–16: "In your book were written all the days that were formed for me, when none of them as yet existed." The notion of heavenly books is also continued in New Testament times as we see in the book of Revelation (5.1, 3; 6.1–17; 8.1–10.11; and 20.12–15). In the latter of these passages books are opened before the throne of God in heaven and "another book was opened, the book of life. And the dead were judged according to their works, as recorded in the books . . . and anyone whose name was not found written in the book of life was thrown into the lake of fire." Similarly, in the Old Testament, God says that those who have sinned will be blotted out of his book (Exod. 32.33). In the New Testament, Paul speaks of Clement and the rest of his ministry colleagues "whose names are in the book of life" (Phil. 4.3).

In both Judaism and early Christianity, the notion of a heavenly book gave rise to the idea that the repository of divine knowledge and heavenly decrees are contained in a divine book that is conveyed in written scriptures. For Judaism, long before the notion of a biblical canon emerged, the Torah or Pentateuch (the first five books of the Bible) was believed to be a divine collection of sacred texts that came directly from God. Moses, for example, proclaimed the words and ordinances of God (Exod. 24.3) and was commissioned by God to put them in writing (Exod. 34.4, 27). The Jews believed that God was the author of the Ten Commandments or *Decalogue* (Exod. 34.1 and Deut. 4.13; 10.4) and that the Law of God was written down in the form of scripture. It appears that such notions played a significant role in the development of divinely revealed written scriptures.

In antiquity, scribes were highly esteemed holding an almost divine priestly status in the Jewish community. Whatever they wrote was considered highly significant even though much of what they wrote was simply copying what others had said. Nevertheless, writing had a certain authority attached to it. Written documents were highly significant to the ancient Jews and if the words "it is written" were attached to those documents, their divine authority was assumed. This sacred authority attached to written materials emerged in part because it was believed that what was written was now "fixed." This notion can be seen in the Jews' objection to Pilate's placing the inscription "King of the Jews," over the cross on which Jesus was crucified. Pilate responded, "what I have written, I have written" (Jn 19.22), a reference to what is written is fixed.

The citing of Scripture in the New Testament is often introduced with what are often called scriptural formulae, namely "as the Scriptures says," or "as it is written," and such like, but this is not the only way that Scriptures are cited. For instance, Jesus cites Dan. 7.13 as scripture in Mk 14.62, but with no introductory formulae. Similarly, the author of Hebrews writes "with" scripture citing more Old Testament texts proportionately than any other writer of the New Testament, but frequently without the scriptural citation formulae. For instance, in Heb. 1.5–13 the writer cites Ps. 2.7; 2 Sam. 7.14; 1 Chron. 17.13; Deut. 32.43; Ps. 104.4; Ps. 45.6–7; Ps. 102.25–27; Ps. 110.1; and Ps. 8.6–8 without mentioning the usual scriptural designations. That author also cites Wisd. of Sol. 7.22 and 7.25, 26 and 8.1 in 1.2–3. In the Gospel of Mark and the book of Hebrews, the authors regularly anchor their arguments in sacred texts, that is, books that they believed had their origin in God and therefore synonymous with divine authority, but they often do not employ the usual scriptural designations.

Whatever was included in the sacred writings was believed to have come from God and therefore these sacred texts could not be changed, but only believed and obeyed. The writings that were recognized as inspired sacred texts were eventually placed alongside other sacred writings and they took their place in a fixed collection of sacred scriptures, that is, a biblical canon. The story of this recognition, while of special interest to contemporary biblical scholars today, was not sufficiently important to the early churches since they left behind no history of how the Bible was formed—they likely assumed everyone knew it!

The word, "fulfill," or its various forms such as "fulfilled" or "as it is fulfilled," was also used in ancient writings to refer to the sacredness of the ancient literature. Since ancient Jews believed that God inspired written material, it was given special priority. For instance, when prophets claimed that they spoke divinely inspired words, many Jews believed that those words conveyed the very word of God. When prophets wrote down their prophecy from God, it eventually took on a special authority in the religious community. If a prophecy was eventually fulfilled in subsequent history, the prophecy was validated and affirmed as divinely inspired. Prophecy-fulfillment motifs are frequently found in biblical literature and Jews and Christians received them as evidence of their sacred status.

The basic properties of "scripture" for ancient Judaism and Christianity included at least four essential ingredients, namely, scripture is a *written* document believed to have a *divine origin* that faithfully *communicates the truth and will of God* for a believing community, and it *provides a source of regulations for the corporate and individual life* of religious people. When the divinely inspired status of a religious text was recognized, it was treated as authoritative scripture even if it was not yet called "scripture." Sometimes that status was temporary, but in other cases such religious texts were eventually included into a fixed collection of Scriptures. For example, the Gospels were welcomed initially as authoritative documents of the church because they told the story of Jesus, the Lord of the church. They were eventually called scripture by the end of the second century and subsequently included in a fixed collection of the church's sacred Scriptures. Some Christians initially accepted the sacred status of several religious texts, but later excluded them from their Scripture collections (*1 Enoch, Eldad and Modad*, the *Epistle of Barnabas, The Shepherd of Hermas, 1 Clement*, and the *Letters of Ignatius*).

While there was initial agreement on the inclusion of many of the books that were included in the Bible such as the Law or Pentateuch and the Prophets or the Gospels and some of the letters of Paul, there were lingering debates about the status of Esther, Ecclesiastes, Ezekiel, Song of Songs, and other books not later included in the Hebrew Bible or the Christian Old Testament.

What do we mean by "Canon?"

"Scripture" and the notion of a biblical "canon" overlap considerably in the sense that both focus on authoritative sacred scriptures, but they are not exactly the same. Because a "biblical canon" is *like* sacred scripture in that it is a normative guide for religious communities, the two are often confused by biblical scholars. Scripture specifically has to do with the divine status of a written book whereas a scriptural canon is a *fixed* collection of sacred writings that defines the faith and identity of religious communities. In this sense, while all scripture has a certain divine authority, a biblical canon is a fixed *collection* of divinely inspired scriptures that constitutes the complete defining authority for a religious body.

The Greek term *kanon* originally derived from a Semitic loan word (*kaneh*) that referred to a "measuring rod" or "measuring stick." The Greeks used the word to refer to a standard or norm by which all things are judged or evaluated, whether the perfect form to follow in architecture or the criterion by which things are to be measured. It was often used for standards of sculpturing, architecture, music, grammar, art, poetry, and even philosophy by which one discovers what is true and false. In Egypt, for example, we find uniform styles of columns in the Karnak Temple with capitals in the form of papyrus plants, both open and closed. We also see this in Egyptian art and architecture. For example, the normal statuary depictions of pharaohs were highly uniform with perfect torsos, often with one foot forward and one arm also extended forward indicating that the pharaoh was still alive when the statue was created. If both feet were together and both arms crossed over the chest, however, it meant that death had occurred. Skin colors of males and females also followed standard canons of art, namely, males have darker skin and females lighter. There was also a canon of books in ancient Alexandria that listed or cataloged the standard works in philosophy and poetry, though they were called *pinakes* (or the singular, *pinax*). In Greek architecture there were uniform styles in temple columns (Doric, Ionic, Corinthian).

There were also religious canons or guidelines among the ancient Greeks. For example, the Greeks worshipped a fixed number of gods, namely, those referred to in Homer's *Iliad* and *Odyssey*. The sacredness of those writings for the Greeks can be seen in the fact that each book has 24 chapters or books and each beginning with a letter in the Greek alphabet. The normal practice was to use numbers or names for sections or chapters. This special use of the alphabet shows that Homer was highly prized among the Greeks and functioned as canon or sacred authority for the Greeks. The writings of Homer also had an important impact on Hellenistic Jews and may have had a significant influence on the canon of the Bible. The Jews, likely following Homer, used the alphabet to divide verses of some Psalms, for example, Pss. 25, 33, 119, and to fix the number of books in their sacred biblical canon. The reference to the risen Christ as the "Alpha and Omega" (the first and last letters in the Greek alphabet) in Rev. 1.8 (see Rev. 22.13) picks up on this use of the alphabet in the ancient world to speak of divinity, divine guidance, and rules for life. The alphabet depicts the holiness and authority of writings, as in the case of Homer, perhaps because the letters of the alphabet are the basic elements of human speech and the scriptures are the basic expressions of the word of God.

There are two essential characteristics of canon, namely, adaptability and survivability. The Jews were able to adapt their authoritative Scriptures to new and changing circumstances and they survived overwhelming challenges facing them (captivity and loss of a nation). Sometimes adaptability continues by creatively spiritualizing (or allegorizing) the scriptural texts. In antiquity, however, religious literature, that no longer spoke to the changing needs of a community of faith and when creative interpretations failed to make the texts adaptable to new situations, it ceased to be scripture in those communities. For both Jews and Christians, writings that ceased functioning as sacred scripture simply dropped out of use.

Canonical literature is repeated in religious communities with confidence in its usefulness in the changing circumstances of the community of faith (adaptability). The primary function of canon, like Scripture, is to aid a community of faith in its own self-definition and to offer to it guidelines for living. Adaptability alone, however, is not sufficient for a writing to be recognized as canon. Those books that eventually formed the biblical canon for ancient Israel also empowered that community for life, that is, they had to give hope even in hopeless situations (e.g., in the Babylonian captivity of the Jews in 587 BCE) and they foster life in the community.

The continual reinterpretation of the Scriptures in both Judaism and Christianity underscores its adaptability, survivability, and ultimately canonicity. An initial important characteristic of canon is therefore not its rigidity, but rather its flexibility. The eventual stabilization of the biblical text, which is the perceived need of a believing community for a fixed tradition, comes much later in the canonical process and at that point creative interpretive method-ologies (hermeneutics) play a significant role in the continuing life of biblical texts.

There are two important realities related to the formation of the Christian Scriptures and I use the terms "canon 1" and "canon 2" to distinguish them, namely the fluid stage (canon 1) and the final fixed stage (canon 2). Canon 1 refers to a flexible or fluid authority when a book was neither fixed nor inviolable. Canon 2 refers to the fixed biblical collection to which nothing is added or taken away. When biblical books became so well established in a community of faith that no doubt existed about its authority thereafter, I call that canon 2. This is when the sacredness of the book is recognized and it becomes inviolable (see Deut. 4.2 and 12.32, cf., Rev. 22.18). In some cases, the temporary recognition of the scriptural status of a book was initially accepted, but eventually the majority of churches rejected it and it did not become part of a *fixed* scriptural collection. Fixed sacred collections (canon 2) are more obvious in the fourth century CE and later and generally reflect a long history of use in the earlier churches. The recognition of the sacred status of the Gospels and their use in the churches may well have emerged in the first century CE (canon 1), but their inclusion in a fixed collection of biblical books (canon 2) is a later development that followed a selection process.

Some biblical scholars contend that the scope of the New Testament Scriptures was largely defined as a result of the church's dealing with heresy in the second century, and if this is so, then the notion of canon is second century. There is no evidence of this, however, and the early churches dealt with the problem of heresy by establishing a list of Christian teachings that defined who they were. Those teachings in their primitive form were called a *regula fidei* (rule of faith) and these were handed down in the churches from the first century. Before establishing a biblical canon, the church first had to establish its core beliefs about Jesus. Broad agreement in such matters came largely (not completely) following the Council of Nicaea (325 CE), after which churches made more conscious decisions about what sacred scriptures reflected their core teachings and which ones did not. This is essential for understanding the origin of a fixed collection of Scriptures for the church.

The origin of "Old Testament" and "New Testament"

In late second century, a few church leaders began to identify their literature in terms of Old and New Testaments. The term "new covenant" (covenant = testament) is found in both the Old Testament (Jer. 31.31) and the New (Lk. 22.20; 1 Cor. 11.25; Heb. 8.8, 13; 9.15; 12.24), but not in reference to a collection of sacred books. Rather, the "*old* covenant" is found only in the New Testament (Heb. 9.1) referring to the covenant of the Law (Exod. 19.5; 24.7–8). "Testament" and "covenant" translate the same Greek word (*diatheke*), but it is not used in reference to a collection of sacred scriptures until the last quarter of the second century CE. It has been argued that the use of the word covenant to identify a collection of sacred writings had its roots in a pseudepigraphal work known as the *Testaments of the Twelve Patriarchs,*[3] a suggestion that is not yet demonstrable, but it is instructive that *some* early Christians identified their sacred books as "testaments," though not *regularly* until the middle-to-late fourth century. The terms Old and New Testament began to be used without clarification in the latter half of the fourth century as we see in canon 59 of the Synod of Laodicea (ca. 360 CE). There we read, "[It is decreed] that private psalms should not be read in the church, neither uncanonized books, but only the canonical [books] of the New and Old Testament."

So far as we can presently determine, the terms first appear in the writings of Irenaeus (ca. 180 CE) who writes:

> . . . *in both Testaments* there is the same righteousness of God [displayed] when God takes vengeance, in the one case indeed typically, temporarily, and more moderately; but in the other, really, enduringly, and more rigidly. . . . *in the New Testament*, that faith of men [to be placed] in God has been increased, receiving in addition [to what was already revealed] the Son of God, that man too might be a partaker of God. (*Adv. Haer.* 4.28.1–2, ANF. Emphasis added)

Similarly, Eusebius (ca. 320 CE) cites Melito, bishop of Sardis (ca. 170–180 CE) saying: "when I came to the east and reached the place where these things were preached and done [Palestine], and learned accurately the *books of the Old Testament*, I sat down the facts and sent them to you" (*Ecclesiastical History* 4.26.13). Tertullian (ca. 200 CE) also writes, "If I fail in resolving this article (of our faith) by passages which may admit of dispute out of the Old Testament, I will take out of the New Testament a confirmation of our view, that you may not straightway attribute to the Father every possible [relation and condition] which I ascribe to the Son" (*Against Praxeas* 15, ANF). The unfamiliarity of these terms in the early third century is seen in Origen's use of "so-called" to refer to both collections:

> It appears to me, therefore, to be necessary that one who is able to represent in a genuine manner the doctrine of the Church, and to refute those dealers [the Gnostics] in knowledge, falsely so-called, should take his stand against historical fictions, and oppose to them the true and lofty evangelical message in which the agreement of the doctrines, found both in the *so-called Old Testament*

and in the *so-called New*, appears so plainly and fully. (*Commentary on John* 5.4, ANF. Emphasis added)[4]

Similarly, Eusebius (ca. 320–330 CE), describing Josephus' canon of scripture, writes: "In the first of these he [Josephus] gives the number of the canonical scriptures of the *so-called Old Testament*, and showed as follows which are undisputed among the Hebrews as belonging to ancient tradition" (*Ecclesiastical History* 3.9.5, LCL. Emphasis added). Later, while speaking of the New Testament he says, "At this point it seems reasonable to summarize *the writings of the New Testament* which have been quoted" (3.25.1, LCL. Emphasis added). While these terms originated in the second century, they were not generally used in the churches until the fourth century CE, but even then it was not completely clear which writings were included in those "Testaments." Because the term "Old Testament" is not used in the Christian community for its earliest scriptures until the end of the second century CE, it is premature to identify that collection of Jewish Scriptures thusly before that time.

THE PROCESSES

The processes that led to the selection of the books that are in the Bible, commonly called the "canonization" of the Bible, are receiving considerable attention today and in part because such questions go to the heart of contemporary Christian beliefs about the inspiration and authority of the Bible. Such inquiries are also relevant to Jewish identity and several Jewish biblical scholars are showing considerable interest in canon questions.

Those inquiring into this subject for the first time are often surprised when they learn that the ancient churches did not leave behind any record of the development and formation of their Scriptures nor how long it took to gain widespread agreement on such matters. This omission is puzzling to modern readers and reflects the largely unconscious development of the churches sacred Scriptures. This untold story in the ancient churches leaves modern scholars with limited bits and pieces of evidence to construct a picture of what took place. This reality also leads us to ask whether we can be certain that the early churches made the right decisions in regard to the scope of their biblical canon. We will return to this question at the end of this volume, but for now what we have in the Bible is *sufficient* for faith even though there are many questions not found in the Bible that puzzle, but must remain open for the time being.

In the formative years of the church, individuals and churches made decisions about which books they acknowledged as their sacred Scriptures. The circumstances facing them eventually led some church leaders to conclude that the time had come to cease adding books to or taking books from their sacred Scripture collections. No evidence suggests that the ancient churches all came to the same conclusions at the same time, or that they used the same criteria to select the writings that they included in their sacred collections. The evidence shows that for centuries they did not always use the same books. The surviving lists or catalogs of sacred books dating from the fourth century show that while there was considerable agreement *on most* of the Old and New Testament books, there was not complete agreement. We will discuss this in more detail later.

Several publishers are now showing considerable interest in making the recent scholarly advances in this field available to nonspecialists and laypersons. Several publishers have asked those of us who write on canon formation issues to produce books on this subject for nonspecialists. I am grateful to the editors of T&T Clark for their invitation to contribute this volume to their *A Guide for the Perplexed* series. It is written in the hope of offering useful information for the interested nonspecialists that allow them to enter into meaningful discussions of this important topic.

I regularly remind students and scholars of canon formation that we are only at the *beginning* stages of this inquiry and how important it is that they become significantly involved in this inquiry in the years ahead. This volume is an introduction to this subject and those seeking more detailed information are encouraged to look more carefully at the critical literature listed in the *For Further Reading* lists at the end of each chapter. Hopefully, this volume will be an important step toward making critical issues about the Jewish and Christian Scriptures available to a larger audience.

For those who want to dig deeper into this subject, they can find on T&T Clark's web site a collection of primary texts and collections of important data that have been used throughout this study. To find those important primary texts, please go to www.biblicalstudies. mcdonald.continuumbooks.com.

Finally, the church's faith and future do not depend on the results of historical inquiry into the origin and development of the Bible, although our understanding of the emergence and growth of early Christianity are considerably enhanced by such studies. Christian faith depends rather on what God has done and continues to do in the life, ministry, death and resurrection of Jesus.

I have prepared this book for those who, like my son Karl, are active laypersons in their churches and regularly read and study their Bibles as well as for those who are interested in this subject but yet do not have access to important scholarly discussions of it. Karl teaches a Bible study in his home, is an active leader in his church, and regularly shows an avid interest in the many intriguing questions about the Christian faith and the Bible. This small volume is dedicated to him and written for the many others like him who are serious about their faith and want a better understanding of this important subject.

Lee Martin McDonald
June 2010

CHAPTER TWO

AN OVERVIEW OF THE STORY

Our study of the formation of the Bible begins with an overview of some important critical issues that are essential in understanding the origins and development of the Bible. These issues will be dealt with in more detail in subsequent chapters, including a number of important citations from ancient texts that bring needed light to the canonization of the Bible.

A STORY THAT GAVE MEANING AND DIRECTION

One of the earliest sacred authorities of the Jews was a story about a people who migrated from Egypt to Canaan under the guidance and protection of God and it is regularly referred to as "the Exodus." Other elements were later added to the beginning and the ending of this story, for example, the Genesis story, the prophetic tradition, and the history of the fall of the nation. The earliest form of the story likely did not include Ten Commandments or other lists of divine commandments (some 613 in number). It consisted of the story of God calling a people to a land and his preservation of those people through his mighty acts. The people's response to these acts of preservation or salvation was their recognition of and obedience to the one true God. There are many references to this story in the Old Testament scriptures, especially in the Prophets, (e.g., see Amos 2.9–11; 3.1–2; 4.10–11; 5.25; 9.7 and 9.11). There are also other early summations of this story in Deut. 26.5–9 and Jos. 24.

In the New Testament, the same story is preserved in several important places (see Acts 7.2–53, Heb. 3.5–19, and to some extent also 1 Cor. 10.1–11). The initial story clearly expanded over time. For example, after the exile of the Jews to Babylon (586 BCE), this story was reconsidered from the perspective of the classic prophets whose earlier message gave them life and hope. In the message from Ezekiel, for example, because of the faithfulness of the Lord the people could look forward to a resurrection of the nation following its death (Ezek. 36–37). In the exilic sojourn, Ezekiel began to echo the vision of Jeremiah who had earlier spoken about the reforming of the nation (Jer. 18.1–11).

After Israel had lost everything in terms of its national identity, its monarchy, and kingdom, and especially its temple and cultus in the terrible destruction of 587–586 BCE, how could the Jewish people maintain their identity and find hope? Unlike many other peoples before and after them whose religious identity disappeared or dramatically changed as they merged with other nations, that did not happen to the Jews. Why? The Jewish nation was reborn because the Jews held on to a *story* that was transported from Israel to Babylon and back to Israel and it was adapted to the new circumstances of the nation in captivity. During the exile a remnant remembered the witness of the prophets who had predicted accurately what would happen to the nation because of their disobedience to God. This remnant realized that the prophets had told the truth regarding the fate of Israel and came to realize that the message of the prophets before the Exile included a story that also gave them hope.

This story allowed them to survive the terrible judgments that had been inflicted upon them, and unlike other nations that saw in their defeat the failure of their gods as well, the Jews accepted the message of the prophets and took responsibility for their failure as a nation. God did not fail, they did! They accepted their captivity and destruction as a judgment of Yahweh for their misdeeds and their story was regularly repeated to the Jewish people. The earlier prophets had proclaimed this story to warn the people of the consequences of their behavior and were accused of being "madmen, unpatriotic, blasphemous, seditious, and traitorous" (see Jer. 29.26). Now, however, they were remembered because what they proclaimed came to pass. Their core message was contained in the Torah and it was eventually expanded to include both the Former and then the Latter Prophets and finally the Writings. Nevertheless, the *core* story that gave life (Jn 5.39) and identity to Israel was nevertheless the books of the Law.

When a remnant of Jews returned from Babylon, what gave them an identity and purpose with guidelines to follow—was the Law of Moses. This was about God's rescue and preservation of his people, calling them into existence as a nation, setting forth laws that governed the daily life of the people, and offered hope for the future. This story was also adaptable to the new circumstances facing the Jewish people.

The fluidity of this story continued well into the time of Jesus and gave rise to several religious texts that interpreted this story anew. The lack of a fixed or stabilized biblical tradition gave rise to other Jewish religious sects that flourished in the time of Jesus and later (Samaritans, Sadducees, Pharisees, Essenes, Christians) after the destruction of the temple and its cultus in 70 CE. Following the failure of the Jewish Bar Cochba messianic movement and its rebellion against Rome (132–135 CE), the two most important Judaisms that survived these traumatic events were Rabbinic Judaism and early Christianity. In the centuries following, the stabilization of the Jewish Hebrew Bible and Christian Old Testament was *largely* settled.

This story has parallels with the emergence of the New Testament scripture canon. That which first brought the Christian community into existence and gave to it an identity and mission was a story about God's activity in Jesus of Nazareth. Although scholars debate the contents of that initial story, there is no debate that Jesus, his fate, and his significance for faith were at the heart of that story. The story about Jesus was first told in preaching (Acts 2.17–36) and teaching (1 Cor. 15.3–8) and eventually through the medium of writing (Mk 1.1; Lk. 1.1–4). In time the story of God's activity in Jesus and its implications for humanity was expanded and expressed in a variety of literary forms (epistle, gospel, historical narrative, apocalypse, and sermon). That story began with the circulation of oral traditions about Jesus in the first century. It was expanded to include the written traditions of the first and possibly early second centuries and became more stabilized in the third and fourth centuries when the sacred status of this early literature was widely accepted. Almost at the same time, the scriptures of the Old Testament were moving toward their final stages of the stabilization in the Christian community (see Chapters 3 and 4).

The adaptability of the *Christian* scriptures to new circumstances was in part due to the creative hermeneutics—the process of interpretation—of the various surviving churches. These interpretations grew out of the need to adapt a stabilized tradition to new situations facing the Christian communities. The ability to see in the literature something that was not only adaptable, but also highly relevant and useful took place through this hermeneutical process.

Some Jewish and Christian literature eventually fell away from the Christian sacred collections because their usefulness and adaptability was no longer acknowledged. An example of this is the ancient prophecy of *Eldad and Modat* that was for a time an authoritative religious resource for some early Christian communities in the first two centuries (it is quoted as scripture in the second century *Shepherd of Hermas, Vis.* 2.3.4). *1 Enoch, Assumption of Moses, Jubilees, Apocalypse of Baruch* (ca. 70 CE), and *Testaments of the Twelve Patriarchs,* and other books were appealed to variously in the early Christian churches and occasionally cited as Scripture. Eventually these books were left out of Christian sacred collections.

The Christian author of the *Epistle of Barnabas* (ca. 140–150 CE) cites *1 Enoch* three times, and in two of those instances he employs scriptural designations (see 4.3 that begins with: "it was written as Enoch says" and 16.5 citing *Enoch* 89.55, 66, 67 beginning with the words "For the scripture says"). It appears that the letter of Jude gave offense to some Christian teachers in the fourth century not because Jude made use of *Enoch* (Jude 14), as other Christian writers had done, but because it specifically referred to that writing by *name*! The use and citation of *Enoch* by name was common in the church in the second century, but by the fourth century it was less popular and had moved out of bounds. The continued use of *Sirach* in Jewish communities in the fourth and fifth centuries also reflects a persisting ambiguity about the precise parameters of the Jewish scripture collection at that time. Sirach was eventually classified as apocryphal by the rabbinic Jews and excluded from their Bible canon, even though some Jews continued to use these writings, especially Sirach (or Jesus ben Sira), for several centuries after the scope of the Hebrew Bible was largely established by the rabbis.

Why the use and authority of the so-called pseudepigraphal books declined in both Jewish and Christian communities is not clear, but a tendency to sharpen the distinction between canonical and noncanonical writings emerged in the second century and was largely complete by the fourth century CE. Subsequently, there was a tendency toward textual stability of the biblical books and a greater focus on hermeneutic methodologies that allowed Jews and Christians to adapt the biblical tradition to their changing circumstances. The books that were recognized as Hebrew Bible (Tanakh)[1] by Jews and Old Testament by Christians varied for centuries. For example, the rabbinical teachers in Palestine and Babylonia from roughly 200 CE to 500 CE (known as the *Amoraim*) continued to discuss the sacredness of *Sirach*. They debated whether Sirach "defiled the hands" (a Jewish reference used to designate the sacredness of religious texts) well into the fourth and fifth centuries.

Since the reading of a text in worship and teaching it in a religious community implies its sacredness and authority for a believing community, the forbidding of reading a document in public conversely suggests that it was *not* viewed as sacred. The exception to this may be the writings that some Jews believed were reserved for the spiritually elite as in the case of 4 Ezra 14.43–47. The biblical writings that rabbis debated and some even excluded from public reading include Song of Songs (see *Yadayim* 3.5; *b. Megillah* 7a); Ecclesiastes (*Yadayim* 3.5; *b. Shabbat* 100a; see also Jerome on Eccl. 12.14); Ruth (b. *Megillah* 7a); Esther (b. *Sanhedrin* 100a; b. *Megillah* 7a); Proverbs (b. *Shabbat* 30b); and Ezekiel (b. *Shabbat* 13b; *Hagiga* 13a; *Menahot* 45a).

The remnant of Jews in the Diaspora (Jews living outside of the Land of Israel), who defined their identity in terms of the Law of Moses, adapted it to their needs. They were the ones who survived assimilation into other cultures and societies. As the Law was adapted to the Jewish community (Neh. 8.1–8), it also brought new life to them. Scriptural interpretation and application continues unimpeded in both Jewish and Christian communities today and, as the production of many new commentaries that interpret Scripture for new circumstances demonstrates, there is no sign that such activity will soon cease!

The books that comprised the sacred Scriptures of the Jews varied from the period of Hellenistic domination of the Land of Israel through New Testament times and later. The Jewish *story* and its specific traditions were significantly reinterpreted to deal with the absence of the Temple and its cultus. Remarkably, fixing the books that comprised the sacred scriptures of Jews and Christians took place especially in the third and fourth centuries. We will address that issue later.

For the church, while there was broad agreement on the authority of many of the books of the New Testament at the end of the third century, a more fixed collection of sacred Christian books emerged in the fourth century influenced by church clarity in theological positions and major moves toward conformity in the empire. Emphasis on fixing the *text* of the biblical books came much later. Indeed, that process is not complete and continues to this day. While there is widespread agreement on most of the biblical text today, textual scholars have not yet recovered the original text Scripture. The first discernible moves toward stabilizing or fixing the books that comprise the New Testament took place during the Diocletian persecution of the church (303–313 CE) when Christians had to decide which books could be turned over to the Roman authorities to be burned. The second move toward uniformity here was just as compelling and stemmed from Constantine's push for religious unity and conformity within the Christian communities with the threat of banishment for those who did not comply. (This story is summarized in Chapter 7.) At that time, there was widespread (not complete) agreement on the scope of the New Testament. We will now look at the origin of sacred writing.

SACRED WRITINGS AMONG JEWS AND CHRISTIANS

For both Judaism and Christianity the final authority for religious faith has always been God. In the early stages of Old Testament times a belief arose among the Jews that the revelation and will of God were disclosed in God's mighty acts, such as the Jewish Exodus from Egypt. Subsequently, it was also believed that the will of God was disclosed in written documents inspired by God. For example, the writing down of something was often viewed as an important mark of its divine revelation (Exod. 24.12; 31.8; 32.15, 32; 34.1;

Deut. 4.13; 8.10, etc.). Moses wrote down the commandments of the Lord (Exod. 24.4; 34.27), as did Joshua (Josh. 24.26) and Samuel (1 Sam. 10.25). In the book of Deuteronomy, which in its present form was probably written toward the end of the Old Testament times, the king is called upon to write down for himself a copy of the Law of God for reading all the days of his life to remind him of the statutes of God and to be humble in his dealings with his people (Deut. 17.18–20). The people were even called upon to write these words of God on their doorposts (Deut. 6.9; 11.20).

The New Testament writers do not indicate that Jesus ever wrote a book or a letter nor did he command his disciples to write anything. Likewise, with two exceptions, New Testament writers do not make claims that their words came directly from God. The Book of Revelation is the clearest exception where the author claims to be writing a prophecy that comes from the risen Lord (Rev. 1.3, 11; 22.18–19). In the other exception, Paul advises his Corinthian readers that he believes that the Spirit inspired his counsel regarding widows, the unmarried, and those married to unbelievers (1 Cor. 7.25–40).

The writers of the Old Testament do not generally reckon with a written scripture as a major known and acknowledged factor or force in the religious life of Israel. When the prophets say, "Thus says the Lord," they are not usually referring to a Scripture text. In fact, very little in the Old Testament writings suggests that leaders of Israel turned to a collection of sacred scriptures when spiritual guidance was needed. If Scriptures had been widely accepted and accessible in Israel, it is remarkable how infrequent references to sacred books are in the stories of David, Solomon, and Hezekiah and elsewhere in the Old Testament. Rather, it appears that Jews in Old Testament times generally related to God more through persons (such as priests and prophets) and institutions (the tabernacle and temple and its cultus with its sacrifices) than through sacred writings. Israel, however, was not without religious traditions that functioned in an authoritative manner among its people. Indeed, no religious community exists without such religious traditions (rules or guidelines), whether they are expressed in oral traditions, creeds, liturgies, or written scriptures. By their very nature, these traditions are adapted to new circumstances of life or they cease to function as in an authoritative manner.

Generally speaking, the religion of Israel was not governed or influenced by and built upon the Law of Moses much before the reforms of Josiah (621 BCE, see 2 Kgs 22–23; cf. 2 Chron. 34–35), but certainly no later than the reforms of Ezra roughly around 460 to 400 BCE (Neh. 8.1–8; 9.1–3).[2] The Deuteronomic movement in Israel in the eighth to the seventh centuries BCE no doubt played a major role in instituting scriptural awareness. See, for example, the admonition to obey the commandments of God (Yahweh) and not to add to or take anything away from them (Deut. 4.2). Not only are we concerned about the time when the influence of the Jewish sacred writings influenced their life, but also when the religious traditions that were written down in Israel gained a normative religious role among the Jews. It is likely that this took place among the Jews no later than the time of Ezra (460–400?) when these sacred texts (probably the laws of Moses and perhaps also the whole of the Pentateuch) were translated and explained to the Jewish community (Neh. 8.8–11). At that time the notion of scripture was clearly present in Judaism even if the precise name and descriptions of it were not yet present.

We are not suggesting here that there were no sacred written traditions among the Jews before the time of Ezra and Nehemiah, or even Josiah. On the contrary, there are a number of "lost" books mentioned in the Old Testament that clearly influenced some of the biblical writers. While these books are not called "scripture" and did not survive the ancient screening and preserving processes, they are sometimes mentioned with reference to their authoritative status in the nation. These include the following:

A. In the Law or Torah: Book of the Wars of the Lord (Num 21.14)

B. In Joshua, Judges, 1–2 Samuel, 1–2 Kings:

1. Book of Jashar (Josh. 10.12–13; 2 Sam. 1.18–27)
2. Book of the Annals of the Kings of Judah (1 Kgs 14.29; 15.7, 23; 22.45; 2 Kgs 8.23; 12.18; 14.18; 15.6, 36; 16.19; 20.20; 21.17, 25; 23.28; 24.5)

3. Book of the Annals of the Kings of Israel (1 Kgs 14.19; 5.31; 16.5, 14, 20, 27; 22.39; 2 Kgs 1.18; 10.34; 13.8, 12; 14.15, 28; 15.11, 15, 21, 26, 31)

4. Book of Acts of Solomon (1 Kgs 11.41)

C. In Chronicles, Ezra, and Nehemiah:

1. Book of the Kings of Israel (1 Chron. 9.21; 2 Chron. 20.34)
2. Book of the Kings of Judah and Israel (2 Chron. 16.11)
3. Book of Kings of Israel and Judah (2 Chron. 27.7)
4. Annals of the Kings of Israel (2 Chron. 33.18)
5. Records of the seer Samuel (1 Chron. 29.29)
6. Records of the seer Gad (1 Chron. 29.29)
7. Records of the seer Nathan (1 Chron. 29.29)
8. History of the Prophet Nathan (2 Chron. 9.29)
9. Prophecy of Ahijah the Shilonite (2 Chron. 9.29)
10. Visions of the seer Iddo (2 Chron. 9.29)
11. Records of the Prophet Shemaiah and the seer Iddo (2 Chron. 12.15)
12. Annals of Jehu the son of Hanani (". . . which are recorded in the Book of the Kings of Israel." 2 Chron. 20.34)
13. Records of the seers (2 Chron. 33.19)
14. Story of the prophet Iddo (2 Chron. 13.22)
15. Commentary on the Book of the Kings (2 Chron. 24.27)
16. A book written by the prophet Isaiah son of Amoz containing the history of Uzziah (2 Chron. 26.22)
17. A vision of the prophet Isaiah son of Amoz in the Book of the Kings of Judah and Israel (2 Chron. 32.32; cf. Isa. 1.1)
18. Annals of King David (1 Chron. 27.24)
19. Annals of your ancestors (Ezra 4.15)
20. Book of the Annals (Neh. 12.23)

D. Additional book: "Laments" in 2 Chron. 35.25 is not a reference to Lamentations, but rather to a book evidently produced by or for Josiah that is now lost.

We should observe that the titles given to several of these books, such as "seer," "prophet," "vision(s)" and "commentary," all suggest a sacred role that they played at an earlier stage in Jewish history.

EMERGING COLLECTIONS OF
JEWISH SCRIPTURES

In recent years, biblical scholars have come to some agreement on various aspects of the origins of the Bible and more are likely in future publications. Some of these include the recognition that the Pentateuch (Law or Torah = the first five books of the Old Testament) was largely recognized as sacred literature among the Jews returning from Babylon under the leadership of Ezra (ca. 450–400 BCE). Affirmation of this recognition is also obvious later when the Pentateuch was translated into Greek (ca. 281–280 BCE). Had other books in the Hebrew Scriptures been widely accepted as sacred scripture at the beginning of the third century BCE, it is likely that they too would have been included in the first Greek translation of the Jewish Scriptures (commonly called the LXX or Septuagint). Many of the other books of the Old Testament were translated into Greek by at least 130 BCE as we see in the Prologue to the Wisdom of Jesus ben Sira (this text is cited in Chapter 3). Not only these books, but others also were eventually included in Jewish sacred scripture collections and translated into Greek. It is not clear when the translation of all of the books that now comprise the Greek translation of the Old Testament took place, but it is likely that it was no later than the first century BCE.

Some of those excluded writings that were recognized as sacred texts among the Jews and subsequently among the Christians include what we now call "apocryphal" (Heb. = "hidden" or "secret" now referring to any book of doubtful authority) and pseudepigraphal (a book written under a false superscription or pseudonymous name) writings. Some of these books are included in the Old Testaments of Roman Catholics and the Orthodox Christians and are oftenidentified as "Deuterocanonical" books (see these lists at the end of Chapter 4). Only the Protestant Christians use the term "Apocrypha" for those additional writings in the Roman Catholic and Orthodox Church Old Testaments. Some pseudepigraphal writings were widely accepted as sacred scripture by some early Christians up to the mid-third century CE (especially *1 Enoch, Psalms of Solomon, and Testaments of the Patriarchs*). The most popular of the apocryphal or Deuterocanonical books included the Wisdom of Jesus ben Sirach (or Ecclesiasticus), the Wisdom of Solomon, and 1 and 2 Maccabees, but others also such as Tobit, Judith, and Baruch.

Protestant Christians have accepted these same books as those in the Hebrew Bible for their Old Testament, but *not in the same order*. The specific books in the Jewish collection are *first* identified in a rabbinic tradition called *b. Baba Bathra* 14b (likely produced in Babylon between 150–180 CE, possibly 200 CE). This *baraita*[3] text (*b. Baba Bathra* 14b) lists *for the first time* the books of the Tanakh (the Law is omitted here, but it is clearly assumed in context) and places them in a threefold category (Law, Prophets, and Writings). Most, if not all of this collection of Jewish sacred books, was widely recognized among Jews and Christians in the first century CE, but at that time the collection was not closed or fixed and other religious books were also circulating among Jews and Christians. For most Jews in the first century CE, the broad contours of their sacred scriptures (Law and Prophets) were widely recognized at that time, but other Jewish religious texts were also circulating among Jews and Christians at that time and were often treated like "scripture." We see this in the New Testament, but also in later Christian writings as well.

The popular terms "Hebrew Bible" and "Old Testament" are regularly used anachronistically to make clear what literature we are talking about, that is, sacred scripture collections in the time of Jesus and earlier, but these designations did not exist at that time to identify these Scripture collections. They are later terms and there is no evidence that a widely accepted *fixed* collection of Jewish scriptures existed before the second and following centuries CE for the rabbinic Jews or for the Christians. Josephus, the Jewish historian, speaks of one at the end of the first century and the *b. Baba Bathra* 14b text offers early moves in that direction.

These "additional books" in the various sacred scripture collections were welcomed by some Jews of the first century and later also by many Christians. There are at least 70 of these Jewish apocryphal and pseudepigraphal books. Some of them include Christian additions and, in the case of the *Odes of Solomon*, some may have been completely written by Christians. It is possible that more excluded books will be found in the future. The best *known* include the following:

1. Apocalyptic and Related works:

    1 (Ethiopic Apocalypse of) *Enoch* (Jewish, ca. 200 BCE–50 CE)

    2 (Slavonic Apocalypse of) *Enoch* (Jewish, ca. 75–100 CE)

    3 (Hebrew Apocalypse of) *Enoch* (Jewish, in present form from ca. 5th to 6th cent. CE)

    Sibylline Oracles (both Jewish and Christian, ca. 2nd cent. BCE–7th cent. CE)

    Treatise of Shem (ca. near end of first cent. BCE)

    Apocryphon of Ezekiel (mostly lost, original form ca. late 1st cent. BCE)

    Apocalypse of Zephaniah (mostly lost, original form ca. late 1st cent. BCE)

    4 Ezra (original Jewish form after 70 CE, final Christian additions later)

    Greek Apocalypse of Ezra (present form is Christian ca. 9th cent. CE with both Jewish and Christian sources)

    Vision of Ezra (a Christian document dating from 4th to 7th cent. CE)

    Questions of Ezra (Christian, but date is imprecise)

    Revelation of Ezra (Christian and sometime before 9th cent. CE)

    Apocalypse of Sedrach (present form is Christian from ca. 5th cent. with earlier sources)

    2 (Syriac Apocalypse of) *Baruch* (Jewish, from ca. 100 CE)

    3 (Greek Apocalypse of) *Baruch* (Christian utilizing Jewish sources, ca. 1st–2nd cent. CE)

    Apocalypse of Abraham (Jewish primarily, ca. 70–150 CE)

    Apocalypse of Adam (Gnostic derived from Jewish sources from ca. the 1st cent. CE)

    Apocalypse of Elijah (both Jewish and Christian, ca. 150–275 CE)

Apocalypse of Daniel (present form ca. 9th cent. CE, but contains Jewish sources from ca. 4th cent. CE).

2. Testaments:

Testaments of the Twelve Patriarchs (current form is Christian, ca. 150–200 CE, but Levi, Judah, and Naphtali are Jewish and date before 70 CE and probably 2nd–1st cent. BCE)

Testament of Job (Jewish, ca. late 1st cent. BCE)

Testaments of the Three Patriarchs (Jewish Testaments of *Abraham, Isaac,* and *Jacob* from ca. 100 CE which are linked with the Christian *Testament of Isaac* and *Jacob*)

Testament of Moses (Jewish, from ca. early 1st cent. CE)

Testament of Solomon (Jewish, current form ca. 3rd cent. CE, but earliest form ca. 100 CE)

Testament of Adam (Christian in current form ca. late 3rd cent. CE, but used Jewish sources from ca. 150–200 CE).

3. Expansions of Old Testament and other legends:

The Letter of Aristeas (Jewish, ca. 200–150 BCE)

Jubilees (Jewish, ca. 130–100 CE)

Martyrdom and Ascension of Isaiah (has three sections, the first Jewish from ca. 100 BCE, and 2nd and 3rd sections are Christian. The second from ca. 2nd cent. CE, and the third— Testament of Hezekiah, ca. 90–100 CE)

Joseph and Asenath (Jewish, ca. 100 CE)

Life of Adam and Eve (Jewish, ca. early to middle 1st cent. CE)

Pseudo-Philo (Jewish, ca. 66–135 CE)

Lives of the Prophets (Jewish, ca. early 1st cent. CE with later Christian additions)

Ladder of Jacob (earliest form is Jewish dating from late 1st cent. CE. One chapter is Christian)

4 Baruch (Jewish original but edited by a Christian, ca. 100–110 CE)

Jannes and Jambres (Christian in present form, but dependent on earlier Jewish sources from ca. 1st cent. BCE)

History of the Rechabites (Christian in present form dating ca. 6th cent. CE, but contains some Jewish sources before 100 CE)

Eldad and Modat (forged on basis of Numbers 11.26–29, before the 1st CE is now lost, but quoted in *Shepherd of Hermas* ca. 140 CE)
History of Joseph (Jewish, but difficult to date).

4. Wisdom and Philosophical Literature:

Ahiqar (Jewish dating from late 7th or 6th cent. BCE and cited in Apocryphal Tobit)
3 Maccabees (Jewish, ca. 1st cent. BCE)
4 Maccabees (Jewish, ca. before 70 CE)
Pseudo-Phocylides (Jewish maxims attributed to 6th cent. Ionic poet, ca. 50 BCE–100 CE)
The Sentences of the Syriac Menander (Jewish, ca. 3rd cent. CE).

5. Prayers, Psalms, and Odes:

More Psalms of David (Jewish psalms from ca. 3rd cent. BCE to 100 CE)
Prayer of Manasseh (sometimes in Apocrypha, Jewish from ca. early 1st cent. CE)
Psalms of Solomon (Jewish, ca. 50–5 BCE)
Hellenistic Synagogal Prayers (Jewish, ca. 2nd–3rd cent. CE)
Prayer of Joseph (Jewish, ca. 70–135)
Prayer of Jacob (mostly lost Jewish document from ca. 4th cent. CE)
Odes of Solomon (Christian but influenced by Judaism and probably also Qumran, ca. 100 CE)

Besides these, there are many known *Christian* books that were eventually excluded from scripture collections by the ancient churches and identified as Christian or New Testament Apocrypha and sometimes books "spoken against" (Greek = *antilegomena*). Most are from the second or third centuries CE. The best known of these include the following:

Gospels:

The Protoevangelium of James
The Infancy Gospel of Thomas
The Gospel of Peter
The Gospel of the Nicodemus

The Gospel of the Nazoreans
The Gospel of the Ebionites
The Gospel of the Hebrews
The Gospel of the Egyptians
The Gospel of Thomas
The Gospel of Philip
The Gospel of Mary.

Acts (The first five of these are called the "Leucian Acts" and circulated together):

The Acts of John
The Acts of Peter
The Acts of Paul
The Acts of Andrew
The Acts of Thomas
The Acts of Andrew and Matthias
The Acts of Philip
The Acts of Thaddaeus
The Acts of Peter and Paul
The Acts of Peter and Andrew
The Martyrdom of Matthew
The Slavonic Act of Peter
The Acts of Peter and the Twelve Apostles.

Epistles:

Third Corinthians
The Epistle to the Laodiceans
The Letters of Paul and Seneca
The Letters of Jesus and Abgar
The Letter of Lentulus
The Epistle of Titus.

Apocalypses (visionary writings on the imminent intervention of God in human affairs and the end of all evil in the world):

The Apocalypse of Peter
The Coptic Apocalypse of Paul
The First Apocalypse of James
The Second Apocalypse of James

The Apocryphon of John
The Sophia of Jesus Christ
The Letter of Peter to Philip
The Apocalypse of Mary[4]

None of these Christian books were initially identified as "apocryphal" or "pseudepigraphal" writings and it is most likely that all of them were recognized as Christian scripture by some early Christians. By calling this literature apocryphal or pseudepigraphal often prejudices their investigation, but those terms now conveniently identify nonbiblical literature from antiquity. Readers should remember, however, that Jews and Christians welcomed many of these nonbiblical writings as sacred literature. This is demonstrated in their considerable use in those communities. They believed that these religious texts along with the Old Testament books disclosed the will of God, the identity of the people of God, and often their mission in this world. While the collection of Christian books that were not included in the New Testament *currently* contains some 80 books, that number may increase as more discoveries are made and brought to our attention. In recent years several ancient books have come to light that were only known by name.

Among the most common books in this so-called Christian non-canonical collection are the various gospels, acts, and letters that were put forth in the names of the apostles identified in the canonical Gospels. They informed the faith of some Christians in some cases for centuries before being left behind in favor of the writings that now comprise the Christian Bible.

As we observed earlier, those who wrote the books that were included in the New Testament generally did not write as if they were producing sacred literature. Nevertheless, from the early stages of the churches several New Testament writings were highly valued, frequently cited, and used in the churches for catechetical instruction and to advance their mission. The Gospels, because they told the story of Jesus and his teachings, and the letters of Paul, because they contained many practical teachings and significant doctrinal teachings for early churches, were widely used in many churches from the first century on. From the last third of the second century, Christian writings were beginning to be called "scripture" often including the usual scriptural designations "as it is written" or "as the scripture says."

EMERGING COLLECTIONS OF *CHRISTIAN* SCRIPTURES

By around 160 CE, the Gospels were read and cited alongside of the Old Testament writings (sometimes corporately called the "Prophets") in Christian worship services. The earliest witness to this practice is found in Justin's *1 Apology*, the first known book to describe the basic components of early Christian worship. Justin did not specifically call for a new collection of Christian scriptures, even though he unquestionably recognized the authority of what he called the "memoirs of the Apostles"—the Gospels, for Christian faith. Justin writes: "For the apostles, in the memoirs composed by them, which are called Gospels, have delivered unto us what was enjoined upon them . . . (*1 Apology* 66, ANF). He frequently cited them to establish and defend Christian doctrine (*Dialogue with Trypho* 100.1–2 and 101.3), and shows that the Gospels were used in Rome in liturgical readings (see *1 Apology* 66, 67). He also refers to the Gospels as "memoirs of all things concerning our Savior Jesus Christ" (*1 Apology* 33 and 66). These "memoirs" were for him an authoritative guide to the teaching of Jesus on church matters, including the Eucharist (*1 Apology* 67). That these "memoirs" were read "as time allowed" along with and sometimes instead of the "writings of the prophets." The description of worship is as follows:

> After these [services] we constantly remind each other of these things. Those who have more come to the aid of those who lack, and we are constantly together. Over all that we receive we bless the Maker of all things through his Son Jesus Christ and through the Holy Spirit. And on the day called Sunday there is a meeting in one place of those who live in cities or the country, and the *memoirs of the apostles* or the writings of the prophets are read as long as time permits. When the reader has finished, *the president in a discourse urges and invites [us] to the imitation of these noble things.* Then we all stand up together and offer prayers. And, as said before, when we have finished the prayer, bread is brought, and wine and water, and the president similarly sends up prayers

and thanksgivings to the best of his ability, and the congregation assents, saying the Amen; the distribution, and reception of the consecrated [elements] by each one, takes place and they are sent to the absent by the deacons. Those who prosper, and who so wish, contribute, each one as much as he chooses to. What is collected is deposited with the president, and he takes care of orphans and widows, and those who are in bonds, and the strangers who are sojourners among [us], and, briefly, he is the protector of all those in need. We all hold this common gathering on Sunday, since it is the first day, on which God transforming darkness and matter made the universe, and Jesus Christ our Savior rose from the dead on the same day. For they crucified him on the day before Saturday, and on the day after Saturday, he appeared to his apostles and disciples and taught them these things which I have passed on to you also for your serious consideration. (*1 Apology* 67, *ECF.* Emphasis added)

Notice that immediately after these "*memoirs of the apostles* or the writings of the prophets" were read, "the president in a discourse urges and invites [us] to the imitation of the *noble* things." This "imitation" of the "noble things" implies the recognition of their value in the church life, a prelude to scriptural recognition. Also, reading these "memoirs" along with the Prophets strongly suggests that they were viewed in a scriptural manner. This practice anticipated the later recognition of this literature as *Christian* scripture. Because this literature served the worship and instructional needs of the churches, it was shortly thereafter called "scripture" in some churches. Elsewhere Justin speaks of "our writings" to bolster his theological arguments (*1 Apology* 28.1) referring to the Old Testament and Christian writings, especially the "memoirs" or Gospels. When he mentions the "memoirs" *first* in the above text, Justin may be suggesting that the Christian writings were given preference in worship over the Old Testament prophets. This is certainly the practice of second and third century writers who regularly cited Christian texts more frequently than the Old Testament writings.

By around 170 CE, recognition of the prominence of the apostles and esteem for their role in the mission of the churches had grown considerably. As a result, the Gospels began to be identified by apostolic names (Matthew and John) or by those associated with the Apostles (Mark and Luke). At the same time, Irenaeus (cs. 170–180) called the four Gospels (Matthew, Mark, Luke, John), and some of Paul's letters "scripture." These writings were often cited in a scriptural manner before then, but generally they were not yet called "scripture" until toward the end of the second century. We should hasten to say that this does not mean that all of the New Testament writings had either achieved the same level of recognition or that the recognition took place at the same time in all churches. The recognition of other New Testament books as Christian scripture took place variously and over longer periods of time in the churches.

By the end of the third and early fourth centuries, many churches had already largely agreed on the sacredness of some New Testament books, though full agreement was not present in these matters. Other Christian books, for example, continued to have broad circulation and acceptance in various churches (especially *The Shepherd of Hermas, The Epistle of Barnabas, The Didache,* the *Letters* of Ignatius of Antioch and *1 & 2 Clement*). In other words, initially the churches widely accepted the New Testament Gospels and seven or more letters of Paul, but did not agree on many others. The eventual acceptance of all of the New Testament books did not take place at the same time or in the same locations. Now, of course, the three major church bodies that exist today (Catholic, Orthodox, and Protestant) accept all 27 books that now make up the New Testament. Christians have never fully agreed, however, on the scope or contents of their Old Testament scriptures.

By the end of the fourth century, various church councils began to draw up lists of sacred books, but that did not mean that there was universal agreement on the scope of the New Testament at that time. There was broad agreement on the acceptance of the four canonical Gospels, the book of Acts, and the writings of Paul, as well as 1 Peter and 1 John, but there was no *complete* agreement on the scope of the New Testament for sometime to come. For example, even after the late fourth and fifth century church council decisions on the scope of the Christian Scriptures, a number of ancient scriptural manuscripts produced subsequently continued to include books that were not eventually included in the New Testament (see Chapter 7). A number of factors went into the selection of the books that now comprise the New Testament, as we will see later in this volume, but we hasten to say that the earliest churches did not agree on which books to include in their Bibles, whether Old or New Testament. As we will observe later, it is not until around 1000 CE that we find the first Christian manuscripts containing all of the New Testament books and only those books. Most of the manuscripts have fewer books and some at a relatively late time still contain some noncanonical writings. Interestingly, the Ethiopian Christians, unlike the Catholics, Orthodox, and Protestants, have both a larger collection of Old and New Testament books. Even as late as the mid-sixteenth century, Martin Luther rejected several New Testament books, namely Hebrews, James, Jude, and Revelation, though he included them at the end of his New Testament. For him they added nothing to Christian doctrine and were even contrary to essential Christian teaching. His rejection of the importance and significance of these books and the Deuterocanonical books reflects the freedom in his generation to question books in the biblical canon.

FOUR FAULTY ASSUMPTIONS

In telling the canonical story, it is important to identify four common assumptions that often account for faulty conclusions about the formation of the biblical canon. *First*, it is often assumed that if one ancient writer in one location acknowledged a particular writing as sacred scripture, then all writers of the same era and elsewhere throughout the Roman Empire drew the same conclusion. There is, of course, no evidence to support this and the early churches were often at odds on a number of issues whether in regard to organization, baptism, the Eucharist (or Lord's supper), who Jesus was (Christology), when Jesus Christ would return, and the future for the church. The greater church largely decided some of these issues in the fourth century, even if some Christians continued to debate them for centuries after that. Given this diversity, it would be strange indeed if all Christians were nevertheless uniform in their thinking about the scope of their biblical canon. It took several centuries for the churches to settle major theological issues and it would have scarcely been possible to fix the scope of the sacred literature before the theological issues were largely settled. When church leaders in the fourth and fifth centuries considered the scope of the Christian Scriptures, we can hardly expect full agreement from them.

Second, it is often assumed that the early Christians responded to the heresies that emerged in the second century by producing a fixed collection of sacred scriptures, that is, a biblical canon. There is nothing in the history of the second and third century churches to support this view. What we see in the writings of that period is that they answered theological challenges (heresy) by setting forth a *canon* (or rule) of faith (in Latin = *regula fidei*). In other words, they answered theological challenges with theological teachings that most Christians believed to be true and passed along to them through apostolic succession, that is, passing the apostolic Christian teachings from one generation to the next through its church leaders, the bishops. (See discussion of this in Chapter 5.) Second century Christians responded to heresy with a canon of faith, not a biblical canon.

Third, it is often assumed that whenever an ancient writer cited or quoted a particular text, that the writer regarded it as scripture. This cannot be demonstrated, however, and each quotation or citation must be considered in its own context to determine how it was used. In some cases, ancient writers cited both biblical and nonbiblical sources as they would sacred texts, but that is not always the case. One must determine if the cited text is used in an authoritative manner to establish Christian belief or order behavior.

Fourth, and similarly, some Bible scholars assume that the books cited by the early church fathers constituted the books that they believed were sacred scripture, namely, their biblical canon. Apart from asking whether a particular writer cited noncanonical sources, what is often forgotten is that a citation of texts was produced in a specific context to address specific problems. In such cases, authors appealed only to those writings that would advance their perspectives *in those situations*, but this cannot be used to imply that the ancient writers cited *all* of the literature that they considered sacred and inspired. If the ancient writers had addressed other situations, they would have likely employed other sources to argue those cases. Since most of the ancient writings are *ad hoc* in nature, that is written to address specific situations or circumstances, it is unlikely that any compiling of the sources these writers used will enable us to produce their biblical canons unless they made a specific list of books that comprised their Scriptures.

These common assumptions often skew the results of otherwise important research on the biblical canon. However, these assumptions must be tested by the evidence that we find in the Bible and in the primary artifacts of antiquity, namely, the biblical and non-biblical books, early church history, and the surviving biblical manuscripts.

SOME IMPORTANT PRELIMINARY OBSERVATIONS

As we begin our story of how the Bible came to be, we should be aware that even though the church inherited the notion of sacred scripture, *it did not inherit the notion of a fixed collection of sacred scriptures.* The fixing of the biblical canon, that is selection of books for inclusion in it and excluding all others took centuries to decide even though the church was born with a large collection of Jewish sacred books available to it. The early Jewish and Christian communities often included other books that were not eventually included in their sacred Scriptures. The early churches saw themselves as inheritors of the Jewish scriptural traditions and also living in the age of the Spirit in which the living Word of God regularly addressed them. The earliest Christians believed that the prophetic voice was very much alive in their midst through the power of the Spirit (Acts 2.17–21). During the time of the Reformation in the 1500s and later, some scholars of the church assumed in practice (not in theory) that the Holy Spirit no longer speaks a new word from God for the church, but only through the closed collection of Old and New Testament Scriptures.

That view prevailed especially in Protestant theology since the Reformation, but on what grounds? How did some teachers of the church come to believe that the Spirit of God stopped speaking newly inspired utterances when the last apostle died? The early church did not teach that view, of course, but in time it became a common assumption in the reformation era. When that view emerged, Christians developed a variety of interpretive steps to enable them to apply biblical teaching to ever-new situations facing them.

Christians believed that whatever was written in their sacred Scriptures came from God and it could not be changed, but rather believed and obeyed. The writings that were recognized as inspired sacred texts were placed alongside other sacred writings and were eventually placed in a fixed collection of sacred scriptures, that is, a biblical canon.

WHICH *TEXT* AND *TRANSLATION* OF THE BIBLE IS SCRIPTURE?

In the history of the formation of the Bible, not only is the selection of *books* important, but also which *text* of those books should function as sacred scripture for the church. Not until the later development of what is now called the "textus receptus" or "received text" of the Scriptures was there any broad agreement on the text of the Bible and that did not last long! That text was the basis for the King James Bible in the early 1600s. Students of the Bible and many contemporary Christians, however, are well aware of the subsequent discovery of hundreds of ancient biblical manuscripts with consider-able variation in their texts. Over the last 120 years or more, many ancient biblical manuscripts were discovered in Egypt, Israel, muse-ums, libraries, and other places and the study of them has shown that the text of these manuscripts are often at considerable variance with each other. This is true at times with regard to the books that are in them, and also with reference to the specific texts in them. No two biblical manuscripts have exactly the same words! Further, all of these manuscripts functioned as "scripture" for the communities of faith that possessed and read them. The Greek texts of the New Testament that were used to produce the so-called received text were quite late and that text has been largely replaced. Modern translators and textual critics now have much earlier manuscripts available to them that are hundreds of years closer to the original writings of the New Testament. Likewise, because of the modern discovery of the Dead Sea Scrolls, biblical scholars and textual critics are even closer to the original manuscripts of the Old Testament. While no one believes that the text critical scholars have now produced the elusive "original" biblical text, we are certainly much closer to it than before. There are many thousands of variants in the surviving biblical manuscripts and biblical scholars are working to produce a text of both Old and New Testaments that is more accurate and much closer to the original text of the biblical books. This should not take away from the fact that there are hundreds of thousands of variants, both accidental and intentional, in the biblical manuscripts that have survived antiquity. Indeed, there are more variants than words in the Bible! Scholars are working to resolve these and to produce a more accurate text of the Bible, but they are not there yet!

Before the invention of the printing press in the fifteenth century, the Scriptures were all individually hand copied by scribes with varying degrees of skill. Those copyists who produced biblical manuscripts before the fourth century were often less skilled than were the later copiers. In the earlier copies, many variants, both accidental and intentional, were included in these handwritten manuscripts. While scholars have been able to make reasonable assessments of the surviving texts and have resolved most of the textual variants, some uncertainty and ambiguity still remains about the original text of some passages of both the Old and New Testament Scriptures. As noted above, some of these texts are significantly different from others and so it is appropriate to ask which texts translators should follow today?

Another related subject is also a challenge for biblical scholars today. All of our modern translations of the Bible are based on a critical assessment of the hundreds and even thousands of copies of biblical texts that have survived antiquity. Since most Christians do not speak or read Hebrew, Aramaic, or Greek, the languages of the biblical books, which translation of the Bible should Christians read in their churches and in private study and devotion? As translators know, many of the ancient translations are poor in quality and produced by amateur translators. St. Augustine, in the early fifth century wrote about the poor quality of Latin translations (which could also be said of most others) saying: "For in the early days of the faith every man who happened to get his hands upon a Greek manuscript, and who thought he had any knowledge, were it ever so little, of the two languages, ventured upon the work of translation" (*On Christian Doctrine* 11). This, of course, raises the question of whether there is an authoritative translation of the Scriptures for the church. There were a number of ancient translations of the Jewish and Christian scriptures and while there is a core of books that most include, most do not contain the same books and the quality of translation is generally poor. Nevertheless, these translations were the Scriptures of the early churches that had them.

In a church that I visited not long ago, I heard a discussion of the inspiration of the Bible that tied the inspiration of the Bible to the "original inerrant manuscripts." I was asked my opinion on the matter and I answered that since we do not have the autographs, or original manuscripts, and since no translation of the Bible today is based on them, we need to ask about the status of the only Bibles that we have and circulate in our churches. Are they inspired even though they are not based on original manuscripts and the manuscripts they are based on have many errors in them? Further, we know that the books of the Bible were originally written in Hebrew, Aramaic, and Greek, but the Bibles that I saw in the auditorium were all in English and not even the same English translation. I saw the King James Version, the New International Version, the Revised Standard Version, and the New American Standard Version, and there may have been others present. I asked the people whether the King James Version of the Bible that an elderly lady was clutching in her hand was inspired since her Bible was in no way based on the original manuscripts of the Bible (we know which ones were available then) and her Bible was not in the original languages of the biblical books. I suggested to them that they should consider as more relevant a discussion of the only Bibles that we do have, none of which are based on "inerrant original manuscripts!" All of our Bibles are based rather on ancient manuscripts that have many textual variants and even errors in them. Further, our translations are revised regularly based on a growing collection of data from ancient manuscripts. Which translations are inspired? Perhaps all of them since many persons have come to faith and grown in their faith as a result of using them, but none of them are without error.

While no one responded to my comments in the meeting, there seemed to be considerable unease about the issues I raised. It is not irrelevant to ask which translation is the most authoritative for the church today and why. My initial response is that we should seek a translation that most accurately reflects the earliest and most reliable manuscripts that we possess, but one that also communicates carefully the message intended by the authors of Scripture. That, of course, also involves some discussion of what a translation is and which audience it is designed to reach. Most translations today are aimed at or around the tenth grade level, but some more loosely translated Bibles (paraphrases) and others aimed for an audience with somewhere between a sixth to eighth grade level of education. Which translation should become the authoritative biblical text for the church in the English-speaking world and which one for the French, or the Germans, or Chinese, or others who speak a different language than ours? Again, while I favor an accurate and carefully translated Bible based on the best and earliest manuscripts, I also choose to read the one that is easiest to read and teach in the churches where the average education is considerably lower than it is in the academy of scholars. I modify it where needed to bring clarity. A more useful habit for those persons who do not have the skills to look at the Bible in its original languages (Hebrew, Aramaic, and Greek) is to read the Bible in two translations. Not infrequently one will help clarify the other.

A "CANON WITHIN THE CANON"

Many Christians today, as throughout church history, ignore large segments of the Scriptures that they acknowledge as divinely inspired literature. Does this matter? At a recent church where I was lecturing, a woman of the church mentioned that she got very little out of the book of Leviticus and so she regularly ignored it. Others nodded their heads in agreement with her. I have heard similar comments about several books of the Bible, including Hebrews and Revelation. We sometimes describe this practice as having a "canon within the canon." We mean by it that Christians often ignore large segments of the Bible in favor of others. For many years now, I have spoken to church groups about this matter of selective Scripture reading and have tried to make more of the biblical literature relevant in their worship services and Bible study. This selective practice is common though seldom acknowledged or discussed in many churches. For example, many churches today follow a liturgical calendar and use the standard lectionaries for Scripture readings, preaching, and teaching or catechetical instruction in the church. These lectionary guides seldom include more than small portions of most of the books of the Bible but never all of the books of the Bible, even over a long period of years. Nevertheless, Christians who use the lectionaries regularly affirm the whole canon of Scriptures that has been handed down to them in the church. The lectionaries seldom include selections from the Chronicles, Nahum, Habakkuk, Hebrews, 2 Peter, 2–3 John, Jude and Revelation and other books as well. If they do, it is only rarely and generally only small portions are read. Maybe this is deliberate and has some justification, but it should be openly acknowledged and discussed in the churches.

If we regularly ignore some of the books of the Bible because it involves more study to understand them, should they be *excluded* from the Bible? On the other hand, in the last century or more, many discoveries were made of ancient books that were earlier included in Christian Scripture collections but later excluded (e.g., the *1 Enoch*, *Psalms of Solomon*, *Didache* (or *Teaching of the Twelve Apostles*), *Gospel of Thomas,* and others). Should these now be reconsidered for inclusion in Christian collections of sacred texts? While not a lot would be gained by changing the current biblical canons in terms of Church teaching, this reading of other texts can provide useful information on the context and development of Judaism and early Christianity. Back to the earlier question on lectionaries, what books should be included in them? Do those who construct the lectionaries always get it right?

Those Christians who do not follow the traditional church lectionaries are often not better off in terms of reading, preaching, and teaching the whole biblical canon. They too often ignore even *larger* portions of the Scriptures. This is not necessarily to be critical of those who ignore portions of the Bible, since many recognize that not all portions of the Bible have an equal relevance for the modern congregations. I agree that what Jesus said has more relevance for the church today than those portions of Leviticus that list regulations about Sabbath, dietary, and purity regulations. Most Christians ignore these laws and regulations and focus more on grace and freedom in Christ, but is it appropriate to ignore several books of the New Testament as well? As noted above, Christians often ignore several New Testament books. Should we take these books out of the New Testament? Would we have more unity in the churches with or without the Book of Revelation because it is difficult to understand and because some Bible teachers contend that it does not present a credible picture of Jesus or the faith of the early church? Should it be excluded because many of its prophecies apparently have not yet come to pass (e.g., Rev. 1.3; 22.20)? Or, should it be discarded simply because it depends on a worldview that some believe is largely incredible by modern standards? Biblical scholars and church leaders are divided over such matters.

In principle, most Christians and Jews affirm the whole of their sacred Scriptures, but in practice they often teach or preach only small portions of it. For example, the late Donald Grey Barnhouse, former pastor of the Tenth Presbyterian Church in Philadelphia, reportedly preached Sunday after Sunday for years only on Paul's letter to the Romans. His successor also, the late Reverend James Montgomery Boice, did the same except that he selected instead the Gospel of John for an even longer period! These are admittedly rare examples, but they illustrate a tendency of some ministers to affirm in principle the inspiration and authority of the whole biblical canon, but in practice are quite selective of the texts that they utilize in their proclamation and teaching in the churches. While the intention of those pastors was good, namely, they demonstrated that there is much to be gleaned in the biblical books, still, there was much that was ignored in the process.

It is also quite possible today that seminary students will graduate with a theological degree without having had one course on any of the so-called marginal books of the New Testament or Old Testament listed above except for a few pages quickly read in an Old or New Testament introduction. Likewise, there is little attention given to the "excluded books," that is, to those early contenders that were eventually excluded.

In the Old Testament, it is highly unlikely that students in seminary will be exposed to a careful interpretation of most of the books of the Minor Prophets or, as we noted above, Ecclesiastes, Song of Songs, and even Esther, except for a fleeting familiar passage cited in support of something else that might be considered more important. Although survey courses lightly touch on these books, I seldom find seminary courses on Ecclesiastes, the Song of Songs, Nahum, or

Zephaniah! Most Old Testament courses with which I am familiar focus on the Pentateuch, touch lightly on Leviticus and give more attention given to Genesis, Exodus, and Deuteronomy. Ultimately, if these or other books of the Bible are "canonical," marginalizing them makes very little sense. It is not uncommon for seminary students and members of congregations to receive only very light discussions of several biblical books. The other books that were *not* included in the biblical canon are now beginning to get some attention in survey courses in most seminaries regardless of their perspective (liberal, moderate, or conservative) and many professors are finding these books useful both in advancing their understanding of the biblical books and the contexts of early Christianity and early Judaism.

Jews and Christians who acknowledge the authority of the Bible generally adopt something like a "canon within the canon," that is, in *practice* they follow only some of the biblical admonitions, or they adopt creative ways to interpret the more obscure or more challenging biblical texts. How can the Bible continue to be authoritative scripture if we acknowledge its authority and sacredness but selectively ignore many of its admonitions and messages?

For believing communities, the Bible is never simply an ancient historical document that is useful for understanding the emergence of Jewish and Christian communities of faith. For them it is a practical understanding of the identity and will of God for them and it exercises a certain level of authority in their conduct and mission in the world. Some biblical scholars have suggested recently that some of the biblical books could be excluded without much loss to the church and that some of the books that were initially excluded in the canonization of the Bible might be included with considerable profit to the churches. Today there are more assaults on the validity of the biblical canon than at anytime in the last 400 years. Is it time to reconsider the biblical canon again? Is it regardless of what scholars do "a done deal" that cannot be changed?

If the scope of the Bible were changed, as some Bible scholars have encouraged, what difference would it make? What difference would it make in the churches' understanding of God, their identity, their community life, and mission if some books were taken away and others added? These are all questions about the biblical canon, that is, about the *books* that make up the Bible, and they focus on sacred books that both Christians and Jews around the world believe are foundational to their faith, conduct, and mission.

Some Christians today are asking which collection of Old Testament scriptures best reflects the Scriptures of Jesus and his earliest followers. Is it the one adopted by the rabbinic Jews in mid to late-second century CE, or was it a larger and less precisely defined collection that included both biblical books and several "apocryphal" and even "pseudepigraphal" writings? If the latter, what does that mean in regard to biblical authority today?

We will now turn to more specific issues related to the formation of the Old and New Testaments.

FURTHER READING

Auwer, J.-M. and H. J. De Jonge, eds. *The Biblical Canons*. BETL clxiii. Leuven: Leuven University Press, 2003.

Barr, James. *Holy Scripture: Canon, Authority, Criticism*. Philadelphia, PA: The Westminster Press, 1983.

Barton, John. *Holy Writings, Sacred Text: The Canon in Early Christianity*. Louisville, KY: Westminster John Knox Press, 1997.

Campenhausen, Hans von. *The Formation of the Christian Bible*. Trans. J. A. Baker. Philadelphia, PA: Fortress, 1972.

Davies, Philip R. "The Jewish Scriptural Canon in Cultural Perspective," in *The Canon Debate*, ed. Lee M. McDonald and James A. Sanders. Peabody, MA: Hendrickson Publishers, 2002, pp. 42–44.

Gamble, Harry Y. *Books and Readers in the Early Church: A History of Early Christian Texts*. New Haven, CT/London: Yale University Press, 1995.

Guillory, John. *Cultural Capital: The Problem of Literary Canon Formation*. Chicago, IL: University of Chicago Press, 1995.

Hallberg, Robert von, ed. *Canons*. Chicago, IL: University of Chicago Press, 1985.

Kraemer, David. "The Formation of the Rabbinic Canon: Authority and Boundaries," *JBL* 110 (1991), 4:613–630.

Leiman, Sid. Z. *The Canon and Masorah of the Hebrew Bible: An Introductory Reader*. New York: Ktav, 1974.

McDonald, Lee M. *The Biblical Canon: Its Origin, Transmission, and Authority*. Peabody, MA: Hendrickson Publishers, 2007 (3rd printing with corrections, March, 2008).

McDonald, Lee M. *Forgotten Scriptures: The Selection and Rejection of Early Religious Writings*. Louisville, KY: Westminster John Knox Press, 2009.

McDonald, Lee M. and James A. Sanders, eds. *The Canon Debate*. Peabody, MA: Hendrickson Publishers, 2002.

Metzger, Bruce M. *The Canon of the New Testament: Its Origin, Development, and Significance*. Oxford: The Clarendon Press, 1987.

Sanders, James A. *From Sacred Story to Sacred Text*. Philadelphia, PA: Fortress Press, 1987.

Sheppard, Gerald T. "Canon," in *The Encyclopedia of Religion*, Mircea Eliade, Editor in Chief. New York: Macmillan Publishing Co., 1987, Vol. 3, pp. 62–69.

Smith, J. Z. "Canons, Catalogues, and Classics," in *Canonization and Decanonization: Papers Presented to the International Conference of the Leiden Institute for the Study of Religion*. SHR 82, ed. A. van der Kooij and K. van der Toorn. Leiden: E. J. Brill, 1998, pp. 300–307.

Sundberg, Albert C. Jr., *The Old Testament of the Early Church*. Cambridge, MA: Harvard University Press, 1964.

Sundberg, Albert C. Jr. "The Septuagint: The Bible of Hellenistic Judaism," in *The Canon Debate*, ed. Lee M. McDonald and James A. Sanders. Peabody, MA: Hendrickson Publishers, 2002, pp. 68–90.

Theron, Daniel J. *Evidence of Tradition*. Grand Rapids, MI: Baker Book House, 1980.

Ulrich, Eugene. *The Dead Sea Scrolls and the Origins of the Bible*, ed. M. Abegg, P. Flin, SDSSRL. Grand Rapids, MI: Eerdmans, 1999, pp. 51–61, 73–78.

CHAPTER THREE

THE EMERGENCE OF AN OLD TESTAMENT CANON

MOVING FROM SCRIPTURE TO SCRIPTURES

The origin of the Old Testament Scriptures emerges within a context where the notion of sacred literature had moved to the recognition of authoritative written collections of scriptures or sacred books. By the first century CE the notion of scripture was already well established, and so were collections of sacred scriptures even if the boundaries of those collections were still fluid and imprecise at that time. There was no question among the Jews of the first century that the word and will of God had been transmitted through written words, but there is doubt over the scope of those collections. All religious parties of Israel and Jesus himself had accepted multiple Jewish religious texts as sacred scripture. In the previous chapter, we discussed how this notion developed among the Jews, but when did it end, and what was included in the earliest collections and how similar were they to our current Bible?

There is considerable disagreement among biblical scholars over whether the final collection that comprised the Old Testament or Hebrew Bible was complete in the time of Jesus and before. The Law (or Pentateuch) was undoubtedly complete by this time, but it is difficult to establish the full contents of the Prophets, the second major category of Jewish Scriptures. It appears that in the first century CE, generally speaking, all sacred books except the Law (or Pentateuch) were categorized as "the Prophets" as we see throughout the New Testament literature. Many of the books that were later placed in the third part of the Old Testament (the Writings or

Ketubim) were also acknowledged as "Prophets." By the second century, this third category began to take shape for the rabbinic Jews.

It is likely that most of the books that the Jews now call the "Prophets" (*Nebiim*) and the "Writings" (*Ketubim* or *Hagiographa*) were recognized as sacred scripture in the first century CE. That is certainly true for books in those collections that are cited as scripture in the New Testament writings, but likely also for most of the rest of the Old Testament books that are not cited in the New Testament. The third part of the Hebrew Bible, the Writings, was not likely separated from the Prophets before the second century CE and it is unclear whether all of the writings were acknowledged as sacred scripture. Almost a third of the Old Testament writings were not cited in the New Testament and the scriptural status of some of those books that were not cited in the New Testament was often debated among the Jewish rabbis in the second century and later (e.g., Song of Songs, Esther, Ezekiel, and Ecclesiastes). The boundaries between the second and third parts of the Jewish Scriptures were not clear for rabbinic Jews much before the middle to the end of the second century CE. At least, there is no evidence that those boundaries existed before the second century CE.

Also, the sacred books and the categories of those books were not so clearly defined by the Jews living in the diaspora (outside of the Land of Israel and especially those Jews living to the west of the Land of Israel). Those Jews adopted the Greek translation of the Jewish scriptures, but those scriptures were neither limited to the books that now make up the Hebrew Bible nor were they put in the three groups of Jewish scriptures that currently comprise the Hebrew Bible. There is no evidence that the Jews living in the Diaspora accepted the more limited collection of scriptures circulating among the Jews in the Land of Israel and in Babylon in the second century CE and later. In fact, the available evidence points in the opposite direction. The Diaspora Jews were unfamiliar with the Hebrew text of their scriptures and only used the more inclusive Septuagint (Greek) translation of their scriptures including the books widely known among Protestants as the Apocrypha and among the Roman Catholics as the Deutero-canonical scriptures.

The discovery of the Dead Sea Scrolls and other religious texts discovered in the Judean Desert leads us to believe that the sacred writings that comprised the Jewish scriptures were fluid in the first century CE and broader in scope than the current Hebrew Bible or Protestant Old Testament. These other Jewish religious books that were produced between the late fourth century BCE and the first century CE, and widely circulated in the Land of Israel, were welcomed as sacred literature by many the Jews of the first century and by the early Christians as well. What makes it difficult to believe that the sacred books in the Hebrew Bible or Old Testament were in a fixed collection long before the time of Jesus is that a large collection of other Jewish religious texts were produced mostly in the second and first centuries BCE in the Land of Israel and they were welcomed as sacred writings both by Jews and later by Christians in the first century and later. If there was a closed biblical canon present in Israel before the time of Jesus and accepted by the majority of Jews, how could more sacred texts emerge and find acceptance among the Jews in the first centuries BCE and CE?

Again, it is safe to say that most of the books in our current Old Testament scriptures were widely circulated and accepted as sacred scripture by many Jews in the time of Jesus, but there were many *other* sacred books, both apocryphal and pseudepigraphal, that were widely circulated and read as scripture among the various Jewish sects of the first century. These same books also informed the emerging followers of Jesus in the first and second centuries, and some of them remained in the church's sacred literature.

Generally speaking, the scriptures adopted by the Pharisaic Jews were the same ones accepted by Jesus and his followers. That collection, however, was rather fluid in the first three centuries CE and it often included several apocryphal and pseudepigraphal books. It took the churches several centuries before they came to a broad agreement on the scope of their Bible, though there has never been a complete agreement in the churches on the contents of their Old Testament scriptures in the churches. By the fourth and fifth centuries, a significant amount of the literature was no longer included in the Jewish and Christian biblical canons. Today, Protestant Christians accept as the first part of their Bibles the 39 books of the Protestant Old Testament. They accept the same books that comprise the 24 books in the Hebrew Bible canon though in a different sequence and with different divisions.

As we saw in Chapter 2, the canonical processes started with a *story* that gave to the people of Israel a sense of identity, mission, and a reason to continue in the face of overwhelming odds. They had been taken away into captivity, their cities and temple had been destroyed, and the kingdom abolished. The Babylonian captivity and many of the challenges from Israel's neighbors and foreign occupiers of their land would normally have completely destroyed a nation, but that did not happen! The story that gave hope and led the nation to continue in the midst of overwhelming odds grew and often changed to meet the continuing needs of the religious community, but its core was the same. It was eventually accepted as sacred scripture when written down and was at the core of the sacred texts acknowledged by the Jews. This sacred story was also told in more and more religious texts that emerged after the last books of the Old Testament were written, including in several New Testament books. We will now examine a number of the ancient texts that show awareness of collections of sacred Jewish texts and then we will assess their significance for clarifying the origin and development of the Bible.

SCRIPTURE COLLECTIONS IN EARLY JUDAISM

There are numerous places in the Old Testament when a prophet speaking a word of admonition to ancient Israel could have strengthened his case considerably by citing a text (prescription or proscription) from the Law. Amos, for instance, could have made an argument for his reproof of the house of Israel if he had enlisted commandments from the Law to support his accusations against Israel (see 2.6–16; 5.1–6.14; and the five visions in 7.1–9.15), but he did not. Similarly, Hosea might have intensified his argument against Israel if he had cited sacred texts from the Decalogue about having no other gods before the Lord (Exod. 20.4–6), but he did not. Finally, Nathan the prophet could have been more specific about David's murder of Uriah and his adultery with Bathsheba as violations of specific commandments of the Law. He could have cited "you shall not kill" and "you shall not commit adultery" from the *Decalogue*

(Exod. 20.13–14), but, instead, he told David a parable about an injustice done to a disadvantaged man to reinforce the case against David (2 Sam. 12.1–15). He does say that David broke the word of the Lord (12.9), but does not indicate what that word of the Lord was. It is difficult to read into this passage a reference to a codified Law that prohibited such conduct, since there are no other references to such laws in the rest of 1 and 2 Samuel. Even if the Law of Moses did stand *behind* the prophet's message (a disputed assumption), citing a specific violation of the Law would have greatly added to the impact of the message on the writer's audience.

While Joshua appeals to keeping the "Book of the Law" (1.8), references of this sort are rare in Judges. See for instance a reference to the word of the prophet in Judg. 6.8–11, but even there we see no clear recollection of a sacred text or scripture in Judges. There are many examples of silence about a sacred text elsewhere in the Old Testament, but some scholars suggest that this lack of scriptural citation raises the question of whether and how the Law actually functioned in ancient Israel. When did the Old Testament scriptures take on a canonical authority in Israel? Why did they not function as canon more prominently before the reforms of Josiah, where their use becomes more explicit (2 Kgs 22.1–3.25 and 2 Chron. 34.14–33)?

In the earlier stages of Israel, its religion was obviously not yet informed by the scriptural texts that later dominated its religious life, but there is evidence that just prior to the Babylonian captivity and destruction of Jerusalem and its surrounding environs (597–585 BCE), there was a renewal of faith in the Jewish nation prior to the loss of the nation's independence. That renewal came as a result of the discovery of the book of the Law (probably the book of Deuteronomy) by Hilkiah the high priest in the temple (2 Kgs 22.8–23.20) and the subsequent reforms led by King Josiah. At the end of this "first Temple" period, there was a concerted effort to show the relevance of the laws of Moses to the people, and the early stages of acknowledging both them and some of the Prophets as sacred authority in the religious life of Israel (2 Kgs 17.13, perhaps written between 450–400 BCE). With the later reforms of Ezra (ca. 458–390 BCE), however, there is a clear call to observe and obey the "Laws of Moses" (Ezra 10.2–3; Neh. 8.1–8), but it is not clear at that time whether that is equal to the whole Pentateuch (or the first five books of the Old Testament) or simply to the laws of Moses (the Ten Commandments and other commandments).

Later, similar but never equal authority was conferred upon the Prophets or some of them (perhaps by around 400 BCE and possibly earlier). An early reference to the authority of other prophets, as noted above, can be seen in the warning from the Lord to his people. The Lord had frequently warned Israel in the north (the House of Israel headquartered in Samaria) to keep his commandments. When they did not, the Assyrians destroyed their nation and took them captive in 721–720 BCE. The commentator of 2 Kings says that the Lord said to them: "Yet the Lord warned Israel and Judah by every prophet and every seer saying, 'Turn from your evil ways and keep my commandments and my statutes, in accordance with all the law that I commanded your ancestors and that I sent to you by my prophets'" (2 Kgs 17.13). Subsequently, following the destruction of Judah and its capital in Jerusalem, and the nation exiled in Babylon, the authority earlier attributed to the Law was also attributed to other writings, namely the Former Prophets (Joshua, Judges, 1–2 Samuel, 1–2 Kings). Thereafter, authority was gradually attributed to the Latter prophets as well (Isaiah, Jeremiah, Ezekiel, and the Twelve, that is, the twelve Minor Prophets). For example, by ca. 160 BCE, the Prophet Daniel cites an earlier prophet (Jeremiah) as a religious authority (see Dan. 9.2 and compare with Jer. 29.10). In the next section we will look briefly at several of the most important ancient texts that reflect knowledge and authority attributed to several collections of sacred writings.

IMPORTANT TEXTS REFLECTING THE AUTHORITY OF ISRAEL'S SCRIPTURES

Recognition of the value and authority of the books identified in the Law and the Prophets may have begun by the sixth or fifth century BCE, but the clearest evidence of their recognition begins to appear more consistently around 200 to 180 BCE. There was no doubt among most Jews about the sacredness of these two collections of scriptures even though there is little evidence of the contents of the latter (Prophets) until the second century CE. Several other ancient texts were produced in this time frame as well and many if not most were received as sacred scripture by Jews in the first centuries BCE and CE and also later by the early Christians. In the following collection of primary ancient texts, we will first see the praise of the prophets and subsequently several instances referencing their writings also. These 12 significant witnesses to various collections of sacred Jewish literature reflect the progress of recognition of the Jewish scriptures and also the ambiguities that remain.

1. *Sirach* (ca. 180 BCE). The first primary witness for this is Sirach (Jesus ben Sira or Ecclesiasticus), who shows an awareness of the books of Ezekiel, Job, and the "Twelve Prophets." In an important passage (44.1–50.24), *Sirach* refers not so much to written books by the prophets as he does to their heroic deeds. The exception comes in *Sirach* 49.8–10:

It was Ezekiel who saw the vision of glory, which God showed him above the chariot of the cherubim. For God also mentioned Job who held fast to all the ways of justice. May the bones of the Twelve Prophets send forth new life from where they lie, for they comforted the people of Jacob and delivered them with confident hope. (NRSV)

Sirach's longer section on the "History of Famous Men" (*Sir* 44.1–50.24) tells the story of the famous persons or activists in his list. Knowledge of the books of the Former and Latter Prophets and of the book of Job seems obvious in the extended passage. Minimally there is a "canon 1" status or recognition of sacred literature. *Sirach* shows possible awareness of the books of Joshua (46.1–6), Samuel (46.13–47.11), and possibly also the Kings (47.12–49.3), including David and Solomon, as well as mentioning Hezekiah and Isaiah (48.20–25), Josiah (49.1–4); besides Jeremiah (49.6), Ezekiel, Job, and the Twelve Prophets (49.9–10). This suggests that the twelve Minor Prophets may already have been circulating in one volume (scroll) in Israel by this time (200–180 BCE) and possibly the Major Prophets (Isaiah, Jeremiah, and Ezekiel) were circulating in single volumes or scrolls.

2. *Prologue to Sirach*. When Sirach's grandson, or possibly someone else (the authorship is uncertain), wrote the *Prologue* for the

book of the Wisdom of Jesus ben Sirach (Ecclesiasticus) and translated it into Greek for those in Alexandria (ca. 130 BCE), he described the literature that had already been translated for them as the "Law and the Prophets and *the others that followed them.*" Subsequently, while describing the difficulty of translating sacred Hebrew texts into Greek, he states that there are differences that remain in the translation of the Law, Prophets, and some other books, including the translation of his grandfather's work. For our purposes, the text of the most relevant part of that Prologue is italicized as follows:

> Many great teachings have been given to us *through the Law and the Prophets and the others that followed them,* and for these we should praise Israel for instruction and wisdom. Now, those who read the scriptures must not only themselves understand them, but must also as lovers of learning be able through the spoken and written word to help the outsiders. So my grandfather Jesus, who had devoted himself especially to the reading of *the Law and the Prophets and the other books of our ancestors,* and had acquired considerable proficiency in them, was himself also led to write something pertaining to instruction and wisdom, so that by becoming familiar also with his book those who love learning might make even greater progress in living according to the law.
>
> You are invited therefore to read it with goodwill and attention, and to be indulgent in cases where, despite our diligent labor in translating, we may seem to have rendered some phrases imperfectly. For what was originally expressed in Hebrew does not have exactly the same sense when translated into another language. Not only this book, *but even the Law itself, the Prophecies, and the rest of the books differ not a little when read in the original.* (NRSV)

We do not know for certain what these "other books" were, but that has not stopped many scholars from speculating. It is tempting to assume that they were the same books that comprised the third part Hebrew Bible, but they could also include some of the so-called apocryphal or Deutero-canonical, or pseudepigraphal writings that were eventually left behind. The "Prophets" or "Prophecies" could well have included some or all of the books that later comprised the Writings (Ketubim). We simply cannot be sure at this time, but since the grandson was willing to include Sirach's book in the collection of sacred books, how do we know that other noncanonical books were not included in "the others" as well? In the following paragraphs, we will list several other well-known references to collections of sacred texts among the Jews in the time before Jesus, but their identity cannot be clearly established. I will list them here and then offer a few comments on what I think they reveal about the contours of the biblical canon before the time of Jesus.

3. *1 Macc. 1.56–57.* This passage, produced in Israel (ca. 100–64 CE, probably closer to the former), reflects how the Seleucid (Syrian) king, Antiochus IV Epiphanes plundered the temple in Jerusalem in 167 BCE and directed his troops to destroy the sacred books of the law. The question about this text centers on the meaning of the words in italics. The text in question reads:

<54> Now on the fifteenth day of Chislev, in the one hundred forty-fifth year, they erected a desolating sacrilege on the altar of burnt offering. They also built altars in the surrounding towns of Judah, <55> and offered incense at the doors of the houses and in the streets. <56> *The books of the law that they found they tore to pieces and burned with fire.* <57> *Anyone found possessing the book of the covenant,* or anyone who adhered to the law, was condemned to death by decree of the king. (1 Macc. 1.54–57, NRSV)

4. *2 Macc. 2.13–15.* This controversial text is often cited in reference to canon formation. It was written sometime between 104 and 63 BCE (see 2 Macc. 15.37) and reflects a time following the Jewish rebellion when the Jews were back in control of their own land for a brief period of time (until 63 BCE when Pompey invaded Palestine and the Jews were subsequently subject to the will of Rome). It reads as follows:

<13> The same things are reported in the records and in the memoirs of Nehemiah, and also that he founded a library and collected the books about the kings and prophets, and the writings of David, and letters of kings about votive offerings. <14> In the same way *Judas [Maccabeus] also collected all the books that had been lost on account of the war that had come upon us, and they are*

in our possession. <15> So if you have need of them, send people to get them for you. (NRSV. Emphasis added)

5. **4QMMT** (= 4Q394–99 or 4QHalakhic Letter, sometimes called "A Sectarian Manifesto") or *Miqsat Ma'seh ha-Torah* translated as "Some Works of the Law" (ca. 150 BCE). In this recently translated Qumran text there is a reference to three and possibly four categories of sacred writings. The text in question is fragmented and consequently difficult to decipher having several omissions of words in the text that scholars have to supply in the bracketed portions. The elevated numbers in this text refer to the lines in the discovered Hebrew text. A portion of this recently released "epistle" (*Halakhic Letter*), some argue, appears to offer evidence of an early threefold division of the Hebrew canon. There are no two translations of this passage that are exactly the same because of the fragmentary nature of it. Sometimes the gaps in the original text have been supplied with words of the same approximate length that appear to fit the context of the passage. We include the brackets here to show the reader the amount of uncertainty of the text in question. The supplied material is consistent in both translations, but not the same and some of the supplied texts are merely educated guesses. The appropriate portion of this fragmented and reconstructed text in 4Q398 14–17 is as follows:

> for concerning [these things] we give [. . .]to you we have [written] that you must understand the book of Moses [and] the book[s of the pr]ophets and Davi[d . . .] [the annals of] each generation.

And subsequently in 4Q397 14–17, we see this similar comment:

> [. . . for concerning these things we gi]ve [. . .]we have written that you must understand the bo]ok of Moses [and the books of the prophets and David and the annals of each] generation [and in] the book is written [. . .] and the former times . . .

The most significant parts of this reconstructed text and translation are, of course, the references to the "Book of Moses," the "books [or words] of the prophets," "David," and "annals of each generation."

Does the third category, "David," refer to the Psalms as we have them now or to a different collection of psalms such as we find at Qumran that are quite different from the book Psalms, especially in the last third of that collection? Likewise, is there a fourth category, namely "annals of each generation" that refers to the Chronicles, Ezra–Nehemiah and possibly Esther, or to something else? Neither Philo's text (below) nor 4QMMT present a clear statement about the contents of what is later identified in rabbinic writings as the *Ketubim* or *Hagiographa* ("Sacred Writings"), nor do they clarify the contents of the Prophets. They do show us, however, that both the Therapeutae in Egypt and those addressed by this 4QMMT text may have acknowledged some three or four categories of sacred writings. Whether these possible categories are comprised of the writings that were later discovered at Qumran, or if they are like the more precise divisions of the Scriptures mentioned in 4QMMT or the Prologue to Sirach, and even Josephus (see below) is uncertain. We must also be cautious about whether such categories infer a *closed* collection of sacred writings (canon 2) with clearly defined boundaries. Nothing thus far suggests a closed collection of sacred scriptures among the Jews in the first century CE or before.

6. *De Vita Contemplativa (On the Contemplative Life)* **3.25–28**. While discussing a Jewish sect in Egypt known as the Therapeutae, Philo (ca. 20–35 CE) identifies *collections* of the Jewish sacred writings that were read by this sect of Jews in their sacred shrines, though he does not specify the contents of those collections. We can see, however, the possible emergence of a three- or four-part collection of sacred scriptures emerging among the Jewish people. Philo, for example, mentions the holy books of the "Therapeutae" who were similar to but distinct from the Essenes who produced or preserved the now famous Dead Sea Scrolls. He claims that this sect of Jews took with them into their sacred shrines or holy places several sacred texts. The text is question reads as follows:

> (3.25) And in every house there is a sacred shrine which is called the holy place, and the monastery in which they retire by themselves and perform all the mysteries of a holy life, bringing in nothing, neither meat, nor drink, nor anything else which is indispensable towards supplying the necessities of the body, *but*

*studying in that place the laws and the sacred oracles of God enunci-
ated by the holy prophets, and hymns, and psalms, and all kinds of
other things by reason of which knowledge and piety are increased
and brought to perfection.*

(26) Therefore they always retain an imperishable recollection
of God, so that not even in their dreams is any other object ever
presented to their eyes except the beauty of the divine virtues and
of the divine powers. Therefore many persons speak in their sleep,
divulging and publishing the celebrated doctrines and sacred
philosophy. . . .

(28) And the interval between morning and evening is by them
devoted wholly to meditation on and to practice virtue, for they
take up the sacred scriptures and philosophize concerning them,
investigating the allegories of their national philosophy, since
they look upon their literal expressions as symbols of some secret
meaning of nature, intended to be conveyed in those figurative
expressions. (*On the Contemplative Life* 3.25–26, 28, trans.
C. D. Yonge, 1993. Emphasis added)

7. *Lk. 11.48–51 and Matt. 23.34–35.* These New Testament passages are often cited by scholars who press them to say that they
acknowledge a fixed biblical canon that begins with Genesis (Abel,
Gen. 48) and concludes with the last book of the Hebrew Bible
(Zechariah in 2 Chron. 24.20). The passages are as follows:

<48> So you are witnesses and approve of the deeds of your
ancestors; for they killed them, and you build their tombs. <49>
Therefore also the Wisdom of God said, "I will send them prophets and apostles, some of whom they will kill and persecute," <50>
so that this generation may be charged with the blood of all the
prophets shed since the foundation of the world, <51> from the
blood of Abel to the blood of Zechariah, who perished between
the altar and the sanctuary. Yes, I tell you, it will be charged against
this generation. (Lk. 11.49–51, NRSV)

And the parallel passage in Matthew:

Therefore I send you prophets, sages, and scribes, some of whom
you will kill and crucify, and some you will flog in your synagogues

and pursue from town to town, so that upon you may come all the righteous blood shed on earth, from the blood of Zechariah son of Barachiah, whom you murdered between the sanctuary and the altar. (Matt. 23.34–35, NRSV)

Zechariah (see 2 Chron. 24.20–24) was the last canonical prophet to be killed, and since Zechariah was the last prophet to die in 2 Chronicles, so the argument goes, and since 2 Chronicles was the last book in the Hebrew Scriptures, then Jesus had in mind the whole biblical canon by sharing these two examples. The argument continues that Jesus' words in Lk. 11.49–51 were intended to cover the whole of the Hebrew scriptures from Genesis to 2 Chronicles as it appears in the Hebrew Bible. If so, does this not suggest that the third part of the Hebrew Bible was complete when Jesus spoke these words? Interestingly, regardless of whether 2 Chronicles was the first book in the Writings or the last book in the Hebrew Bible, it would not affect the accuracy of the statement made in Lk. 11.49–51. There are simply no other martyred prophets after this time in the third part of the Hebrew Bible. We should be aware that Jerome's Bible canon, which scholars widely recognize was heavily influenced by Judaism, does not conclude with Chronicles. Also, he only has a 22-book canon (no doubt based on the number of letters in the Hebrew alphabet) instead of the more commonly accepted 24-book biblical canon (based on the number of letters in the Greek alphabet).

Interestingly, the most commonly cited Hebrew text today, the famous Aleppo texts from which the Masoretic Text of the Hebrew Bible is derived, places Chronicles at the *beginning* of the third division and Ezra–Nehemiah were placed at the end. Also, the concluding sentences of 2 Chronicles 34 are the same as the opening sentences of Ezra 1. It therefore appears that the writer/editor of this collection of sacred books at least wanted to have Chronicles in first place and Ezra–Nehemiah in last place, even if they were separated in the collection. Jerome's Old Testament translation in the fifth century, the Vulgate, preserves somewhat the threefold division of the Hebrew Bible, though without the designations (Law, Prophets, and Writings) and he has Job in first place in the third category and Chronicles in seventh place followed by Esdras (Ezra and Nehemiah). He concludes with Esther.

8. **Lk. 24.44**. Israel's tripartite canon was only *beginning* to close when the Evangelists were writing their Gospels, that is, at a time when Christianity had essentially ceased being another Jewish sect heavily influenced by Judaism. Even then, however, the boundaries of the third part of the Old Testament canon were not yet firmly fixed. Can "psalms" in what follows refer to the whole of the third part of the Hebrew Bible, the Writings (Ketubim)? Written in 65–70 CE, Luke tells about Jesus' meeting with his disciples after his resurrection and explaining his fate from the Scriptures. In that story he writes: "These are my words that I spoke to you while I was still with you—that everything written about me in the law of Moses, the prophets, and the psalms must be fulfilled" (Lk. 24.44, NRSV).

9. **Josephus, *Against Apion*.** One of the most frequently cited texts in discussions of the development of the Hebrew Bible canon is Josephus' defense of the Jewish people against the earlier verbal attacks by Apion in Egypt (ca. 93–95 CE). In his apology, *Against Apion*, he claims that the Jews had only a 22-book biblical canon and that its contents had been settled for most Jews for a long time. In his defense before Caligula (the Roman Emperor, ca. 100 CE), Josephus claimed that the Jews' sacred scriptures were 22 books in number and he identified them by *classification* or category, not by name. The relevant portions are italicized in the following passage:

> It therefore naturally, or rather necessarily, follows (seeing that with us it is not open to everybody to write the records, and that there is no discrepancy in what is written; seeing that, on the contrary, the prophets alone had this privilege, obtaining their knowledge of the most remote and ancient history through the inspiration which they owed to God, and committing to writing a clear account of the events of their time just as they occurred)— it follows, I say, that we do not possess myriads of inconsistent books, conflicting with each other. *Our books, those which are justly accredited, are but two and twenty, and contain the record of all time.*
>
> Of these, *five are the books of Moses*, comprising the laws and the traditional history from the birth of man down to the death of the lawgiver. This period falls only a little short of three thousand

years. *From the death of Moses until Artaxerxes*, who succeeded Xerxes as king of Persia, *the prophets subsequent to Moses wrote the history of the events of their own times in thirteen books. The remaining four books contain hymns to God and precepts for the conduct of human life.*

From Artaxerxes to our own time the complete history has been written, but has not been deemed worthy of equal credit with the earlier records, *because of the failure of the exact succession of the prophets.*

We have given practical proof of our reverence for our own Scriptures. For although such long ages have now passed, *no one has ventured either to add, or to remove, or to alter a syllable;* and it is an instinct with every Jew, from the day of his birth, to regard them as the decrees of God, to abide by them, and, if need be, cheerfully to die for them. Time and again ere now the sight has been witnessed of prisoners enduring tortures and death in every form in the theaters, rather than utter a single word against the laws and the allied documents. (*Against Apion* 1.37–43, LCL, trans. H. St. J. Thackeray. Emphasis added)

Josephus' division of the 22 books differs considerably from the later threefold division, especially with regard to the contents of the *Hagiographa* in *Baba Bathra* 14a-15b that is cited in full below. On its surface, this passage is one of the strongest arguments in favor of a closed canon of the Hebrew Scriptures in the first century, as some scholars argue, but there are four important observations that should be kept in mind. The first is that Josephus's *twenty-two* book canon did not eventually obtain in Judaism, but rather the *twenty-four* book canon became more popular even in Josephus's own day (see 4 Ezra 14.44–48 cited below). Secondly, and more importantly, it is well known that Josephus was given to exaggeration. The passage listed above was written in an apologetic context, that is, it was written as a vigorous rebuttal not only against Apion, but also against all who denied the antiquity of the Jews and their sacred literature. In it Josephus is contending for and defending the accuracy of the Hebrew Scriptures as reliable history, and not arguing for them as Scripture. Thirdly, Josephus' comment that "no one has ventured to add, or to remove, or to alter a syllable" cannot be defended historically, since it is highly unlikely that Josephus was unaware of the wide range of textual divergence common to the Hebrew, Greek, and Aramaic versions of the Hebrew Scriptures current in first century.

Josephus' frequent exaggeration especially in the defense of Judaism, which is, of course, the context of *Against Apion*, has led some to question his reliability. He is generally considered reliable in the areas of topography and geography of the land of Israel and also in matters of economics, but he is widely recognized as a propagandist in regard to the defense of Judaism against the pagan intellectuals of his day. It is more likely that Josephus's 22-book canon revealed his wish rather than the actual state of affairs regarding the biblical canon in his day. Finally, what Josephus claimed in terms of a fixed collection of Jewish scriptures was clearly not uniform throughout the Jews in the rest of the Roman Empire in the first century and later.

Although Josephus does not specify which books he has in mind for his three- or four-division scripture canon, some of the books can probably be assumed, namely Genesis to Deuteronomy, Joshua to the Kings, and the Psalms or at least parts of the Psalms. It is also possible that he included other books, but their identity is not clear in the text above. It may be that in Josephus' collection Ruth is assumed to be combined with Judges and Lamentations with Jeremiah, but that cannot be established on the basis of Josephus' comments. Such conclusions are inferences drawn from later witnesses to the biblical canon when these matters were of far more interest both to Judaism and to the early Christian Church, but they may not necessarily have been in the mind of Josephus!

We should note that there is no evidence from the Jews of the Diaspora, that is, those Jews living outside of the land of Israel and especially to the west of the land of Israel, that they held to the same collections of Jewish sacred scriptures. As late as the eighth century CE, a geniza (a storage place for old sacred manuscripts) in a Cairo synagogue contained copies of both Tobit and Sirach (Ecclesiasticus) in Hebrew and Aramaic! That suggests that the biblical canon of the rabbinic Jews in the Land of Israel and to the east in Babylon did not find immediate acceptance among the Jews of the Diaspora, especially because they continued to use the Greek translation of the Jewish sacred literature that included a number of the so-called apocryphal books.

Since Josephus claims that the exact succession of prophets ceased with Artaxerxes, the son of Xerxes, whom he identifies in *Antiquities of the Jews* (11.184) as Ahasuerus from the book of Esther, it is obvious why he concluded his biblical canon as early as he did, but this was not the only view about prophecy circulating among the Jews of the first century (see the discussion of *4 Ezra* 14 below). Prophecy was still present in the first and second century for some Jews and for the early Christians and consequently a number of other sacred religious books were produced by the Jews well after some of those that were believed to have been produced before the Spirit supposedly had left Israel. That view, though a popular view among some Jews (see 1 Macc. 14.41, ca. 140 BCE), was not shared by all Jews and certainly not shared by the early Christians or the residents at Qumran. In the 1 Maccabees text, for instance, Simon of the Hasmonean Dynasty (ca. 140 BCE) was chosen as "leader and high priest forever, *until a trustworthy prophet should arise*."

Where did Josephus get his understanding of the biblical canon, if it was not a widely held information in his day? Some scholars have suggested that *Jubilees* 2.23–24 is the first reference to a 22-book scriptural canon, and may stand behind the reference in Josephus, *Against Apion* 1.37–43. The original text of Jubilees was probably written ca. 150 BCE but it has been corrupted in transmission. The earliest texts that we have of the passage do not mention the 22 books. The Jubilees text as we *now* have it reads as follows:

> There were twenty-two chief men from Adam until Jacob, and twenty-two kinds of works were made before the seventh day. The former is blessed and sanctified, and the latter is also blessed and sanctified. One was like the other with respect to sanctification and blessing. And it was granted to the former that they should always be the blessed and sanctified ones of the testimony and the first law just as he had sanctified and blessed sabbath day on the seventh day. (Trans. Wintermute, OTP 2.57)

Several versions of *Jubilees* 2.23–24, including the Ethiopic text of that book, have survived in antiquity. The earliest form of the text that we possess, however, does not have the reference to a 22 sacred book collection. The reference may have been an insertion placed in the text during a time when the notion of a 22-book canon had subsided in Israel, but the tradition of the 22 books was well known among the church fathers, who frequently referred to it. For example, Origen referred to it according to Eusebius (*Ecclesiastical History* 6.26.1, 2). If the tradition were a late first-century invention, it is easy to see how a reference to it by Josephus would impact Christian writers of the fourth century who had high respect for Josephus and continued to publish his works.

They apparently passed it along in the Church longer than it continued in the rabbinic traditions. It is likely, therefore, that the 22-book canon did not originate with Josephus, and that he may have depended on an earlier form of the text of *Jubilees*, but this is not obvious or certain. Whatever the source of this 22-book canon, however, it is difficult to affirm by the available evidence that Josephus's scriptural canon was as widespread and inviolable as he claims. For example, Epiphanius (315–403 CE) in his *On Weights and Measures twenty-two* mentions the sacred number 22 that circulated in tradition in Israel and he includes the reference to the 22 books of the Hebrew Scriptures. But again, the earliest form of this text from Qumran does not include the 22 books.

10. **4 Ezra 14.22–48** (or 2 Esdras). *4 Ezra* is a pseudonymous Jewish writing written around 90 CE and later interpolated by Christians who likely added chapters 1–2 and 15–16. The writer tells the story of how Ezra miraculously recovered the scriptures of Israel following the return of the Jews from Babylon and the process of the recovery involved God inspiring the scribes to write down the books that had been lost. The books mentioned included 24 books to be read by all Jews, but also an additional collection of 70 sacred writings that were reserved for those who were "wise." The passage reads as follows:

<22> "If then I have found favor with you, send the holy spirit into me, and I will write everything that has happened in the world from the beginning, the things that were written in your law, so that people may be able to find the path, and that those who want to live in the last days may do so." <23> He [God] answered me and said, "Go and gather the people, and tell them not to seek you for forty days. <24> But prepare for yourself many writing tablets,

and take with you Sarea, Dabria, Selemia, Ethanus, and Asiel—these five, who are trained to write rapidly; <25> and you shall come here, and I will light in your heart the lamp of understanding, which shall not be put out until what you are about to write is finished. <26> And when you have finished, some things you shall make public, and some you shall deliver in secret to the wise; tomorrow at this hour you shall begin to write."

<27> Then I went as he commanded me, and I gathered all the people together, and said, <28> "Hear these words, O Israel. <29> At first our ancestors lived as aliens in Egypt, and they were liberated from there <30> and received the law of life, which they did not keep, which you also have transgressed after them. <31> Then land was given to you for a possession in the land of Zion; but you and your ancestors committed iniquity and did not keep the ways that the Most High commanded you. <32> And since he is a righteous judge, in due time he took from you what he had given. <33> And now you are here, and your people are farther in the interior. <34> If you, then, will rule over your minds and discipline your hearts, you shall be kept alive, and after death you shall obtain mercy. <35> For after death the judgment will come, when we shall live again; and then the names of the righteous shall become manifest, and the deeds of the ungodly shall be disclosed. <36> But let no one come to me now, and let no one seek me for forty days."

<37> So I took the five men, as he commanded me, and we proceeded to the field, and remained there. <38> And on the next day a voice called me, saying, "Ezra, open your mouth and drink what I give you to drink." <39> So I opened my mouth, and a full cup was offered to me; it was full of something like water, but its color was like fire. <40> I took it and drank; and when I had drunk it, my heart poured forth understanding, and wisdom increased in my breast, for my spirit retained its memory, <41> and my mouth was opened and was no longer closed. <42> Moreover, the Most High gave understanding to the five men, and by turns they wrote what was dictated, using characters that they did not know. They sat forty days; they wrote during the daytime, and ate their bread at night. <43> But as for me, I spoke in the daytime and was not silent at night.

<44> So during the forty days, ninety-four books were written. <45> And when the forty days were ended, the Most High spoke to me, saying, "Make public the twenty-four books that you wrote first, and let the worthy and the unworthy read them; <46> but keep the seventy that were written last, in order to give them to the wise among your people. <47> For in them is the spring of understanding, the fountain of wisdom, and the river of knowledge." <48> And I did so. (NRSV)

This text shows that *twenty-four* books of the Hebrew Bible, whose identity is not clear, were acknowledged as holy books at the end of the first century CE. The number is a sacred number that reflects divine participation at the least, but it is also obvious from that passage that there were "seventy" other sacred books given to Ezra and his scribes by divine revelation the identity of which is also not clear to us but they were also deemed to be inspired by God and authoritative, even if they were reserved for the "wise." The fact that it took "forty days" (14.36) to complete the whole assignment of copying the lost sacred books, including the 70 books, and that God transmitted all of them (4 Ezra 14.19–48) to Ezra and his scribes provides evidence of the belief and acceptance of the sacredness of that collection. The "forty days" has widespread biblical precedence for the presence and activity of God (days of the flood on the earth, Moses at Mt. Sinai, Elijah at Mt. Horeb, the temptation of Jesus, time of Jesus' appearances in Acts 1, etc.). The number "seventy" for the special books for the wise in the 4 Ezra text reserved points to their sacredness and spiritual insight for the readers. If they were not considered scriptural or inspired, would the author of 4 Ezra have claimed that God transmitted them to Ezra and his scribes (14.22–26)? His claim that these additional books were to be given only to the wise among them, "for in them [the seventy books] is the spring of understanding, the fountain of wisdom, and the river of knowledge" (14.48, NRSV), reflects clear affirmation of their authority.

Many early Christians welcomed 4 Ezra into their sacred collections, and even made significant additions to it by transforming parts of its legend into a Christian text. This would be strange indeed, as some scholars argue, if the contents of the Jewish biblical canon had been settled well before the time of Jesus and if Jesus had given to his disciples a closed collection of sacred scriptures.

11. **Melito.** Melito was bishop of Sardis (ca. 170–180 CE), who was asked by a member of his church about the contents of the scriptures accepted by the church and remarkably, he did not know the answer and so he made a trip to the Land of Israel to find out. It is unthinkable that the bishop of a large church at the end of the second century would not know the scope of the church's sacred scriptures if that were known in his day and settled well before the time of Jesus. Eusebius later (ca. 320–330 CE) relates this story and goes on to list the books in the collection that he discovered on his journey. The list does not include Esther and it strangely includes the apocryphal book, the *Wisdom of Solomon*. The list is as follows:

> . . . when I came to the east and reached the place where these things were preached and done, and learned accurately the books of the Old Testament, I set down the facts and sent them to you. These are their names: five books of Moses, Genesis, Exodus, Numbers, Leviticus, Deuteronomy, Joshua the son of Nun, Judges, Ruth, four books of Kingdoms, two books of Chronicles, the Psalms of David, the Proverbs of Solomon and his Wisdom, Ecclesiastes, the Song of Songs, Job, the prophets Isaiah, Jeremiah, the Twelve in a single book, Daniel, Ezekiel, Ezra. From these I have made extracts and compiled them in six books. (Eusebius, *H.E.* 4.26.14, LCL)

One of the values of this text is that it reveals the fluidity of the Old Testament Scriptures of the church at the end of the second century. Again, if such matters had been settled for the Jews and Christians in the time of Jesus or before and that they looked like the scriptures that are in the current Hebrew Bible and Protestant Old Testament, then we have to conclude without justification that the disciples of Jesus or their successors lost track of that collection. That seems more unthinkable than to say that the Christian Old Testament and the Jewish Hebrew Bible had not yet been finalized and that some fluidity in the collection continued well past the time of Jesus. If there was a clear cut collection whose parameters were well known in the first century, as some scholars contend, then we have to find some way to account for its loss in subsequent years and for the fact that the church has never agreed on the scope of its Old Testament canon. I will refer to this text again in the next chapter.

12. *b. Baba Bathra* **14b.** A rabbinic text, *b. Baba Bathra* 14b, is the first Jewish tradition that identifies specifically the books of the Hebrew Bible. This tradition had its origin *in Babylon* and is commonly acknowledged as a *baraita,* (pl., *baraitot*) an Aramaic term meaning "external" referring to a Jewish *tannaitic* text or tradition (ca. 10 BCE to ca. 200 CE) that was not included in the Mishnah.[1] *Baraitot* are often accorded special authority in the Babylonian Talmud[2] equal to that of the Mishnah. The *Baba Bathra* 14b text was written in Babylon sometime around the middle (likely) to the end of the second century CE (less likely). Significantly, this tradition was not included in the Mishnah, which suggests that by the end of the second century CE it had not yet obtained sufficient prominence among the rabbinic Jews either in Israel or Babylon where it originated to be included in the Mishnah. The passage in question here is preserved only in the Babylonian Talmud. While a few scholars date the text before the time of Josephus (end of the first century CE), more cautiously, others say that it was written no later than 200 CE. It is a very important reference because it clearly identifies for the first time the writings that make up the 24-book collection of the Jewish sacred writings and it assumes a threefold division of the biblical canon.

The Law is not mentioned in this text, but is clearly assumed in the context. This is the first text that clearly identifies the three-part collection that includes the 24-book collection of sacred writings that formed the Hebrew Bible. It reads as follows:

Our Rabbis taught: the order of the Prophets is, Joshua, Judges, Samuel, Kings, Jeremiah, Ezekiel, Isaiah, and the twelve Minor Prophets. Let us examine this. Hosea came first, as it is written (Hos. 1.2): *God spoke first to Hosea.* But did God speak first to Hosea? Were there not many prophets between Moses and Hosea? R. Johanan (250–290), however, has explained that [what it means is that] he was the first of the four prophets who prophesied at that period, namely, Hosea, Isaiah, Amos, and Micah. Should not then Hosea come first?—Since his prophecy is written along with those of Haggai, Zechariah and Malachi, and Haggai, Zechariah and Malachi came at the end of the prophets, he is reckoned with them. But why should he not be written separately and placed first?—Let us see again. Isaiah was prior to Jeremiah and Ezekiel. Then why should not Isaiah be placed first?—Because the book of Kings ends with a record of destruction and Jeremiah speaks throughout of destruction and Ezekiel commences with destruction and ends with consolation and Isaiah is full of consolation; therefore we put destruction next to destruction and consolation next to consolation. [Our Rabbis taught:] The order of the Hagiographa is Ruth, the book of Psalms, Job, Proverbs, Ecclesiastes, Song of Songs, Lamentations, Daniel and the Scroll of Esther, Ezra and Chronicles. Now on the view that Job lived in the days of Moses, should not the book of Job come first?—We do not begin with a record of suffering. But Ruth also is a record of suffering?—It is a suffering with a sequel [of happiness], as R. Johanan said: Why was her name called Ruth?—Because there issued from her David who replenished the Holy One, blessed be He, with hymns and praises.

Who wrote the Scriptures?—Moses wrote his own book and the portion of Balaam and Job. Joshua wrote the book which bears his name and [the last] eight verses of the Pentateuch. Samuel wrote the book which bears his name and the book of Judges and Ruth. David wrote the book of Psalms, including in it the work of the ten elders, namely Adam, Melchizedek, Abraham, Moses, Heman, Yeduthun, Asaph, and the three sons of Korah. Jeremiah wrote the book which bears his name, the book of Kings, and Lamentations. Hezekiah and his colleagues wrote (mnemonic YMSHQ) Isaiah, Proverbs, the Song of Songs and Ecclesiastes. The Men of the Great Assembly wrote (mnemonic QNDG) Ezekiel, the Twelve Minor Prophets, Daniel and the scroll of Esther. Ezra wrote the book that bears his name and the genealogies of the book of Chronicles up to his own time. This confirms the opinion of Rab (220–250), since Rab Judah (250–290) has said in the name of Rab: Ezra did not leave Babylon to go up to Eretz Yisrael until he had written his own genealogy. Who then finished it [the book of Chronicles]?—Nehemiah the son of Hachaliah. (Trans. Leiman, 52–53)

The books identified in this passage constitute the biblical canon that finally obtained canonical status in rabbinic Judaism, probably first in Babylon, the place of its origin, and subsequently in the Land of Israel. However, even after the writing of this text there was debate and discussion among the rabbis about the books on the "fringe" of the biblical canon. These books include the Song of Songs, Ecclesiastes, Esther, Ezekiel, and Proverbs and, although their sanctity was never questioned among the early rabbis, inclusion of them in the sacred Jewish collection apparently was. We should also note here that Wisdom of Jesus ben Sira (Sirach, or Ecclesiasticus) was initially included as sacred scripture by some rabbis, but only later rejected. In regard to the *Baba Bathra* text above, it appears that it was not mentioned in the Mishnah because in the second century it had not obtained sufficient or widespread support among the Jews either in the Land of Israel or in Babylon, at least not before the closure and codification of the Mishnah at the end of the second century CE and the beginning of the third.

No one can dispute that *some* second-century sages accepted as canon the list of books in *Baba Bathra* 14b as a fixed list of sacred writings among the Jews, even though we have no evidence that other Jews drew the same conclusions. In the second century this particular *baraita* was most likely a minority view among the Jews or simply an insignificant matter *at that time.* In the second century CE, apart from Melito's similar but not identical list of Old Testament books (see above), this *baraita* has no parallels.

THE DEAD SEA SCROLLS AND THE OLD TESTAMENT CANON

For more than 60 years, biblical scholars and the world community have known of the very important discovery of a collection of ancient manuscripts discovered in the vicinity of a community of Essene Jews living at Qumran on the northwest shore of the Dead Sea. This collection is regularly identified as the Dead Sea Scrolls, though more recently, scholars have studied alongside this corpus of manuscripts the discovery of several other smaller collections of ancient manuscripts from approximately the same time and general vicinity. As a result, scholars of these other Judaean discoveries now regularly identify all of these collections as "Discoveries of the Judaean

Desert" (or DJD) because they have included more recent discoveries of Jewish religious texts at Masada, Naḥal Ḥever, and Muraba'at that also reflect the status of sacred texts among the Jews in the time of Jesus and before. In terms of the Dead Sea Scrolls that were discovered in 11 caves in the vicinity of Qumran between 1947 and 1952 on the northwest shore of the famous Dead Sea, almost three-fourths of the more than 900 manuscripts discovered there are of books that did *not* find a place in the *later* collection of books that comprise the Hebrew Bible or the Christian Protestant Old Testament. The exact number of manuscripts discovered at Qumran remains imprecise since many of the manuscripts are in very small fragments, some of which may represent one or several books and consequently, it is not possible yet to be more precise.

Of those approximately 900 or more books, only around 200 of them are copies of biblical books. The rest are copies of noncanonical books. On what basis can we say that the earlier collections listed above contained none of these so-called noncanonical books? Except in the two cases of Melito of Sardis and the *b. Baba Bathra 14b* listed above and both stemming from the second century CE, we have no idea what was in any of the collections listed in the previous section. Since the number "twenty-four" is used in reference to sacred books in the *4 Ezra* 14.22–28 text cited above, we can assume that some Jews, like Josephus (*Against Apion* 1.43–47), had some agreement on scope of their sacred books, though in the *4 Ezra* passage the status of the other "seventy" books is not clear but certainly not negligible. Historically, Melito, and the *Baba Bathra* texts are the first to identify clearly the specific books included in the Jewish Scriptures and Christian Old Testament. What is also important here is that they identify similar but not exactly the same books in their collections.

The other noncanonical books discovered at or near Qumran and placed in sacred collections by the Essenes, often placed side-by-side with canonical books in the nearby caves, encourages caution about identifying which books were part of a sacred scripture and which were not. To put it in the reverse, while there were 200 fragments of Old Testament books discovered in the vicinity of Qumran, including fragments of all the books of the Old Testament except Esther, this does not rule out the significance of the more than 700 portions of books that were not eventually placed in the Hebrew Bible canon. On what basis can we say that none of the latter was included in any of the collections mentioned in the previous section? It is an argument from silence, though not an inappropriate one, and we simply do not know what was in the earlier noted collections.

Likewise, there is nothing to suggest that the sacred books valued by the Therapeutae in Egypt have exactly the same books as the ones that now comprise the Hebrew Bible or the Protestant Old Testament canon. Scholars of antiquity sometimes make unwarranted leaps in logic here and more caution is needed. We simply do not know what was in the previous collections, but we are aware of the books in the Dead Sea Scrolls and the other discoveries of the Judaean Desert. Most of those books were imported into Qumran from elsewhere and only a few of them can be considered sectarian, that is, specifically produced by the Essene Jews at Qumran. If they came from elsewhere, then it is likely that other Jews in the time of Jesus in the Land of Israel were aware of this literature and found it important enough to make multiple copies. Because some Christians were also aware of and made use of this literature, it is likely that we have to postpone notions of an early widespread biblical canon among the Jews in the time of Jesus. The manuscripts that were copied there date from approximately 150 BCE to 68 CE, but some manuscripts may be dated earlier and were transported to Qumran by the Essenes.

With the exceptions of Josephus (*Against Apion*) and the *Baba Bathra* 14b text, nothing in the texts cited above suggests a *closed* or *fixed* collection of sacred scriptures among the Jews in the first century CE or before, nor do they identify what was in their collections. Those who want to find a closed biblical canon among the Jews in the first century during or before the time of Jesus should be reminded of the reasonable dictum of the Jewish scholar, Jacob Neusner, who has often challenged scholars over the years with the words: "what you cannot show, you do not know!"

Some scholars have rightly observed that all of the books of the Old Testament except Esther and Nehemiah were found at Qumran and only one book of the Apocrypha (*Tobit*) was found, but drawing conclusions about the scope of the later Hebrew Bible from this is misleading. There were many other books found there and there may have been reasons for excluding Esther. Since Ezra and Nehemiah often circulated in one book and since the copy of Ezra that was found is fragmentary, we cannot be sure that Nehemiah was purposefully excluded. Similarly, only a small fragment of Chronicles was discovered at Qumran. Following the wisdom of Harvard professor, Frank More Cross, we could also say: "an additional hungry worm, and Chronicles, too, would have been missing!"

No Dead Sea Scroll scholar claims that all of the books that were *originally* stored in caves at Qumran have been found, nor even that all of the caves have been discovered, though extensive excavations have been made in the area. There could be a "cave 12" (or more) that will be discovered someday and it may contain many more surprises, but we are far from certain that the collection that now comprises the Dead Sea Scrolls is all that was there originally. Regularly, manuscripts or fragments of manuscripts are placed on the international market for sale that came from the vicinity of Qumran or elsewhere. In recent years several significant manuscripts have been sold and are likely be published in the near future. While we do not have the complete picture of all the books that were at Qumran in the first century or in that vicinity, the manuscripts that have been discovered in the caves that we know about lead us to a different story than what was earlier believed about the scope of the Jewish scriptures in the time of Jesus.

Some of the other documents found at or near Qumran, include the *Damascus Document* (CD), the *Manual of Discipline* (1QS), the *Messianic Rule* (1QSa), *Book of Blessings* (1QSb), *War Scroll* (4QM), the *Hymn Scroll* (*Hodayot*), the *Genesis Apocryphon*, and the *Temple Scroll*. Besides these, portions of Sirach, *Epistle of Jeremy*, *Jubilees*, *1 Enoch*, and *Testaments of the Twelve Patriarchs*. The variety of literature discovered there suggests that it is not possible to draw firm conclusions about the boundaries of the Jewish scriptures *at that time*—or that the sacred collection was considerably larger than what was obtained later in Judaism and in Christianity.

The noncanonical books found at Qumran that were not later included in the later *Tanakh*[3] (the Jewish Bible), or the Old Testament of the Protestant churches, appear alongside the biblical books with little or no distinction. *Some* of the biblical books discovered in the caves at Qumran were written with an older or earlier Hebrew script (often called the "*paleo*-Hebrew" script, or the early Hebrew style of writing before the adoption of Aramaic "square" script that the Jews brought back with them from Babylonian). This was the preferred script for some of the biblical books, especially the books of the Law (Genesis, Exodus, Leviticus, Numbers, and Deuteronomy), but only 12 of the books discovered at Qumran are in this script. These 12 paleo-Hebrew texts were also copied more carefully and this suggests correctly that at Qumran, a priority was given to the books of the Law over other books. This script is seen in the citations in the 4QMMT passage cited above, but *generally* there is no distinction in script between the other books of the Hebrew Bible and the so-called nonbiblical books. Other than that, it is difficult to distinguish biblical books from nonbiblical books among the Dead Sea Scrolls. It is more likely that all of this literature at Qumran was viewed as sacred texts for that community.

Nothing discovered at Qumran suggests that the residents there adopted a three-part canon or three collections of the Jewish sacred texts (Law, Prophets, and Writings). The closest that we have in the first century comes in the Luke's Gospel when after Jesus' resurrection, he appeared to his disciples and said: "These are my words that I spoke to you while I was still with you—that everything written about me in the law of Moses, the prophets, and the psalms must be fulfilled" (Lk. 24.44, NRSV). This Gospel may have been written as early as 65–70 CE and may suggest an emerging third part of the Jewish scriptures at that time, but not necessarily. Whether the last category ("psalms") should be taken to include all of the books that later came to be known as the Psalms of the Old Testament and the Hebrew Bible is not clear. Some scholars have also tried to make "psalms" in this passage refer to the whole of the third part of the later Hebrew Bible, namely the Writings, but there is no evidence for that in Luke or early Christianity. The references to the "psalms" or "David" in 4QMMT, Philo (*Contemplative Life* 3.25), and Lk. 24.44, probably refer only to "psalms" but which ones we do not know. It is not clear, however, that "David" refers to psalms rather than simply to the deeds or activities of David.

The Gospels of Matthew and Mark indicate that Jesus cited the book of Daniel (see, for example, Dan. 4.26 in Matt. 4.17 and Dan. 7.13 in Mk 14.62), and Daniel was considered a part of the

Prophets in the Septuagint (or LXX) and only *later* was placed in the Writings section of the Hebrew Bible in the second century CE. Some scholars have advanced the notion that if Jesus referred to one part of the Writings (Daniel), then he must have recognized the whole of it. That argument can only have merit if we can show that the Writings existed as a fixed collection in the time of Jesus, and thus far, no one has demonstrated that. As we noted above, that third category and its contents are *first* referred to in the middle to late second century in the Babylonian text known as *b. Baba Bathra* 14b. When Jesus referred to the "psalms" in Lk. 24.44, there is no evidence that he knew and approved all of the other literature later placed in the Writings. Some scholars contend that only the book at the beginning of a larger collection needed to be listed in order for it to refer to all of that collection, but again, there is no evidence of this in the New Testament or in the time of Jesus. We should note that Jesus favored citations from the Old Testament books of Deuteronomy, Isaiah, and the Psalms. There is no indication that "psalms" otherwise covered everything else in that later collection.

If the "psalms" did include the rest of the third part of the Hebrew Bible, and if it was so understood in the same was in the first century (these are big and unsubstantiated if's), then it could be argued that Jesus endorsed the whole Hebrew biblical canon. The problem with this view, of course, is that there is no evidence that "psalms" ever referred to anything more than psalms in the first century. There are no other references in the time of Jesus or in the New Testament to three categories of sacred scripture. In the first century CE, the categories Law and the Prophets were the most common designations for Israel's sacred scriptures, not only in Israel, but also in the New Testament even though what they contained at that time is not altogether clear.

AN ASSESSMENT OF THE EVIDENCE

There are many scholars who continue to argue that the Hebrew Scriptures were completed no later than the second century BCE, and claim that this collection was endorsed by Jesus and accepted by the earliest Christians. This, however, does not square with what we know about Jesus' citations and allusions to biblical and nonbiblical literature. We know that some early Christians were informed by a number of the apocryphal and even pseudepigraphal Jewish writings as in the case of Jude citing a pseudepigraphal writing (Jude 14 citing *1 Enoch* 1.10). Interestingly, as late as 200 CE Tertullian (*De cultu Fem. 1.3*) cites Jude 14 to support the scriptural authority of *1 Enoch*! In other words, for Tertullian, if Jude cited it then it must be scripture! A major difficulty with the notion that Jesus passed on to his disciples a fixed biblical canon equal to our current Protestant Old Testament is the widespread use of apocryphal and pseudepigraphal writings in the New Testament (where considerable familiarity is shown) and apostolic fathers and other church fathers after them who often cite them as scripture. Some scholars account for this phenomenon by claiming that the early church fathers simply lost the biblical canon that Jesus left to them, but since the early Christians were so inclined to pass on the traditions of Jesus both orally and in written form, and since they never mention that Jesus gave to his disciples a biblical canon and they never attribute one to him, it is reasonable to conclude that he never gave them one. Also, since there is no consistency in the order of the writings in the third division of the Hebrew Bible it is difficult to argue that such a category existed in the time of Jesus.

Similarly, the continuing imprecision in the scope of the Hebrew Bible as late as the second and early third century is seen in the disputes reflected in the Mishnah over the sacredness of the Song of Songs and Ecclesiastes (*Qohelet*). For instance, see how the Mishnah tractate, *Yadayim* 3.2–5, describes what is clean and unclean and related this to the controversy of which writings are sacred and which are not.

Yad. 3.2

    A. Whatever imparts unfitness to heave offering imparts uncleanness to hands, putting them into the second remove of uncleanness.

    B. "One hand imparts uncleanness to the second," the words of R. Joshua.

    C. And sages say, "That which is unclean in the second remove does not put [something else into uncleanness at] the second remove."

D. He said to them, "And do not sacred scriptures, unclean in the second remove, impart uncleanness to hands?"

E. They said to him, "They do not draw inferences about rulings of the Torah from rulings of scribes, nor about rulings of scribes from rulings of Torah, nor about rulings of scribes from rulings of scribes."

Yad. 3.3

A. The Straps of *tefillin* [while they are still attached] to the *tefillin* impart uncleanness to hands.

B. R. Judah says, "The straps of *tefillin* [under any circumstances] do not impart uncleanness to hands."

Yad. 3.4

A. The blank spaces in a scroll, whether above or below or at the beginning or at the end impart uncleanness to hands.

B. R. Judah says, "That which is at the end does not impart uncleanness unless one will affix the roller to it."

Yad 3.5

A. A scroll which was erased and in which remain eighty-five letters—

B. such as the paragraph, *And it came to pass when the ark set forward* [Num. 10.35f.],

C. imparts uncleanness to hands.

D. A scroll in which eighty-five letters are written,

E. such as the paragraph, *And it came to pass when the ark set forward,*

F. imparts uncleanness to hands.

G. All sacred scriptures impart uncleanness to hands.

H. The Song of Songs and Qohelet [Ecclesiastes] impart uncleanness to hands.

I. R. Judah says, "The Song of Songs imparts uncleanness to hands, but as to Qohelet there is dispute."

J. R. Yose says, "Qohelet does not impart uncleanness to hands, but as to Song of Songs there is dispute."

K. Rabbi Simeon says, "Qohelet is among the lenient rulings of the House of Shammai and strict rulings of the House of Hillel."

L. Said R. Simeon b. Azzai, I have a tradition from the testimony of the seventy-two elders,

M. on the day on which they seated R. Eleazer b. Azariah in the session,

N. that the Song of Songs and Qohelet do impart uncleanness to hands.

O. Said R. Aqiba, "Heaven forbid! No Israelite man ever disputed concerning Song of Songs that it imparts uncleanness to hands."

P. For the entire age is not so worthy as the day on which the Song of Songs was given to Israel

Q. For all the scriptures are holy, but the Song of Songs is holiest of all.

R. "And if they disputed, they disputed only concerning Qohelet."

S. Said R. Yohanan b. Joshua the son of R. Aqiba's father in law, according to the words of Ben Azzai, "Indeed did they dispute, and indeed did they come to a decision." (Neusner, *The Mishnah: A New Translation* 1126–1127)

We should also observe that the three-part division that has finally obtained in the organization of the Hebrew Bible (Law, Prophets, and Writings) is not found in any Greek translation of the Hebrew Scriptures (the LXX). The Greek Bible was the Bible of the majority of the early Christian churches, especially those that spoke only Greek. It was also cited in over 94 percent of the instances of the New Testament's use or citation of the Old Testament writings. Since it is clear that the early Christians accepted the Jewish Scriptures (those currently cited as scripture in the time of Jesus) as their Old Testament, it is important to know that the Christians did not accept the Jewish three-part organization of those Scriptures. Why? If it was popular among the Jews in the first century when Christians and Jews still met together, why did the Christians not follow it? There is nothing wrong with the Jewish three-part division of their scriptures, even though it does communicate a different message than the order and divisions of books in the Christian Bibles. The point is obvious in that had the Jewish three part biblical canon been in place at the time of Jesus or before, it would be odd if the early churches made no use of it. Why would the early Christians make use of the same books, but not the same divisions and sequence of books if the order in the Hebrew Bible had been in place and widely accepted in the time of Jesus as some scholars argue?

In regard to Josephus' claim that the biblical canon was well established and any Jew would know it and would even die for it, one cannot imagine why Melito, bishop of Sardis, would have made a long trip to the Land of Israel to discover the contents of the biblical canon if he could have walked across the street and asked a local Jew in Sardis at the end of the second century. Evidently, he could not find sufficient knowledge of the scope of the biblical canon in his own city to answer the questions about it, so he therefore made that special trip to the east to discover the contents of the Hebrew Scriptures/Christian Old Testament.

There is no evidence that the Jews living in the diaspora held to the same collection of sacred texts adopted by the rabbinic Jews of the second century and later. As late as the eighth century CE, a geniza in a Cairo synagogue contained copies of both Tobit and Sirach (Ecclesiasticus) in Hebrew and Aramaic! That suggests that the biblical canon of the rabbinic Jews in the Land of Israel and to the east in Babylon did not find immediate acceptance among the Jews of the diaspora, especially those who continued to use the Greek translation of the Jewish sacred literature that included a number of the so-called apocryphal books.

If the church had received a closed biblical canon from Jesus, it would be especially odd and highly improbable that a bishop of a prominent church at the end of the second century, Melito of Sardis, would not know which books were in his Bible! This would be strange indeed if the matter had been settled for a long time in the church and if such a closed or stable collection of sacred literature had been recognized by Jesus and handed on to his disciples. It would not be so strange, however, if the matter of the contents of the Christian Old Testament scriptures was still unresolved in the time of Jesus and throughout the first century before the Jews and Christians had parted ways.

In light of the above evidence, it appears that the scope of the Old Testament as it is now constituted was not the scope of the Jewish scriptures in the time of Jesus. It is also apparent that discussions of the contents or scope of a biblical canon were not raised in that day. Had the contents of a biblical canon, as we now know it, been of considerable interest to Jesus or his earliest followers, it seems reasonable that at least one tradition about its contents or some discussion of it would have been preserved in the early churches. It has not. It is theoretically possible that such a canon may have been so well established that no one ever thought to defend it or discuss it, a claim made by a few biblical scholars, but the surviving historical evidence points in the opposite direction. In the next chapter we will focus on the closing of the Old Testament canon.

FURTHER READING

Ackroyd, P. R. and C. F. Evans, eds. *The Cambridge History of the Bible: From Beginnings to Jerome*. Vol. 1. Cambridge, England/New York: Cambridge University Press, 1970.

Auwer, J.–M. and H. J. De Jonge, eds. *The Biblical Canons*. BETL clxiii. Leuven: Leuven University Press, 2003.

Barr, James. *Holy Scripture: Canon, Authority, Criticism*. Philadelphia, PA: The Westminster Press, 1983.

Barrera, Julio Trebolle. *The Jewish Bible and the Christian Bible: An Introduction to the History of the Bible*. Trans. Wilfred G. E. Watson. Leiden, New York and Köln: E. J. Brill; Grand Rapids, MI: Eerdmans, 1998.

Barton, John. *Holy Writings, Sacred Text: The Canon in Early Christianity*. Louisville, KY: Westminster John Knox Press, 1997.

Barton, John. *How the Bible Came to Be*. Louisville, KY: Westminster John Knox Press, 1997.

Beckwith, Roger. *The Old Testament of the New Testament Church and Its Background in Early Judaism*. Grand Rapids, MI: Eerdmans, 1985.

Bruce, F. F. *The Canon of Scripture*. Downers Grove, IL: InterVarsity Press, 1988.

Campenhausen, Hans von. *The Formation of the Christian Bible*. Trans. J. A. Baker. Philadelphia, PA: Fortress, 1972.

Chapman, Stephen B. *The Law and the Prophets: A Study in Old Testament Canon Formation*. Forschungen zum Alten Testament 27. Tübingen: Mohr Siebeck, 2000.

Childs, Brevard S. *Biblical Theology of the Old and New Testament: Theological Reflection on the Christian Bible*. Philadelphia, PA: Fortress Press, 1993.

Childs, Brevard S. *Introduction to the Old Testament as Scripture*. Philadelphia, PA: Fortress Press, 1979.

Cross, Frank Moore. *From Epic to Canon: History and Literature in Ancient Israel.* Baltimore, MD and London: Johns Hopkins University Press, 1998.

Davies, Philip R. *Scribes and Schools: The Canonization of the Hebrew Scriptures.* Library of Ancient Israel. Louisville, KY: Westminster John Knox Press, 1998.

Ellis, Earle E. *The Old Testament in Early Christianity: Canon and Interpretation in the Light of Modern Research.* Grand Rapids, MI: Baker Book House, 1991.

Jones, Barry Alan. *The Formation of the Book of the Twelve: A Study in Text and Canon.* SBL Dissertation series 149. Atlanta, GA: Scholars Press, 1995.

Leiman, Sid. Z. *The Canon and Masorah of the Hebrew Bible: An Introductory Reader.* New York: Ktav, 1974.

McDonald, Lee M. *The Biblical Canon: Its Origin, Transmission, and Authority.* Peabody, MA: Hendrickson Publishers, 2006.

McDonald, Lee M. *Forgotten Scriptures: The Selection and Rejection of Early Religious Writings.* Louisville, KY: Westminster John Knox Press, 2009.

McDonald, Lee M. and James A. Sanders, eds. *The Canon Debate.* Peabody, MA: Hendrickson Publishers, 2002.

Miller, John W. *The Origins of the Bible: Rethinking Canon History.* Theological Inquiries. New York: Paulist Press, 1985.

Sanders, James A. *From Sacred Story to Sacred Text.* Philadelphia, PA: Fortress Press, 1987.

Sanders, James A. *Torah and Canon.* Philadelphia: Fortress Press, 1972.

Sawyer, John F. A. *Sacred Languages and Sacred Texts.* Religion in the First Christian Centuries. London/New York: Routledge, 1999.

Schniedewind, William M. *How the Bible Became a Book.* Cambridge, England and New York: Cambridge University Press, 2004.

Seitz, Christopher R. *The Goodly Fellowship of the Prophets: The Achievement of Association in Canon Formation.* Acadia Studies in Bible and Theology. Series editors: C. A Evans and Lee M. McDonald. Grand Rapids, MI: Baker Academic, 2009.

Silver, Daniel Jeremy. *The Story of Scripture: From Oral Tradition to the Written Word.* New York: Basic Books, Inc. Publishers, 1990.

Swete, H. B. *An Introduction to the Old Testament in Greek.* Revised by R. R. Ottley with Appendix by H. St. J. Thackeray. Cambridge: Cambridge University Press, 1914, reprinted by Hendrickson Publishers, 1989.

VanderKam, James C. *From Revelation to Canon: Studies in the Hebrew Bible and Second Temple Literature.* JSJSup 62. Leiden/Boston, MA: E. J. Brill, 2000.

Wise, Michael, Martin Abegg, Jr., and Edward Cook, *The Dead Sea Scrolls: A New Translation.* San Francisco, CA: Harper Collins, 1996.

CHAPTER FOUR

THE COMPLETION OF THE OLD TESTAMENT CANON

The rabbinic Jews of the second century CE and following were the first to set fixed boundaries on the scope of their sacred scriptures. Within a short time, the same process was taking place among the Christians. This does not mean that all Jews or all Christians everywhere made the same decisions about the scope of their scriptures at the same time. On the contrary, among the Jews in the first centuries BCE and CE as well as in early Christianity the fluid state of the scripture canon was obvious. There was considerable division over the books that formed the contents of the sacred scriptures of Jews and Christians well into the fourth and fifth centuries. In recent years, it has become more clear that the views of the later rabbinic Jews on the scope of the Hebrew Bible (and Protestant Old Testament canon) do not reflect the views of the Jews and Christians in the first century about the books that comprise their sacred scriptures. We will begin with an examination of rabbinic notions about the scope of the Hebrew Scriptures and conclude with a focus on the scriptures of Jesus and the early Christian churches.

THE BIG DIVIDE: RABBINIC AND DIASPORA JEWS

As we have observed earlier, there seems to have been something like a "continental divide" among the Jews over the fixing of the param-eters of their sacred collection. The case has been convincingly made that, up to about the end of the eighth century the scriptures of the diaspora Jews were larger in number than those in the rabbinic Hebrew Bible. Indeed, the scriptures of the diaspora Jews included the books circulating in the LXX, which included the apocryphal and pseudepigraphal books in it.

It is an overstatement to conclude that the Jews in the Land of Israel had no affect on the Jews living in the diaspora, but Jews in the diaspora had relative independence from their homeland. The Jews of the dispersion were well aware that the dispersion was seen in their scriptures as a punishment for sin (Lev. 26.33; Deut. 28.63–64; Jer. 5.19; 9.15). Those who were taken from their land by force and compelled to live elsewhere were seen as judged by God or living in the judgment of God. This perspective is also reflected in the *Letter of Aristeas* in which the king of Egypt asks one of the wise men how one could express love of country and the response from one of them to the king clarifies how banishment from one's country was perceived. He states, "Keep in mind that it is good to live and die in one's country. Residence abroad brings contempt upon poor men and upon rich—disgrace, as though they were in exile for some wickedness" (*Ep. Arist.* 249). Diaspora Jews were also used to being judged for the sins of their brethren in the Land of Israel (see Tob. 1.18; *3 Macc.* 2.21–24). Cicero, for instance, justified confiscation of Jewish money in Asia Minor because their fellow Jews in Judaea went against Pompey in battle (*Pro Flacco* 28.69).

There are several references in rabbinic literature that speak of God's judgment on Jews living in exile (see *b. Ned.* 32a; *b. Ta'an* 29a; *Lev R.* 29.2). At times it appears that their banishment and exile was due to their lack of faith in the divine promise of blessing in their homeland. Again, dispersion was a bad thing and perceived as the result of sins. Because those in the Land of Israel often looked down with contempt on those who lived in exile because they were believed to be facing the judgment of God, it is easy to see the origin of this contempt for those living in exile (see also *The Testament of Levi* 10.3–4; *Testament of Asher* 7.2–7; Tob. 3.4; Jdt. 5.18; *2 Baruch* 1.2–4; *Third Sibylline Oracle* 267–76; the *Midrash on Psalm* 71.4). These texts all reflect the well-known Jewish view that exile was a judgment from God and this perspective also affected the attitudes of the Jews in the Land of Israel toward diaspora Jews in the west who did not speak their language.

While matters of circumcision, observance of the Passover meal, observance of the Law and the practice of prayers were common features of Jewish activity in both the East and West in the time of Jesus, and for centuries after him, the sacred texts that Jews recognized in the East were fewer and different after the destruction of Jerusalem in 70 CE. Those in the West continued for centuries to affirm the scriptures of the Septuagint that contained books from the Apocrypha and Pseudepigrapha, but those books and even the Greek translation of the Pentateuch were rejected by many Jews in the east. By the end of the second century Jewish rejection of the translation of the Law into Greek by later rabbis can be seen in the following: "It is related that five elders wrote the Torah in Greek for King Ptolemy. And that day was as intolerable for Israel as the day the golden calf was made, for the Torah cannot be translated adequately" (*Massekhet Soferim*, 1). The Jews to the east and those to the west became separated by language and eventually by various interpretations of the traditions and sacred books that they held in common.

These two different strands of Judaism, along with the early Christian community, survived after the destruction of the Temple in 70 CE. Jews in the east and west both continued to celebrate the Passover and other traditions present in the sacred books that they held in common, but some aspects of their faith and its interpretation were different. The Jewish oral tradition that was eventually codified by Judah the Prince (Judah Ha-Nasi, ca. 200–220) was not translated into Greek, the language of the Jews to the north and west of the Land of Israel. All Jews continued with their daily prayers, but because of the language barrier between east and west, the prescribed prayers from the Mishnah and two Talmudim in the east (e.g., *Eighteen Benedictions*), did not make their way into the prayer habits of the western Jews. The scriptures of the Jews in the east (Israel and eastward to Babylon) were eventually limited to the ones that now comprise the Hebrew Bible, but at least until the middle to the end of the eighth century CE the sacred books of the Jews to the west also included apocryphal and some pseudepigraphal books. In this regard, the Jews in the western diaspora were much like the early Christians who initially regarded not only the books of the Hebrew Bible as scripture, but also many apocryphal and pseudepigraphal books. This may have contributed to many of the successes of the Christians in gaining a number of early converts from the diaspora Jews.

As noted earlier, a factor that reflects the differences in the scriptures of Jews in the east and those in the west is the discovery of several copies of the books of Tobit and Sirach in both the Hebrew and Aramaic languages in the ninth to the tenth century Cairo Geniza (a storage room in Jewish places of worship for sacred texts that were no longer usable). There were few binding connections between the Jews in the east and those in the western part of the Roman Empire especially after the destruction of the Temple in 70 CE. The Temple in Jerusalem had been the center of connectedness for the Jews of the diaspora in the east and west with Jews in the Land of Israel. After its destruction, the central feature of that connectedness was missing.

After the destruction of the Temple, the rabbinic Jews in the east focused especially on the oral Torah traditions that were codified in the Mishnah and those in the west focused more on the scriptures that the Jews in the east had earlier (by or before 150 CE) given to them. Those sacred texts included the apocryphal and pseudepigraphal books along with the books of the Hebrew Bible, some of which of which were likely the same as the noncanonical books found in the caves at Qumran. What further supports the division between east and west noted above is that there are no known *yeshivot* (Jewish schools) in the west where rabbis from the east came to teach western diaspora Jews the teachings of the rabbinic sages from the east. It is remarkable that there is very little comment in the rabbinic literature about the Jews in the west.

THE ORDER OF THE HEBREW BIBLE AND
THE OLD TESTAMENT

Another difficult issue in the formation of the Hebrew Bible and the Old Testament has to do with the differences in the ordering of the books in each collection. James A. Sanders ("Spinning the Bible") has made a positive contribution to the study of the origins of the biblical canon by considering the causes for the two orderings or sequences of the same sacred books. These differences are often overlooked and their significance is ignored in most studies on canon formation, not to mention in most theological seminaries and academic inquiries today. The books that make up the Christian Old Testament scriptures, except for the inclusion of the Apocryphal or Deutero-canonical books in the Catholic and Orthodox Bibles, are the same books as those in the Hebrew Bible. The books differ considerably, however, in their placement in the Jewish and Christian collections (see the listing of these books below for Jews and Christians). The order or sequence of books is a later development in both of these two religious traditions and comes after the various books were selected to be a part of these collections. Although in all collections of biblical books the Law or Pentateuch has the place of priority, the oldest ordering of books is a Common Era development and not something that goes back to or before the first century. In other words, recognition of the sacredness of these books is a prior step to their inclusion in the two different Bibles, but the location of the various books in these collections has significant meaning in how those collections are interpreted by their respective communities of faith.

The Hebrew Bible (*Tanakh*), for example, begins with the books of the Law (Torah), followed by the Former and Latter Prophets (*Nebi'im*), and finally the Writings (*Ketubim*). The last group (Writings) begins with an emphasis on individual piety (the Psalms) and concludes with the story that shows how Israel's history declined from its former glorious days. Those days peaked during the reign of Solomon (1 Kgs 10) but eventually caused the destruction of the nation, its temple, captivity of its leaders to Babylon, and finally a restoration of the Jews to their land. The final part of this canon in its current location appears to call each individual to personal faithfulness to the Lord (Yahweh), but there is no significant focus in this final collection on the future, a coming kingdom, or the blessings of God for his people, or any other great promises for the nation of Israel. The call is to be faithful to Yahweh, the Lord. Judgment came to the nation because of their faithlessness and hope comes in a renewal of faithfulness to the Lord.

The current ordering of the Hebrew Bible took place in the second century. Even if the Law and Prophets (in that order and regardless of their contents at that time) had a place of prominence among the Jews, the changing circumstances of the Jewish people after their tragic defeat in 70 CE, and the subsequent failure of the messianic Bar Cochba rebellion against Rome, led to a rejection or down play of the messianic fervor one present in Israel. There was very little among the circumstances of those disasters that offered hope, joy, or excitement for the Jewish nation. These are the historical circumstances in which the Jews decided the ordering or sequence of the books in the third part of their Hebrew Bible. What is reflected in the ordering of the Hebrew Bible is also similar to the circumstances that prevailed among the Jews in the post-70 CE period. There was an important search for identity once again in the face of the destruction of the nation, its Temple, and many of its leaders.

The story line of the Hebrew Bible begins with Genesis and ends at 2 Kings with the defeat of the tribes of the north (the House of Israel) and those of the south (the House of Judah) at the hands of the Assyrians and Babylonians, respectively. Many Jews were forced into exile from their land. Even after the decree of Cyrus that allowed the Jews to return to their homeland (532–530 BCE), many if not most Jews did not return. They either stayed in Babylon and its environs or migrated to others lands as a diaspora community whether in Asia Minor, Rome, Greece, Egypt, or other places.

On the other hand, the Christian Old Testament extends this time line considerably by inserting Ruth behind Judges and making it a historical book. The Chronicles are placed immediately after the Kings; and Ezra, Nehemiah, and Esther are also included in this historical timeline. In the Catholic and Orthodox Bibles, this timeline is extended to include Judith, Tobit, and 1 and 2 Maccabees. In the Jewish canon, the Latter Prophets, beginning with Isaiah, Jeremiah, Ezekiel, and the Twelve Minor Prophets, follow the historical narrative to explain the tragedy that has come to the nation of Israel. The prophets clarify what has happened to the nation and why Israel is in her current condition given the earlier promises of God (Gen. 12.1–3; 2 Sam. 7.10–17). The Writings, or the third part of the Hebrew Bible, was put in its final form in the second century CE under the influence of the rabbinic leaders, many of whom had influenced the recent terrible tragedies that befell the nation in 70 CE and 135 CE. The Writings encourage persons to serve God and above all to be faithful to God even in difficult times. This was believed to be the most appropriate way to conclude their sacred Hebrew Bible. Given the tragedies that had befallen the nation as a result of their faithlessness, the call to faithful obedience to the Law of God had special relevance for the Jews of the post-70 CE period.

The Christian Old Testament, on the other hand, had a focus on the future unfolding activity of God that was soon to break forth, they believed, in the activity of Jesus the Christ. In the Christian canon, the first part of the Old Testament, following the rabbinic order has the books of the Law (the Pentateuch which has place of priority in all Old Testaments), followed by the historical books of Joshua, Judges, Ruth, Samuels, Kings, Chronicles, Ezra, Nehemiah, and Esther. The historical books are followed by the poetic books (Job, Psalms, roverbs, Ecclesiastes, Song of Songs), and finally the prophetic books follow them (the "Major Prophets": Isaiah, Jeremiah, Ezekiel, Daniel; and the Twelve "Minor Prophets"). The Roman Catholics and Orthodox include the Apocryphal or Deutero-canonical books among these books. Some Jews have occasionally complained that this grouping in the first instance does not highlight adequately the primacy of the Law in a class by itself, but instead puts prophecy as the climax of the Scriptures.

The Christian ordering of the Old Testament books has four major parts: the Pentateuch, the historical books, the wisdom or poetic books, and finally the Prophets. The Pentateuch is always identified by itself and given primacy in the Christian Bibles. Daniel, one of the books in the Writings or third part in the Hebrew Bible, became one of the Prophets in the Christian Bible. In the Christian Bibles, Chronicles were generally placed after the Samuels and Kings and they were followed by Ezra, Nehemiah, and Esther.

The Prophets' role of last place in the Christian Old Testament was not so much to explain the adversity that had befallen the Jews, as we see in the Hebrew Bible, as it was to point forward to the hope promised in the Old Testament that Christians believed found fulfillment in Jesus Christ. By concluding the Old Testament where it did, the church claimed that the prophetic literature pointed to hope for a new day in which those who are faithful to God will be blessed and judgment will come to those who are disobedient. Those days, according to this ordering of books, would be anticipated by the coming of Elijah the prophet (Mal. 4.1–6) who would prepare the people of God for the time of the coming rule of the Lord. In the very next book in the Christian Bible, Matthew says that Elijah has come in the person of John the Baptist (Matt. 11:7–15) and Jesus is the promised one who will bring in the Kingdom of God.

How the books of the Hebrew Bible and the Christian Bible are ordered is very important in interpreting what it was that each community was trying to say about this literature and what it was that they believed God was doing in their respective communities of faith. The Christians believed that they were living in the last days of fulfillment that was promised in their Old Testament scriptures and that the blessings of the new age had descended upon them (Acts 2.17–36). The Hebrew canon, on the other hand, has a much more sober perspective and very little focus on a hopeful future for the nation as its sacred scripture canon closes. It appears from the ordering of their canon that this was no longer the object of the nation's hope. Unlike in the Christian Old Testament, messianic fervor was marginalized by the rabbis. The stabilization of the biblical texts in the second century CE for many rabbinic Jews, coupled with the emerging technological ability to expand the size of the scroll to include all of the books of the Hebrew Bible, allowed the canonization process to advance. The circumstances were considerably different for the Christian communities, however, and the ordering of the same books in a different sequence reflects those differences.

THE BIBLICAL CANON OF JESUS AND THE EARLIEST CHRISTIANS

There is little doubt that the core component of the earliest sacred writings of the initial followers of Jesus was the Law and the Prophets, but also most, if not all, of what the rabbis later identified as the Writings. The many citations of two-thirds of that literature in the New Testament is considerable, even though books like Judges, Ruth, and Esther are not mentioned and many others do not appear to have played much of a role in the formative ministry and witness of the early churches. There are numerous references to the Law and the Prophets, or to Moses and the Prophets, in the New Testament as we see in Matt. 7.12 and Rom. 3.21. These designations are sometimes confusing, however, as we see in Jn 10.34 when Jesus says "is it not written in your law," referring to Ps. 82. Similarly, Paul also speaks of the "law" (3.19) when he cites a series of references from the Psalms in Rom. 3.10–18 (see also Lk. 4.17; Jn 1.45; Acts 13.27 and 28.23 for references to the use of the Law and the Prophets in the early Christian community). According to the Book of Acts, both the Law and the Prophets were regularly read in the synagogue and nothing is said of a third category or even "psalms" as we see earlier in Lk. 24.44, even though Psalms are clearly included in the scriptural citations of Acts. For instance, according to Acts 13.15, "After reading of the law and the prophets, the rulers of the synagogue sent to them [Paul and Barnabas], saying, 'Brethren, if you have any word of exhortation for the people, say it'" (NRSV). As we noted earlier, there is only one reference to a third part of the scriptures in the New Testament (Lk. 24.44) and that is not as clearly intended to refer to a third category of scripture as some scholars have argued. In that passage the reference to the third part of the scriptures is simply to "psalms" without any qualifications or definite article that might suggests a specific collection and certainly not a broader collection of books.

The numerous references to a two-part collection of sacred writings (Law and Prophets) in the New Testament and only one verse that may refer to a limited third part made up of psalms leads us to surmise that there was not *at this time* any widespread recognition of a three-part biblical canon, even if many of the books that make up that third part were already in use and incorporated in the "Law and the Prophets." As we saw in the last chapter, even Melito (ca. 180 CE), the earliest known Christian writer to produce a list of the Jewish scriptures that made up the Old Testament, refers to the whole collection of Old Testament scriptures including books that were later included in the third part of the Hebrew Bible (omitting Esther) as the "Law and the Prophets." Writing to a Christian "brother" named Onesimus, Melito describes as follows his reason for making his journey to the land of Israel to find out the contours of the Old Testament:

> "Melito to Onesimus his brother, greeting. Since you often desired, in your zeal for the true word, to have extracts from *the Law and the Prophets* concerning the Saviour, and concerning all our

faith, and moreover, since you wished to know the accurate facts about the ancient writings, how many they are in number, and what is their order, I have taken pains to do thus, for I know your zeal for the faith and interest in the word, and that in your struggle for eternal salvation you esteem these things more highly than all else in your love towards God. Accordingly when I came to the east and reached the place where these things were preached and done, and learnt accurately the books of the Old Testament, I set down the facts and sent them to you. The books in this text are listed above in Chapter 3, p. 72. These are their names: five books of Moses, Genesis, Exodus, Leviticus, Numbers, Deuteronomy, Joshua the son of Nun, Judges, Ruth, four books of Kingdoms, two books of Chronicles, the Psalms of David, the Proverbs of Solomon and his Wisdom, Ecclesiastes, the Songs of Songs, Job, the prophets Isaiah, Jeremiah, the Twelve in a single book, Daniel, Ezekiel, Ezra. From these I have made extracts and compiled them in six books." Such are the facts about Melito. (*Ecclesiastical History* 4.26.13, 14, LCL. Emphasis added)

This letter allows us to see that there was no three-part Old Testament canon *for the church* before or during Melito's time and it was not a conscious division for the church after that either. Again, Melito includes all of the books of the Hebrew Bible except Esther and identifies them all as the "Law and the Prophets." He also adds the Wisdom of Solomon to the list. We should add that the authenticity of Melito's list is less suspect in Eusebius than when he lists the biblical canons of Clement and Origen. In the later cases he seems to be compiling the list of books that they cited in their works and concludes that this was their biblical canon. In the case of Melito, he is making an actual quote of a letter from Melito.

The Gospel writers indicate that Jesus frequently cited various Psalms, for example, in Mk 15.34 Mark indicates that Jesus referred to Ps. 22.1, and probably the following verses, and John tells of Jesus citing Ps. 69.4–9 in reference to the temple cleansing incident in Jn 2.17. In the Gospels, Jesus cites the Psalms more frequently than all of the other Old Testament books, but for our purposes, did Jesus and the early Christians also appeal to any books other than the Old

Testament literature in an authoritative manner? For example, did they appeal to some of the apocryphal and pseudepigraphal literature in a scriptural-like manner, that is, authoritatively? That seems to be beyond reasonable doubt, though many scholars today continue to deny it. Whatever might be the traditions behind *Against Apion* 1.37–43, 4 Ezra 14.44–47, and *Baba Bathra* 14b–15a, the three most important traditions reflecting a more fixed collection of sacred Jewish writings from the end of the first century to the middle or end of the second century CE, their interest in a fixed collection of scriptures had no obvious impact on the writers of the New Testament.

The New Testament books betray no special interest in limiting the books of the Bible to a fixed number. What supports this conclusion is the fact that there are many references to noncanonical literature in the church fathers often referring to it as "scripture" or using it in an authoritative manner. Before looking at the early church's apparent lack of interest in the scope of its sacred scriptures, let us examine some of the apparent uses of noncanonical literature in the New Testament itself.

It is likely in Rom. 1.24–32, that Paul makes use of *Wisdom* 14.22–31 and in Rom. 5.12–21 he apparently makes use of the ideas present in *Wisdom* 2.23–24. The question of Wisdom's canonicity does not appear to concern Paul, but only the theological arguments in it. In 1 Cor. 2.9, Paul cites as "scripture" either the *Ascension of Isaiah* 11.34 or a lost *Elijah Apocalypse* derived from Isa. 64.3. Jude 14 expressly cites the pseudepigraphal book *1 Enoch* (1.9). The author of 2 Peter also shows knowledge or awareness of *1 Enoch* in 2.4 and 3.6. The author of Heb. 1.3 makes obvious use of the *Wis. of Sol.* 7.25–26 and Jas 4.5 appears to cite an unknown scripture. These uses of noncanonical literature in the New Testament, and many others, apparently were not matters of concern for Paul or other New Testament writers. The core of the biblical literature for all Jews in the first century and later wasthe Law of Moses. Although the Gospel writers cite the Psalms in telling their story of Jesus more frequently than any other book of the Old Testament, still the Torah or Law of Moses forms the backbone of any "canonical" collection embraced in the first century CE and following, just as it was long before and during the time of Jesus.

In the Apostolic Fathers, the successors of the earliest Christian community, there are a number of even more striking uses of the noncanonical literature. Notice, for example, that Clement quoted Sir. 2.11 in *1 Clement* 60.1, the Wis. of Sol. 12.10 in *1 Clement* 7.5, and Wis. of Sol. 12.12 in *1 Clement* 27.5, which he alluded to in 3.4 and 7.5. In *1 Clement* 55.4–6, both Judith 8 and Esther 7 and 4.16 are cited in the same way, that is, as scripture. *2 Clement* lists a number of quotations from unknown noncanonical writings, as well as a quote from *Tob.* 16.4 (see 11.2–4; 11.7, and 13.2). The *Epistle of Barnabas* also has quotations from Wisdom of Solomon (20.2), *1 Enoch* (16.5), *4 Ezra* (12.1) and other quotations from unknown "scripture" as we see in 7.3, 8 and 10.7. The *Didache* (ca. 70–90 CE), that early on was added to some canonical lists of Christian scriptures, but was excluded by Athanasius in the fourth century, makes use of *Wisdom of Solomon* in 5.2 and 10.3.

Justin in his *Dialogue with Trypho* (ca. 160) may refer to the *Ascension of Isaiah* (see 120.5) but bases his argument on the books accepted as canonical by the Jews. Like Melito, he refers to Genesis, Exodus, Leviticus, the Kingdoms (1 and 2 Kings), the Psalms, Proverbs, and quotes Job. He names the prophets Isaiah, Jeremiah, Ezekiel, and Daniel, as well as the Twelve Minor Prophets and *Esdras* (see *Dialogue with Trypho* 72.1). He also quotes, without referring to them by name, Numbers, Deuteronomy, and 2 Chronicles. This does not necessarily imply a fixed biblical canon, since he is speaking to specific situations in the *Dialogue*, but his example is instructive on the question of the commonly accepted literature among Christians in the middle of the second century.

Justin Martyr is silent about Ecclesiastes, Song of Songs, and Esther, and that may reflect the doubts that existed about these books in the Jewish community and possibly also the Christian community in the second century. Later Christians may have avoided using these writings because they did not address the special concerns of their Christian community unless they were allegorized or spiritualized. Earlier I indicated that the mere citing of noncanonical texts does not necessarily mean that they were received as sacred scripture or placed in a fixed biblical canon. The *manner* of the quotations, however, reveals the significance the writings in the minds of those who used them.

There is no question that the vast majority of the references and quotations in *1 Clement* are from the canonical Old Testament literature and a few references to some New Testament literature. We are not suggesting here that the apocryphal and pseudepigraphal literature was used as much as the Old Testament books in early Christianity. They were not. I am suggesting, that this literature influenced the early churches' teaching and development. Several of the themes of the New Testament have their roots in the apocryphal and pseudepigraphal literature. How the passages from the noncanonical books are cited or alluded to either in the New Testament or in the Apostolic Fathers may be debated, and we are not certain whether there is a specific claim in the New Testament for calling all of these documents "scriptures," but the point here is that these references show that there was no clear tradition in the church about the extent of the Old Testament canon or sacred literature in the first or second centuries. Jude's use of *1 Enoch* 1.9 certainly illustrates the fluidity of the biblical canon in the first century CE.

The additions to biblical books that appear in the LXX that were not accepted by the Jews in the second century also supports this conclusion. The *Song of the Three Holy Children* was added to Daniel, *Susanna* was used by Clement of Alexandria and Origen, and *Bel and the Dragon* (all of these are a part of the LXX) were also accepted by Irenaeus, Tertullian, and Origen. The additions to Esther that are mentioned in Josephus are at the same time regarded as scripture by Clement of Rome, Clement of Alexandria, and Origen. The *Prayer of Manasseh* is found in the Syriac *Didascalia* from the third century CE and the *Apostolic Constitutions* (2.22.12–14) as well as in the fifth century Codex Alexandrinus. An examination of the Apostolic Fathers shows conclusively that they often appealed to the apocryphal and pseudepigraphal literature in much the same way that they appealed to the scriptures of the Hebrew Bible. For example, the only explicit quotation in the *Shepherd of Hermas* comes from the lost *Book of Eldad and Modat* (*Vis.* 2, 3, 4; cf. Num. 11.26). Again, this collection of evidence suggests the fluidity of the early church's Old Testament scripture collection in the time of Jesus and for a considerable time thereafter.

THE CODICES AND THE BIBLICAL CANON
OF THE EARLY CHURCH

One of the peculiarities of the early Christian community is its preference by not later than 100 CE for the codex (pl., codices). The codex is the ancient predecessor of the modern book format, and in time it overtook the use of the roll or scroll that it inherited from the Jews. The Book of Revelation attests to the use of the scroll in the late first century, as we see in its telling the story of the opening of the scroll with seven seals (Rev. 5.1–3; 6.1–17; 8.1–5) and the angel with a little scroll (10.2). In time, and probably by the early second century CE, the church began making use of the codex or book form to copy and transmit its sacred writings. There are many possible reasons for this, for example, compactness, comprehensiveness, convenience of use, ease of reference, the effect of conservatism which was the tendency of the scribes to continue using what they have always used, and possibly other reasons as well, but none of these more obvious reasons answers the question of why the Christians, more than anyone else, preferred the codex to transmit their sacred literature instead of scrolls. The practice for the early church may have begun in Jerusalem with the Christians opting for different means of transmitting their sacred literature than the one used by the Jews (scrolls), but that is uncertain and cannot be substantiated.

There is no evidence either that the early Christians used the codex for economic reasons, a factor that is often shown by the use of cramped letters, unusually narrow margins, or the frequency of palimpsests (erasures). There was, however, a convenience of use and transportability that made use of the codex a valuable medium for a traveling missionary such as Paul. A codex took up much less space and was more convenient to transport on a journey. It was less likely to get crumpled or damaged in route to another city as it was carried on the messenger's back or the back of an animal.

Supporting the greater ability to transport books in a codex format, Martial (ca. 80 CE), the Roman poet, advised his readers to make use of the codex if they wanted to carry his poems on their journeys. It was more of a substitute for the scroll or roll and was more portable taking up less space. Explaining the portability of writings on tablets or "books," Martial writes:

> You who want my little books [tablets] to keep you company wherever you may be and desire their companionship on a long journey, buy these, that parchment compresses in small pages. Give book boxes to the great, one hand grasps me. But in case you don't know where I am on sale and stray wandering all over town, you will be sure of your way under my guidance. Look for Secundus, Freedman of lettered Lucensis, behind Peace's entrance and Pallas' Forum. (*Epigrams* 1.2, lines 1–8, LCL)[1]

Martial indicated in his *Epigrams* that even the great poets' works were transported in this fashion, that is, on tablets, including Homer ("Homer in parchment note books," 14.184), Virgil ("How small a quantity of parchment has comprised vast Maro [Virgil]," 14.186), Cicero ("If this parchment will be your companion, suppose yourself to be making a long journey," 14.188), Livy (14.190),[2] and Ovid (14.192). The codex was clearly more portable than the scroll and by the end of the second century could include more texts than several scrolls. The average length of these full scrolls was about 30 feet. Perhaps what became apparent soon after the regular use of the codex was the convenience of referencing that allowed easy access and rapid use in either teaching or debates with opponents. Because Paul made use of the codex, no doubt for convenience and portability, and because his writings were among the earliest to be acknowledged "scripture" in many churches (2 Pet. 3.15–16), he may have been the instigator of the use of the codex in early Christianity. According to 2 Tim. 4.13, Paul writes: "When you come [to Rome], bring the cloak that I left with Carpus at Troas, also the books [*ta biblia*], and above all the parchments [*membranas*]." When his letters were collected at the end of the first century, it is likely that the very form of transmission was also followed and repeated. This form also made it possible to circulate his writings in one volume. Although the codex may have been used along with the roll or scroll in early Christianity for lists of sayings of Jesus, it was likely the authority of Paul's collected letters circulating in a book or codex format that set the model for its use in subsequent Christian literature in codices. Because of their practicality for everyday use and transportability, by the fourth century CE the codices became standard materials for transmitting all Christian writings. The initial stages of copying of the New Testament writings, however, were often poor in quality, not only because the transcribers were not fully aware that they were transcribing sacred scripture, but also because the early copiers of the church's sacred writings were often unskilled in the art of professional transcription. As some text critical scholars have noticed, the early copiers were generally "literate amateurs" unskilled in the fine art of transcription.

In antiquity there were generally two styles of writing, namely the more literary quality of writing, and the documentary style, that is, a less formal style of writing. This *lower* or more informal style of writing was characteristic of most papyrus manuscripts before the fourth century. In the fourth century, and apparently instigated at the command of the Emperor Constantine, manuscripts of high quality transcription with carefully prepared letters and appropriate spacing were produced on quality parchment. Does this say anything about the understanding by the early Christians of the literature that they had been reading in their churches? Not really. It simply reflects the church's financial state initially and its inability to pay careful transcribers the going rate to make copies of their sacred texts. Those with the skills to do the work had varying levels of competence in the task before them.

Unlike the much more meticulous style of transcription typical in the Jewish communities when copying their scriptures, the Christians were generally (not always) much less meticulous about it until after the time of Constantine's request from Eusebius to produce 50 copies of the Scriptures for use in churches in the New Rome (Constantinople). We will focus more on this request in Chapter 7.

Scholars do not agree on why the Christians adopted the codex instead of the scroll, but portability and perhaps the lack of acknowledging these writings initially as "scripture" probably accounts for the Christians' use of the codex early in the second century, if not sooner. This was at a time when the codex was not common in the rest of the Greco-Roman world, but by the fourth century, the majority of ancient manuscripts began appearing in the codex format. The large-scale substitution of the codex for the scroll for literary documents began to take place in the Roman Empire only in the fourth century.

That the early church did not initially view the New Testament writings as formal literary documents can be seen in the fact that they made so many changes in the texts in the first couple of centuries. Possibly the use of the so-called *nomina sacra* (or sacred names) that were transmitted in abbreviated form in these codices, may suggest the high value the church attached to them. Generally, these abbreviated words included God, Jesus, Lord, and Christ, but some eleven other sacred terms as well. They were often abbreviated as follows: the Greek name God (*theos*), for example, is often substituted with a simple *ths* with a short line drawn over the top of the abbreviated letters. Normally these are a contraction of the first and last letters of the abbreviated word. Well into the fourth century and later, these and other abbreviations were used in copies of the Christian sacred scriptures. They are found, for example, throughout the mid-fourth century Codex Vaticanus. Other common words that received such abbreviations include: spirit, cross, savior, mother, father, man, heaven, Jerusalem, David, and Israel.

The use of the abbreviations may indicate that the church was aware that it was not merely transmitting literary texts, but rather significant religious texts that had considerable value for Christians. Abbreviations were generally not made in standard books or scrolls of a literary quality, but more in tablets or notebooks, such as the codex. Although they were common in secular documentary texts, they were very rare in well-written literary texts. The *nomina sacra* may therefore point to the *practical* use of Christian texts acknowledging that they were not high quality written texts and possibly at first that they were not valued as sacred scripture on par with the Old Testament texts. This is supposition, of course, but there may be some merit in this possibility. In time, however, the *nomina sacra* were used in clearly acknowledged and beautifully prepared sacred scriptures of the churches. Initially, they were used in both religious and nonreligious texts, but clearly only in Christian texts.

More importantly, for our purposes, apart from the simple use of the codex, it appears that the early churches did not have the opportunity to combine all of the books of the New Testament or Old Testament into one book until the fourth century because of the slower development of the codex. Later, the technology for making a codex progressed to the point where all of the books of the Old Testament and New Testament could be included in one volume of more than 1,600 pages. When that was possible, it was more clear what books comprised the sacred scriptures of the churches in both their Old and New Testaments. The story that those fourth century and later manuscripts tell is therefore very important in letting us know which books functioned as scripture in the communities where these large collections were found, and from which other copies were made.

Apart from the simple use of the codex, the early church did not initially have the opportunity, because of the slower development of the codex, to combine all of the books of the New Testament or Old Testament into one book. By the fourth century, however, the significantly improved process of making a codex, especially with parchment, made it possible to combine all of the books of both the Testaments into one book. By the end of the second century, the most that could be circulated together in one book was the four-gospel canon (some 220 pages or 110 leaves with writings on both the front [recto] and back [verso] sides). In the fourth and fifth centuries, four very important codices containing the church's sacred scriptures deserve special recognition. These include: (1) Codex Sinaiticus (א) (ca. fourth century), besides its New Testament collection that we will examine later, the Old Testament collection also includes Tobit, Judith, Wisdom of Solomon, Sirach (Ecclesiasticus) and 1 & 4 Maccabees. (2) Codex Vaticanus (B) (fourth century), besides its New Testament collection the Old Testament collection also includes Baruch, the Epistle of Jeremiah, Wisdom of Solomon, Sirach (Ecclesiasticus), Judith, and Tobit, but not the Maccabees. (3) Codex Alexandrinus (A) (fifth century) includes books from both Testaments and its Old Testament also includes the Epistle of Jeremiah, Tobit, Judith, 1–2 Esdras, 1–4 Maccabees, Psalm 151, Wisdom of Solomon, and Sirach. These additional books are also included in the various other codices along with the books of the Old Testament and without any distinction being made in them. (4) Codex Ephraemi Syri Rescriptus (C) is a fifth century manuscript, which contains some 209 leaves of which 64 are fragments or portions of the Old Testament books. Along with books of the Hebrew Bible, this manuscript also contains Sirach, the Prologue to Sirach, and Wisdom of Solomon. Not all of the Old Testament books are in it, but due to its fragmentary nature, it is difficult to be dogmatic about the full contents of the manuscript except to say that more than the books of the Hebrew Bible or the Protestant Old Testament were included.

It is possible that knowledge of a fixed biblical canon could only have been widespread in the church after the fourth century when it was finally possible to include all of the sacred books into one volume. We can also note that when this was first possible, we do not find a consistent order of the biblical books in these fourth century and later manuscripts. The sequence of books took much longer to fix, but it was only possible after all of the books could be combined in a single volume. For example, in some early Christian manuscripts Matthew is joined with Acts. Also, some canonical books were sometimes circulated with noncanonical books as in the case of the Song of Songs that is bound together with the *Apology of Aristides*. Also, the *Acta Pauli* (*Acts of Paul*) is in Greek and is bound with Song of Songs and Lamentations in Coptic and Ecclesiasticus is in Greek and Coptic, and all are in one volume. That should give some indication about the fluid or unstable collection of sacred books that were circulating in the churches well into the fourth century.

THE CLOSURE OF THE *CHRISTIAN* OLD TESTAMENT CANON

Over the last 80 or more years, one of the most popular views regarding the completion of the Old Testament canon has been that the first two parts (Law and Prophets) were complete before the time of Jesus and likely in the early second century BCE, but the third part of the Hebrew Scriptures, the Writings, was finally defined or closed at a "council" of rabbis that took place at Jamnia (Yavna or Javneh), a city near the coast in Israel and north of ancient Gaza, at or near the end of the first century CE. While there are still a few scholars who hold this view, the majority have challenged its credibility. There is nothing in the surviving Jewish literature from that time that suggests that a council met at Jamnia to determine the scope of its sacred scriptures.

With the widespread demise of that position, some scholars have assumed that if the Jamnia theory was wrong, then the most reasonable time for finalizing the third part of the Hebrew Bible was earlier than Jamnia and perhaps even as early as the time of Judas Maccabees (ca. 165 BCE) or even earlier. During the reign of the Seleucid Dynasty, king Antiochus Epiphanes (ca. 176–163 BCE) tried to force Jews to honor the Greek gods and prohibit them from making sacrifices to their God. During that time he had the sacred book(s) of the Jews destroyed. As we observed in the previous chapter, the story in 1 Maccabees reads as follows: "The books of the Law that they [the Seleucids] found they tore to pieces and burned with fire. Anyone found possessing the book of the covenant, or anyone who adhered to the law, was condemned to death by decree of the king [Antiochus Epiphanes]" (1 Macc. 1.56–57, NRSV). Judas Maccabees, following his successful military campaigns against the armies of the Seleucid king, reportedly collected the Jewish scriptures that remained after the attempts of Antiochus Epiphanes to destroy them and he made them available throughout Israel. This important story builds on the example of Nehemiah who reportedly collected the sacred books in a library and says that Judas Maccabees did something similar. This text is quoted above in Chapter 3, pp. 60–61.

Judas's collecting the scattered and surviving scriptures provides scholars with an obvious place of termination for the Hebrew Bible. However, the passage cited in support of this position (1 Macc. 1.56–57) does not state which sacred texts were destroyed and the second (2 Macc. 2.13–15) does not say which sacred texts were recovered. It is an argument from silence to say that Judas' collection is the same as what eventually comprised the Jewish biblical canon, the Hebrew Bible. Even though some scholars believe that "law" in this text refers to *all* of the sacred Jewish scriptures—and there is precedent for that view as we have seen above. What comprised the "law" at that time is not clear from these passages. It is not clear that the third part of the Bible was completed as a result of Judas Maccabees' activity. What makes it difficult to believe that Judas' collection was the same as the later fixed Hebrew Bible is that other writings, such as those at Qumran, continued to be produced and circulated in the land of Israel and even cited as scripture in Jewish and early Christian communities of faith. Had the matter been settled earlier, it seems highly unlikely that these other noncanonical books could have been produced and welcomed as sacred scriptures among the Jews and subsequently the Christians.

For now, I will suggest that the third part of the Hebrew Bible, and the scope of the Christian Old Testament, had not come to finalization either before the time of Jesus, or even in the early second century CE. Rather, this occurred for some Jews near the end of the first century and later for other rabbinic Jews. This was especially so in the Babylonian area in the second century and for others in the early third century CE, but for some of the Jews it was even later.

For the Christians, this process of determining the scope of their Old Testament scriptures may have begun in the second century CE, but was largely settled sometime in the last half of the fourth century and following. However, the Christians never set forth any argument in antiquity either for a narrower (Protestant) or even for a wider (Catholic or Orthodox) collection of Old Testament writings though the processes of limiting their sacred collections probably began in the second century. There is little doubt that initially they depended on the sacred scriptures that they had inherited from the Jews before the destruction of Jerusalem when more books than those in the current Hebrew Bible were widely recognized as sacred literature among the Jews. However, as we have already said, Christians have never fully agreed on which books belong in their Old Testament.

If, as some scholars claim, the Old Testament scriptures were already in a fixed form in the first century CE, why is it that there are no traditions of the church or synagogue that identify this canonical literature before the late second century (Melito and *b. Baba Bathra* 14b)? Is it simply because it became necessary to construct such lists only later when the scope of the biblical canon became blurred in the churches, as some scholars suggest? If that were the case, it would also be true among the Jews in the first century as well. There are no such Jewish lists until the middle to end of the second century. Does that suggest that the Jews also had lost the list of their sacred scriptures that had been produced earlier? That seems unlikely. It is easier to argue that the matter had not yet been settled in the churches or the synagogues.

More importantly, if the matter were settled earlier in the time of Jesus, or before, how is it possible that there are so many variations in the canonical lists of Old Testament books that were drawn up by the Christians in the fourth, fifth, and sixth centuries? If we must assume that the earliest Christians had a well-defined canon of Old Testament scriptures, we must also conclude that subsequent generations of Christians either lost it or that it was considerably different from the one that churches possesses today!

Since we have no *complete* record of all that Jesus said (observe Jn 20.30), and since what we do have is often specific to concrete situations (for the most part, Jesus' sayings are *ad hoc*, that is, in the Gospels he was responding to specific situations), how can we ever know for sure what his entire biblical canon was? As far as we know today, no one in antiquity ever asked Jesus about the books that comprised his scriptures and no ancient text indicates that he shared such a collection with his disciples.

The lack of an early agreement on the boundaries of the books that comprise the Jewish biblical canon (those that "defile the hands") among the Amoraim, the Jewish rabbinic interpreters of the Mishnah (3rd to 6th cent.), is consistent with the fact that the sacredness of several books in the Hebrew Bible, namely the Song of Songs, Esther, Ecclesiastes, and Proverbs, and even the book of Ezekiel, were still being debated by some of the Amoraim rabbis Jews as late as the fourth and fifth centuries CE. While it is not altogether clear how many of the Jewish religious teachers were involved in such disputes, no rabbi, to our knowledge, attempted to resolve the question by a reference to an earlier fixed collection of sacred writings. Further, the initial acceptance of at least two noncanonical writings as sacred literature (Sirach and Wisdom) and the subsequent rejection of them is evidence that the second and third century rabbis were not in full agreement on the sacredness of these books (for support of this point, see *y. Ber.* 11b; *y. Nazir* 54b; *Bereshith Rabbah* 91.3; *Koheleth Rabbah* 7.11; *b. Ber.* 48a.).

The debates or disputes among some of the rabbis on these matters shows that agreement on the books that make up the Hebrew Bible was still lacking even among the rabbis for several centuries. There is no evidence that all rabbinic Jews accepted the list of books in the *b. Baba Bathra* 14b text as soon as it came out and the evidence from the rabbinic traditions supports this claim. It is interesting that in the collection mentioned by Melito (preserved in Eusebius, *Ecclesiastical History* 4.26.13–14 and cited above), he omits Esther but includes *Wisdom of Solomon* without any commentary on whether such writings belonged in the corpus or not. If Esther is missing and *Wisdom* was included, how fixed could his collection have been especially if he got it from Christians influenced by Jews in the Land of Israel at the end of the second century or if he got it directly from the Jews in the Land of Israel? The "fringe" books continued to be discussed and even debated for considerably longer.

It is almost certain that the framers of the *Mishnah* were the same rabbis who were involved in the initial finalization of the Hebrew Scriptures, but by the time such matters were being openly discussed at the end of the second century, there was also a move to include in their broader sacred collection, not only the Old Testament Scriptures, but also the *Mishnah* and eventually the *Tosephta, Genesis Rabbah, Leviticus Rabbah*, the two Talmudim (Bavli and the Yerushalmi), as well as the various Jewish interpretations of the Law. The expansion of the Torah-based canon to include not only the Hebrew Scriptures but also these other writings occurred when the myth of the "oral Torah"[3] became a part of the sages' teaching. In the fourth century, when the sages mentioned the Torah, they no longer spoke only of a scroll of the laws of Moses, but of both the written and oral teaching that was revealed to Moses at Sinai (the "whole Torah"). This Torah eventually included all that the rabbis taught about the Law as well as the Law. The rabbis also included the Prophets, and the Writings (namely, the Hebrew Scriptures), the Mishnah, the two Talmudim, the various interpretations of the Scriptures, and more. The point here is that the sacred writings of the Jews were expanding and not reducing in size, even though the apocryphal and pseudepigraphal writings for the most part had been dropped from their sacred collections much earlier.

The framers of the Mishnah, however, do not appear to have been that interested in placing a limitation on or expansion of their collection of scriptures, since the matter occupies very little space in their second-century CE deliberations. While it is true that there are some passages in the Mishnah that do focus on the issue, *Yadayim* 3.4–5 (see text cited above) for instance, this hardly qualifies as a significant debate or inquiry into the issue, and at any rate it does not address all divisions or books of the Hebrew Bible but only the Song of Songs and Qohelet (Ecclesiastes). The framers of the Mishnah, with a few exceptions, did not support their various prescriptions and proscriptions for holy living with references to the Hebrew Scriptures. While there are some references to the biblical texts, there is not as much as one would expect from those committed to their sacred scriptures. This relative absence is addressed more extensively later in the two Talmuds, but the example in the Mishnah is not what one would expect from a community that is "willing to die" for its scriptures, as Josephus had argued earlier. This all changed, however, when the Amoraim frequently supported the prescriptions of the Mishnah in their Talmudim with references to the Hebrew Scriptures to undergird each admonition in the Mishnah. This was the Amoraim's way of showing that both the written and the oral dimensions of Torah were the same and did not contradict each other.

It is doubtful that the Hebrew canon was ever closed after the two Torahs became one, and this "whole Torah" (= the Hebrew Scriptures, *Mishnah*, *Tosephta*, the two Talmudim, and various midrashim) became the canon of Judaism. The *basic* contours of the Hebrew Bible were probably defined in the late second century CE for some rabbinic teachers, but we cannot demonstrate that this was true for all Jews of that time both inside and outside of Palestine.

This practice has some parallels in the early Church. As Christians were defining their sacred scriptures, they also saw the need and value of having additional *Christian* scriptures to add to their sacred collection. The core documents that were widely used in the early churches, especially the Gospels and Paul, were eventually supplemented by additional writings that were believed at that time to add clarification to the church's identity and mission. Along with these, the church continued to make use of the Old Testament writings and several of the apocryphal and pseudepigraphal writings.

There was no significant discussion of the contents of the Old Testament canon in the early church, or even the notion of canonization as such, in the second or third centuries CE. Only the canon or "rule of faith" (the *regula Fidei*), which was regularly employed to deal with the heretical challenges facing the Church, was employed to deal with the problems facing the churches. (This will be discussed more carefully in Chapter 6.) Both the Old and New Testament Scriptures were regularly cited by the church fathers to deal with such heresies and crises that were confronting the church, but no focus on which books addressed these problems. When they addressed questions about the nature and identity of Jesus the Christ, there was no special list of writings that made up the Old Testament scriptures to which they appealed, nor did they address the contents of a scriptural collection. The fact that Melito, bishop of a prominent church in Asia Minor (Sardis) in the last third of the second century, did not know for certain which books comprised his Old Testament, strongly suggests that this was not an important issue to most of the churches of his time. Interestingly, Melito's concern is first noted by Eusebius in the fourth century! Furthermore, since only one Hebrew text in the second century mentions the contents of the Hebrew Scriptures (*b. Baba Bathra* 14b), it is not likely that this was an important item for rabbinic Judaism either.

The absence of any discussions about the scope of the Jewish sacred scriptures both before and immediately following the time of Jesus either in the church or in Judaism shows that such notions were simply not a part of the common discourse of Jews or Christians at that time. In the late first century or early second century CE and following, some Jews employed the term "defiling the hands" for their sacred literature. At that time debate *began* among some Jews about which books ritually "defile the hands," that is, which religious texts are sacred scripture. The meaning of this term is somewhat obscure, but it refers to the books that were considered holy by the Jews. Some scholars have argued that the term refers only to the *inspired* status of a particular writing, but not to its *canonical* status;

but this is a form of argument that does not address the nature of canon formation or inspiration. In both cases, if a community believed that a writing came by the inspiration or the moving of God, then it was considered prophetic, that is, inspired. If the writing was accepted as canon—a much later notion, it was also believed to be prophetic and inspired by God. Distinguishing these terms in this part of an inquiry into the Jewish biblical canon only obscures the issue before us. "Defiling the hands" was a reference to the sacredness of sacred books.

The acceptance of the scriptures' ability to defile the hands was a way of accepting their sacredness. To accept a ritual obligation to wash off this holy residue before engaging in any mundane task was a way of recognizing its holiness. In this ceremonial way the divine inspiration of these books was made clear for all to see. The phrase was apparently first used by rabbi Zakkai in a debate withthe Sadducees (see *m. Yad.* 4.6 and also *t. Yad.* 2.19), but it did not become the *lingua franca* of Judaism for distinguishing its sacred literature until the second century CE. The passage reads as follows:

> The Sadducees say: We have a quarrel to pick with you, O Pharisees, for according to you the Holy Scriptures defile the hands whereas the writings of Homer would not defile the hands. Rabban Johanan ben Zakkai (40–80) replied: Have we naught against the Pharisees save this: According to them the bones of an ass are clean while the bones of Johanan the High Priest are unclean? They answered him: Their uncleanness corresponds to their preciousness, so that no man would make spoons out of the bones of his father and mother. He said to them: So too the Holy Scriptures, their uncleanness corresponds to their preciousness. The writings of Homer, which are not precious, do not defile the hands. (*m. Yadayim* 4.6. Trans. S. Leiman, *Canonization* 107–108)

A much later explanation for the origin of the phrase comes from ca. 350–375 CE in *Shabbath* 14a where we read:

> And why did the rabbis impose uncleanness upon Scriptural books? R. Mesharshiya said: Because originally *terumah*[4] foods were stored near Torah scrolls, for they argued: This is holy and

that is holy. When it was seen that the books came to harm, the rabbis imposed uncleanness upon them. (Trans. S. Leiman, *Canonization* 108)

"Defiling the hands" is commonly employed in the second century CE and later as a Jewish designation for sacred literature. In *m. Yadayim* 3.2–5 (quoted in the previous section) we have the primary text for understanding what is meant by this phrase and some of the background for the application of the term. This is, of course, not the only place where the words are used in the rabbinic literature, but it is one of the earliest texts for understanding the phrase and it lets us know, as noted above, that in the second century CE there was a rabbinic debate over the inspired status of Songs of Songs and Ecclesiastes (Qoheleth).

It appears that it is only with the secularization of the scribal profession, which took place in Judaism in the second and third centuries CE, that the designation was regularly used to distinguish between sacred and secular in writings, namely, the writings that "defile the hands" and those that do not. Since most if not all scribal writing was held to be sacred in the earlier and formative time of Judaism, there was a prohibition against writing down of prayers, oral traditions, and legends until the third century CE. When the prohibition ceased, there was a need to distinguish between what was and what was not sacred. This begins to take place in Judaism in the context of the Tannaitic writers of the late second century and following. The shift in the meaning of Torah from referring to a scroll of the Pentateuch to including all that the sages had to say about the Torah began to take place during this time as well. By the fourth century the idea that the Torah was twofold (written and oral Torah) when given to Moses was widely accepted. This change is significant since it effectively and considerably expanded the Hebrew canon of sacred writings.

Christians never used the phrase "defiling the hands" in reference to their sacred scriptures, but in the fourth and fifth centuries they also found meaningful terms of their own to express the sacredness of their scriptures, namely, "canonical" or "encovenanted scriptures [*ton endiathekon graphon*]" (Eusebius, *Ecclesiastical History* 5.8.1). We will speak more about this in Chapter 7.

DECISIONS BY CHURCH COUNCILS

Although it is common to suggest that church councils actually determined what books would be included in the Christian biblical canons, a more accurate reflection of the matter is that the councils recognized or acknowledged those books that had already obtained prominence from usage among the various early and contemporary Christian churches. The examples below of church council decisions demonstrate what the communities recognized. If church councils made any decisions about the scope of the biblical canon, they were made only in regard to books that were *on the fringe* of the collections that had already obtained considerable recognition in some churches though not in others. These decisions came only at the end of a long process of recognition in the churches and they were not unilateral decisions "from the top." Church councils did not so much create biblical canons as they reflected the state of affairs in their geographical locations. Their decisions appear to have been based on what the majority view was at the time the councils met.

The Eastern churches appear to have been more conservative in their selection of writings for a sacred scripture canon. The most important council at the end of the process for the Roman Catholic Church was the Council of Trent. In its fourth cession on April 8, 1546, the church set forth its decision regarding the limits of the Old Testament canon and included in it the books of *Tobit, Judith, Wisdom of Solomon, Ecclesiasticus (Sirach)*, and 1 & 2 *Maccabees*. The 4th session states in part:

> The holy, ecumenical and general Council . . ., following . . . the examples of the orthodox Fathers . . . receives and venerates with a feeling of piety and reverence all the books of the Old and New Testaments, since one God is the author of both; also the traditions, whether relating to faith or to morals, as having been dictated either orally by Christ or by the Holy Ghost, and preserved in the Catholic Church in unbroken succession.

After listing the books it goes on to say, "If anyone does not accept as sacred and canonical the aforesaid books in their entirety and with all their parts, as they have been accustomed to be read in the Catholic Church . . . let him be anathema." This decision was reaffirmed by the First Vatican Council (1869–1870) (Trans. F. J. Stendebach).

In the year 1559, the Reformed Churches set forth their *Gallican Confession* (*Confessio Gallicana*) and later in the *Belgic Confession* (articles IV and V) of 1561 they set forth a biblical canon that excluded the apocryphal books that were included by the Roman Catholics. In England in 1562 and 1571, the church of England accepted or welcomed the apocryphal books, but added that they were not to be used to set forth the church's teaching. After listing the books which belong to the larger Old Testament canon, and affirming the current Protestant Old Testament canon, the document concludes: "And the other books (as Hierome [Jerome] saith) the Church doth read for example of life and instruction of manners, but yet doth it not apply them to establish any doctrine" (Trans. O. Chadwick). After this statement the Apocryphal books are listed.

The popularity of the Jewish biblical canon in the early church is undeniable, but the fact that the lists of Old Testament scriptures from churches of the fourth to the sixth centuries differ from the Jewish biblical canon suggests that Christian dependence on the Hebrew Bible canon was not a determining factor in regard to the books that were placed in the Christian Old Testament canons. Even where there was an attempt to reproduce the Hebrew or Jewish biblical canon, there is still the absence of the book of Esther (see Melito's list) or the addition of the *Epistle of Jeremiah* or *Baruch* in some of these lists. None of the early church lists are exactly the same as the Jewish biblical canon. As late as 1950, the Holy Synod of the Greek Orthodox Church authorized as its Old Testament canon the entire Apocrypha, including *2 Ezra* and *3* and *4 Maccabees*, which were placed in an appendix. The Old Testament of the Russian Bible of 1956 generally has the same contents as the Greek Bible, but *3 Ezra* and *4 Maccabees* are absent.

Among the several council decisions in the early church regarding its biblical canon, two are probably the most important. The first is the council held at Laodicea (ca. 363 CE) that in its Canon 59 decided which Psalms could be used in the churches. Canon 60 of the same council listed the books of the Old Testament canon. These books are the same as those listed in the canon of Athanasius (367 CE), except that Ruth is combined with Judges and Esther immediately follows. A discussion of Athanasius and his influence on the Christian biblical canon will come below in our investigation of the New Testament canon, but we can say here that his canon of scriptures was not universally accepted in his day. Only later with the support of Augustine at the councils of Hippo (393) and Carthage (397) did his collection carry considerably more weight. While all of the three major churches eventually accepted his New Testament canon, his Old Testament canon that included some apocryphal books is another matter.

The second of these most important council decisions, as we just noted, took place in 393 CE when the church council that met at Hippo set forth a biblical canon similar to the one produced by Athanasius and supported strongly by Augustine. Although the deliberations of this council are now lost, they were summarized in the proceedings of the Third Council of Carthage held in 397 CE. The council at Hippo was apparently the first church council to make a formal decision on the scope and contents of the biblical canon.

To conclude, the books now held as sacred scripture by the Jews, namely the Hebrew Bible, were not the only books that informed Jews in the time of Jesus and the churches have never been in complete agreement on the scope of their Old Testament biblical canon, though they all accept the books of the Hebrew Bible. Only the Protestants have restricted themselves to the books in the Hebrew Bible, but not to their sequence or the three-part divisions of that biblical canon.

Jewish Scriptures and Christian Old/First Testament Canons

Hebrew Bible	Catholic	Orthodox	Protestant	Ethiopian
Law/Torah (Pentateuch)	**Pentateuch**	**Historical Books**	**Pentateuch**	**Octateuch**
Genesis	Genesis	Genesis	Genesis	Pentateuch +
Exodus	Exodus	Exodus	Exodus	Joshua
Leviticus	Leviticus	Leviticus	Leviticus	Judges
Numbers	Numbers	Numbers	Numbers	Ruth
Deuteronomy	Deuteronomy	Deuteronomy	Deuteronomy	
		Joshua		Judith
Prophets (Nebiim)	**Historical Books**	Judges	**Historical Books**	Samuels
Former Prophets	Joshua	Ruth	Joshua	Kings
Joshua	Judges	1 Kingdoms (= 1 Samuel)	Judges	Chronicles
Judges	Ruth	2 Kingdoms (= 2 Samuel)	Ruth	1 Esdras + Ezra
1 & 2 Samuel	1 Samuel	3 Kings (= 1 Kings)	1 Samuel	Apocalypse
1 & 2 Kings	2 Samuel	4 Kings (= 2 Kings)	2 Samuel	Esther
Latter Prophets:	1 Kings	1 Chronicles	1 Kings	Tobit
Isaiah	2 Kings	2 Chronicles	2 Kings	1-2 Maccabees
Jeremiah	1 Chronicles	1 Esdras	1 Chronicles	Job
Ezekiel	2 Chronicles	2 Esdras	2 Chronicles	Psalms
The Twelve:	Ezra	Nehemiah	Ezra	5 books of Solomon
Hosea	Nehemiah	Tobit	Nehemiah	
Joel	Tobit	Judith	Esther	**Prophets**
Amos	Judith	Esther (with 6 additions)		*Major Prophets*
Obadiah	Esther (+6 additions)	1 Maccabees	**Poetic Books**	Isaiah
Jonah	1 Maccabees	2 Maccabees	Job	Jeremiah
Micah	2 Maccabees	3 Maccabees	Psalms	Ezekiel
Nahum			Proverbs	Daniel
Habakkuk			Ecclesiastes	
Zephaniah			Song of Songs	
Haggai				
Zechariah				
Malachi				

(Cont'd)

Jewish Scriptures and Christian Old/First Testament Canons (*Continued*)

Hebrew Bible	Catholic	Orthodox	Protestant	Ethiopian
Writings (*Ketubim*)	**Wisdom Books**	**Poetic Books**	**Prophetic Books**	*Minor Prophets*
Psalms	Job	Psalms (with Psalm 151)	Isaiah	Hosea
Proverbs	Psalms	Job	Jeremiah	Joel
Job	Proverbs	Proverbs	Ezekiel	Amos
	Ecclesiastes	Ecclesiastes	Daniel	Obadiah
Five Scrolls (Hamesh	Song of Songs	Song of Songs	Hosea	Jonah
Megillot):	Wisdom of Solomon	Wisdom of Solomon	Joel	Micah
Song of Songs	Ecclesiasticus	Wisdom of Sirach	Amos	Nahum
Ruth			Obadiah	Habakkuk
Lamentations	**Prophetic Books**	**Prophetic Books**	Jonah	Zephaniah
Ecclesiastes	Isaiah	Hosea	Micah	Haggai
Esther	Jeremiah	Amos	Nahum	Zechariah
Daniel	Lamentations	Micah	Habakkuk	Malachi
Ezra-Nehemiah	Baruch + Epistle of Jeremiah	Joel	Zephaniah	Sirach
1-2 Chronicles	Ezekiel	Obadiah	Haggai	Pseud.-Josephus
	Daniel (+3 additions:	Jonah	Zechariah	Jubilees
	Prayer of Azariah & Song of	Nahum	Malachi	1 Enoch
	Three Young Men, Susanna, &	Habakkuk		
	Bel and the Dragon)	Zephaniah		
	Hosea	Malachi		
	Joel	Isaiah		
	Amos	Jeremiah		
	Obadiah	Baruch		
	Jonah	Lamentations of Jeremiah		
	Micah	Epistle of Jeremiah		
	Nahum	Ezekiel		
	Habakkuk	Daniel (+ *Prayer of Azariah, Song*		
	Zephaniah	*of the Three Youths, Susanna,*		
	Haggai	*and Bell and the Dragon*)		
	Zechariah			
	Malachi			

FURTHER READING

Ackroyd, P. R. and C. F. Evans, eds. *The Cambridge History of the Bible: From Beginnings to Jerome.* Vol. 1. Cambridge, England/New York: Cambridge University Press, 1970.

Auwer, J.–M. and H. J. De Jonge, eds. *The Biblical Canons.* BETL clxiii. Leuven: Leuven University Press, 2003.

Barr, James. *Holy Scripture: Canon, Authority, Criticism.* Philadelphia, PA: The Westminster Press, 1983.

Barrera, Julio Trebolle. *The Jewish Bible and the Christian Bible: An Introduction to the History of the Bible.* Trans. Wilfred G. E. Watson. Leiden, New York and Köln: E. J. Brill; Grand Rapids, MI: Eerdmans, 1998.

Barton, John. *Holy Writings, Sacred Text: The Canon in Early Christianity.* Louisville, KY: Westminster John Knox Press, 1997.

Barton, John. *How the Bible Came to Be.* Louisville, KY: Westminster John Knox Press, 1997.

Beckwith, Roger. *The Old Testament of the New Testament Church and Its Background in Early Judaism.* Grand Rapids, MI: Eerdmans, 1985.

Bruce, F. F. *The Canon of Scripture.* Downers Grove, IL: InterVarsity Press, 1988.

Campenhausen, Hans von. *The Formation of the Christian Bible.* Trans. J. A. Baker. Philadelphia, PA: Fortress, 1972.

Chapman, Stephen B. *The Law and the Prophets: A Study in Old Testament Canon Formation.* Forschungen zum Alten Testament 27. Tübingen: Mohr Siebeck, 2000.

Childs, Brevard S. *Biblical Theology of the Old and New Testament: Theological Reflection on the Christian Bible.* Philadelphia, PA: Fortress Press, 1993.

Childs, Brevard S. *Introduction to the Old Testament as Scripture.* Philadelphia, PA: Fortress Press, 1979.

Cross, Frank Moore. *From Epic to Canon: History and Literature in Ancient Israel.* Baltimore, MD and London: Johns Hopkins University Press, 1998.

Davies, Philip R. *Scribes and Schools: The Canonization of the Hebrew Scriptures.* Library of Ancient Israel. Louisville, KY: Westminster John Knox Press, 1998.

Edrei, Arye and Doran Mendels. "A Split Jewish Diaspora: Its Dramatic Consequences," *JSP* 16 (2007), 2:91–137.

Ellis, Earle E. *The Old Testament in Early Christianity: Canon and Interpretation in the Light of Modern Research.* Grand Rapids, MI: Baker Book House, 1991.

Harry Y. Gamble. *Books and Readers in the Early Church: A History of Early Christian Texts.* New Haven, CT/London: Yale University Press, 1995.

Jones, Barry Alan. *The Formation of the Book of the Twelve: A Study in Text and Canon.* SBL Dissertation series 149. Atlanta, GA: Scholars Press, 1995.

Leiman, Sid Z. *The Canon and Masorah of the Hebrew Bible: An Introductory Reader*. New York: Ktav, 1974.

McDonald, Lee M. *The Biblical Canon: Its Origin, Transmission, and Authority*. Peabody, MA: Hendrickson Publishers, 2006.

McDonald, Lee M. *Forgotten Scriptures: The Selection and Rejection of Early Religious Writings*. Louisville, KY: Westminster John Knox Press, 2009.

McDonald, Lee M. and James A. Sanders, eds. *The Canon Debate*. Peabody, MA: Hendrickson Publishers, 2002.

Miller, John W. *The Origins of the Bible: Rethinking Canon History*. Theological Inquiries. New York: Paulist Press, 1985.

Sanders, James A. *From Sacred Story to Sacred Text*. Philadelphia, PA: Fortress Press, 1987.

Sanders, James A. "Spinning the Bible," *BR* 14 (June 1998), 22–29, 44–45.

Sanders, James A. *Torah and Canon*. Philadelphia, PA: Fortress Press, 1972.

Sawyer, John F. A. *Sacred Languages and Sacred Texts*. Religion in the First Christian Centuries. London/New York: Routledge, 1999.

Schniedewind, William M. *How the Bible Became a Book*. Cambridge, England and New York: Cambridge University Press, 2004.

Seitz, Christopher R. *The Goodly Fellowship of the Prophets: The Achievement of Association in Canon Formation*. Acadia Studies in Bible and Theology. Series editors: C. A Evans and Lee M. McDonald. Grand Rapids, MI: Baker Academic, 2009.

Silver, Daniel Jeremy. *The Story of Scripture: From Oral Tradition to the Written Word*. New York: Basic Books, Inc. Publishers, 1990.

Swete, H. B. *An Introduction to the Old Testament in Greek*. Revised by R. R. Ottley with Appendix by H. St. J. Thackeray. Cambridge: Cambridge University Press, 1914, reprinted by Hendrickson Publishers, 1989.

VanderKam, James C. *From Revelation to Canon: Studies in the Hebrew Bible and Second Temple Literature*. JSJSup 62. Leiden/Boston, MA: E. J. Brill, 2000.

Wise, Michael, Martin Abegg, Jr., and Edward Cook, *The Dead Sea Scrolls: A New Translation*. San Francisco, CA: Harper Collins, 1996.

CHAPTER FIVE

THE EMERGENCE OF *CHRISTIAN* SCRIPTURES

The early church from its inception was accustomed to the notion of sacred scripture, the authority of which was indisputable—even if we are unsure of the full extent of that collection of writings. There is no convincing evidence that the early church was born with a *fixed* biblical canon (an Old Testament) in its hands, but the precedent of a sacred scripture was already well established in the Jewish community long before the birth of Jesus. As was noted earlier, in the time of the writing of the New Testament, scripture was generally acknowledged to be the "Law and the Prophets" or simply the "Law." The scope and contents of the sacred scripture collections in the Land of Israel were still fluid in the first century BCE and CE ("canon 1"). The early Christians assumed that the way and will of God were communicated through the written word of Israel's scriptures, but as the church grew, it also saw considerable value in making use in its worship, instruction, and witness of its own collection of writings along with the scriptures that it had inherited from its Jewish siblings.

Well before their own writings were called "scripture" or "Holy Scripture," the early Christians saw the value of the Christian writings. Indeed, soon after, their production and their circulation in the churches were widespread by the end of the first century CE. The church came to believe that the word and will of God were also communicated through inspired writings from the Christian community and eventually (by the end of the second century CE) some Christians began to refer to some of those writings as "scripture."

As previously mentioned, both Christianity and Pharisaic Judaism, the primary Jewish sects in the Land of Israel that survived the destruction of Jerusalem (66–70 CE), as well as the Jews living in the diaspora, saw the need for more sacred literature in addition to "the Law and the Prophets" to meet the needs of their respective religious communities. Christians added the literature that they believed stemmed from the apostolic communities and at roughly the same time that the Jewish community added their codified oral traditions (the Mishnah) to their sacred written collections. Although Christians had a precedent for a written scripture before the time of Jesus, the church did not make a conscious effort to produce its own written scriptures. There is nothing in most of the writings that eventually became the New Testament that suggests that its writers believed that they were producing Holy Scripture as they wrote. The only exception is the author of Revelation who pronounces a curse on those who would change or alter the book (22.18–19; cf. Deut. 4.2), and possibly also Paul in 1 Cor. 7.40 who comes close to claiming that he was speaking (writing) by the power of the Spirit. Paul distinguishes his comments from those of Jesus with the obvious implication that Jesus' words were viewed with greater sacred authority in the churches (see 1 Cor. 7.10, 12).

Just as complexity attended the origins and development of the Old Testament canon, it also attended the formation of the New Testament canon. For more than a century, the origin and development of the New Testament canon has been placed largely in the late second century CE, allowing for minor modifications and adjustments in its scope at a later time. Many well-known scholars accepted the second century as the primary context for the development of a New Testament canon including Adolf von Harnack, R. M. Grant, Hans von Campenhausen, Denis Farkasfalvy, William Farmer, Bruce M. Metzger, F. F. Bruce, and Everett Ferguson (see Further Reading at end of this chapter). They contend that the factors that gave rise to the New Testament canon appeared in that century when Christians addressed the heresies of Marcion, Gnostic Christians, and the Montanists, but there is no viable evidence for a closed or semi-closed New Testament canon in the writings of the second-century fathers and it is highly doubtful that the matter was even discussed, let alone decided in the second century. The strongest argument for a second century dating of canon formation depends on the dating of the Muratorian Fragment in that century. This fragment that was originally produced in Greek and later translated into Latin contains a list or catalogue of Christian books (with the odd addition of the Wisdom of Solomon) that were recognized as authoritative sacred texts among Christians, but this list of sacred books has its only parallels in the fourth and not the second century CE. The theory depends on an early acknowledgment of Christian writings as scriptural texts and that the early church fathers responded to heresies and challenges to Christian tradition by creating a new canon of Christian scriptures, namely, a New Testament canon. In what follows, I will examine these and other assumptions and offer an alternative proposal that situates the stabilization of the New Testament canon in a fourth century context. The logical starting point for the origins of the New Testament writings, however, is with Jesus himself and that is where our discussion will start.

THE AUTHORITY OF JESUS AND EARLY CHRISTIAN WRITINGS

The first and most important authority in the early church was Jesus. Whatever he said or did was considered authoritative and sacred in the church. When the oral traditions circulating in the churches about what Jesus said or did were written down, soon (within 20 to 30 years at the latest) they were readily incorporated into Christian preaching and teaching. When those who followed Jesus most closely (the apostles) spoke, many of the churches believed that they were reflecting what Jesus said and did. The early stories about Jesus that were circulating in the churches were soon put in writing and circulated in the churches. The story of Jesus' activities, preaching or teaching, and his fate were at the center of the life of the early church. The scriptures of the Hebrew Bible, which were not yet finalized in the first century, along with this newly written story of Jesus formed the authoritative base of early Christianity. There was, however, a significant difference in how the Jewish scriptures were not interpreted, namely in light of the activity and preaching of Jesus. For the most part, the Jewish scriptures were viewed as prophetic literature in the sense that they had predicted the life and death and resurrection of

Jesus (e.g., Matt. 2.13–15; 1 Cor. 15.3–4). There is very little in the New Testament that could reasonably be explained as a careful interpretation of the Old Testament scriptures. The longest passage cited from the Old Testament writings in the New Testament is in Heb. 8.8–12 citing Jer. 31.31–34.

Although there are many references to the Old Testament literature in the New Testament books, there are few detailed interpretations of those texts in their original context and meaning. The argument that the earliest followers of Jesus arrived at their understanding of who Jesus was from a careful investigation of the Jewish Scriptures simply cannot be sustained. Their interpretation of those texts came instead from their experience with and knowledge of Jesus, but their perspective of the authority of the scriptures they inherited from their Jewish siblings led them to study them in order to understand better Jesus' identity and mission. The *primary* value of those scriptures for the early followers of Jesus appears to be their predictive witness to his life and work. The early Christians viewed themselves as the new people of God and as such they saw themselves as the recipients of the promises of God in their sacred scriptures that had previously been given to the nation of Israel. They even understood themselves as the "new Israel" (see Gal. 6.15–16) and, as the church became more and more Gentile in its makeup, some of these followers of Jesus believed that the Gentile church had replaced or superseded the Jews, at least temporarily, as the people of God (Rom. 11.11–24).

The starting point in understanding the early church's use of the Old Testament scriptures in the New Testament writings is not so much with a careful understanding of the Old Testament scriptures themselves as it is with a careful understanding of Jesus, that is, who he was and what his mission was in the world. Christian literature itself appears to have begun as a response to Jesus in light of Christian experience (Acts 18.28), and only subsequently as an interpretation of the Old Testament scriptures themselves. Bible scholars today generally agree that the emergence or birth of the early church was not because of a careful interpretation of the Old Testament scriptures, but rather as a result of a new understanding of Jesus that was born out of an experience with the Christ of the church's confession.

It cannot be an overstatement to say that Jesus was the primary authority in the earliest Christian communities. Although the early followers of Jesus recognized the sacredness of the Jewish Scriptures, especially the Law and the Prophets, still it was Jesus' life and death and resurrection that were at the center of their teaching and preaching (1 Cor. 15.3–11). In fact, one of the oldest confessions of faith in the New Testament writings is in the book of Romans where Paul passes on a creed that he himself had received, namely, "that if you confess with your mouth that Jesus is Lord and believe in your heart that God raised him from the dead, you will be saved" (Rom. 10.9). Whatever Jesus said and did was in a very real sense the "canon" (final authority) for his followers. His life was the example par excellence for them to follow (Phil. 2.5; Eph. 5.1–2; Heb. 12.1–3). His death for the sins of the people and his resurrection were not only pivotal in early Christian beliefs, they were also central in the Christians' understanding of their scriptures. Those scriptures were believed to have predicted his life, death, and resurrection (1 Cor. 15.3–11; Acts 2.31–36; Heb. 13.20; 1 Pet. 1.3; Rev. 1.5, 17–18; 2.8). Jesus' life, death, and resurrection were the quintessential presupposition for all Christian faith.

The reports or stories of Jesus' words and deeds, including his fate, no doubt circulated first orally through preaching and teaching (catechetical instruction) within the newly formed Christian communities from the beginning, but in time many of these stories and traditions were written down. At first, only the traditions of the sayings of Jesus along with his death and resurrection were of pivotal importance to the churches, but soon the practical value of several of the Apostle Paul's letters also became apparent to many churches. Before long, a collection of these writings were circulating in churches by the end of the first century containing not only sayings of Jesus (the Gospels), but also their practical implications (Paul's letters) for Christian faith. Some sayings of Jesus continued to be passed on in the churches in oral form even after the written Gospels appeared. Some 266 of these sayings that are not in the New Testament Gospels but have been found in a variety of locations—namely in ancient manuscripts, writings of the early church fathers, and noncanonical writings—are commonly tagged by biblical scholars as the *Agrapha*. Some of those noncanonical sayings that scholars believe are more reliable and may go back to Jesus himself. Many collections of sayings and deeds of Jesus circulated orally at first but subsequently in written form in what we now call "gospels." While we are more familiar with the gospels of Matthew, Mark, Luke and John, there were antecedents to the New Testament Gospels circulating that have been lost. Luke states this much at the beginning of his gospel: "Since many have undertaken toset down an orderly account of the events that have been fulfilled among us . . . I too decided, after investigating everything carefully from the very first to write an orderly account for you . . ." (Lk. 1.1–3). The *agrapha* will be discussed more below.

Some of these accounts may have been sent to various communities of those who followed Jesus, but the ones that were most popular among the early Christians are the canonical Gospels (Matthew, Mark, Luke, and John). The first of these surviving gospels was probably written in the first century in the 60s and is attributed to John Mark, the one time companion of Paul and Barnabas (Acts 13) and later of Peter (1 Pet. 5.13). Since initially there were no names attached to the canonical gospels, they are formally anonymous, but they have come down to us with the names that were attributed to them at the end of the second century and are likely based on earlier oral traditions in the churches. Mark, and subsequently the other Evangelists put the story of Jesus into a narrative form that told of his ministry, teaching and preaching as well as his passion (death) and resurrection.

With the Gospel of Mark, a new genre of literature began that was not altogether a biography nor yet altogether a historical description of Jesus' life and ministry. It was rather a highly selective collection of what the churches believed was most significant about Jesus and they were produced both for catechetical reasons and also for use in drawing persons to follow him (for instance, Mk 8.32–35; Jn 20.30–31). Whatever else may be said about these early Christian writings (Gospels), they were first of all calls to faith in Jesus as the Christ who was the final authority for the churches from the beginning. For example, in Rev. 2–3 the risen Lord is sovereign over the seven churches of Asia Minor and comes to them with divine authority. Jesus has no rivals in the church and he was at the center of and presupposition for all early Christian literature (Matt. 28.19).

Like Mark (Mk 1.1), Paul uses the term "Good News" or ("Gospel") about Jesus and not in reference to a genre of literature about him. Paul claims that Jesus was set apart for the work of the "good news of God which he [God] promised beforehand through his prophets in the holy scriptures, the Gospel concerning his son" (Rom. 1.1–3a; NRSV). Paul used the term to designate the specific oral Christian tradition that he received and shared in the Christian communities about God's activity in the death and resurrection of Jesus (1 Cor. 15.1–5), but also about his coming again or *parousia* (1 Cor. 15.23–28). The preaching of the early church focused on Jesus, his deeds, and the presence of the kingdom of God that was manifested in his words and deeds. In other words, and again, Jesus was the locus of authority of the early Christian movement.

As the church grew in its understanding of its mission and as a result of being scattered by persecution (Acts 82–4; 11.19), it soon became necessary to communicate with the new churches and this often took place in the form of written letters when personal visits were not possible. Paul, the primary missionary to the Gentiles, often wrote letters to churches that he had founded when he could not be with them, (2 Cor. 1.23–2.4). His letters generally tried to clarify issues of Christian faith and conduct that he thought important for his churches. These letters, while not always following the usual Greco-Roman style of writing, have significant parallels with both formal and informal letters in his day. Because of the popularity of this style of writing, later Christians also used this medium to communicate relevant messages for churches (1, 2 Timothy, Titus, 1 Peter, 1–3 John, and James, Jude, but also Rev. 2–3 and subsequently, the *Letters of Ignatius*, ca. 115 CE). Several of Paul's letters have survived antiquity, especially those that were sent to seven churches (Rome, Corinth, Galatia, Ephesians, Philippians, Colossians, Thessalonica) and by the end of the first century at the latest several of them were beginning to be circulated among various churches. One can see even in the Colossian letter an admonition to do this very thing (Col. 4.16–17).

One of the early second century collections of Paul's writings came from Marcion, one of the major "heretics" in the second century, but his collection was not likely the first made of Paul's writings. Marcion, a wealthy businessman from Asia Minor (ca. 140 CE), was an active lay person in the church and was highly influential in many churches throughout the second century. (See a more detailed discussion of Marcion and his influence in Chapter 7.) The letters of Paul were not vested with the authority of Jesus during Paul's lifetime, not even by Paul, but by the end of the second century and after considerable use in the churches, their value and that of the canonical Gospels in the church's life and witness was obvious and they were among the first Christian writings to be recognized as sacred scripture. As we noted in Chapter 3, by the end of the second century these writings were beginning to be called Scripture. This was not the case for several other New Testament writings. Their recognition as sacred scripture took longer.

It is clear that from the beginning of the church the sayings of Jesus had a scripture-like (authoritative) status in the churches whether his sayings and deeds were in written or oral form. See, for example, the higher regard Paul gives to the words of Jesus in 1 Cor. 7.10, 17, and by implication greater than his own in 7.12, 25; 1 Thess. 4.15; Mt. 28.19, and elsewhere. Clement of Rome (ca. 95 CE) likewise acknowledged the authority of the teaching of Jesus for the churches when he wrote:

> Let us, therefore, be humble-minded, brethren, putting aside all arrogance and conceit and foolishness and wrath, and let us do that which is written (for the Holy Spirit says, "Let not the wise man boast himself in his wisdom, nor the strong man in his strength, nor the rich man in his riches, but he that boasts let him boast in the Lord, to seek him out and to do judgment and righteousness"), *especially remembering the words of the Lord Jesus* which he spoke when he was teaching gentleness and long-suffering. For he spoke thus: "Be merciful, that you may obtain mercy. Forgive, that you may be forgiven. As you do, so shall it be done unto you. As you give, so shall it be given unto you. As you judge, so shall you be judged. As you are kind, so shall kindness be shown to you. With what measure you mete, it shall be measured to you." *With this commandment and with these injunctions let us strengthen ourselves to walk in obedience to his hallowed*

words and let us be humble-minded, for the holy word says, "On whom shall I look, but on the meek and gentle and him who trembles at my oracles." (*1 Clement* 13.1–4, LCL. Modified and emphasis added)

In another place he adds:

Why do we divide and tear asunder the members of Christ, and raise up strife against our own body, and reach such a pitch of madness as to forget that we are members one of another? *Remember the words of the Lord Jesus*; for he said, "Woe unto that man: it were good for him if he had not been born, than that he should offend one of my elect . . ." (*1 Clement* 46.7–8, LCL. Emphasis added)

Clement's appeal for order is based on the warnings of Jesus, but he emphasizes and introduces this with his "remember the words of the Lord Jesus." These are the only two references to the words of Jesus in *1 Clement*, but there are over 100 references to the Old Testament literature. Interestingly, Paul is cited in Clement more than Jesus, but this is no doubt because Paul founded the Corinthian church and had himself spoken about the divisions in the church that continued well into the end of the first century and occasioned Clement of Rome's letter to them (1 Cor. 1.10–13). The language of Clement cited in the above passages shows considerable familiarity with the sayings of Jesus, especially those found in the Gospel of Matthew, but there are only a few general references to other traditions in the Synoptic Gospels. Although Clement refers or alludes to Hebrews and Paul's epistles throughout his letter, he never refers to them or the Gospels as "scripture" (Greek = *graphe*). The authority of the words of Jesus no doubt had the authority attributed to them that was not unlike the authority of sacred scripture, but that designation was not yet given to his sayings in the Gospels until later in the second century.

In his well known *Letter to Flora* (ca. 160 CE), Ptolemy frequently refers to the "words of the Savior" (3.5, 8; 4.1, 4; and also 7.5, 10) as the primary authority for his instruction. See, for instance, his devotion to the teaching of Jesus in his explanation of the proper way to understand the Law of Moses and his reference to those who have misunderstood it:

> *That is what happens to people who do not see what follows from the words of the Savior.* For a house or city divided against itself cannot stand, our Savior declared. Furthermore the apostle says that the creation of the world was peculiar to Him and that all things were made through him, and apart from him nothing was made, refuting the flimsy wisdom of these liars; not the creation of a god who corrupts, but of a just God who hates evil. That is the opinion of heedless men who do not understand the cause of the providence of the Demiurge [a name given to an inferior deity who created the material world], who are blind not only in the eye of the soul but also in that of the body.
>
> How they have strayed from the truth is clear to you from what has been said. Two groups have gone astray each in their peculiar fashion, the one through ignorance of the God of justice, the other through ignorance of the Father of All, whom only he who alone knew him revealed at his coming. Now it remains for us who have been granted the knowledge of both of these, to explain the Law to you with accuracy, what its nature is and the one by whom it has been given, the Lawgiver, *proving our demonstrations from the words of our Savior, through which alone it is possible without error to travel toward the comprehension of reality.*
>
> First one must learn that the whole Law which is contained in the Pentateuch of Moses has not been decreed by some one person, I mean by God alone; but there are also some command-ments in it given by men; *and that it is tripartite the words of the Savior teach us.* For one part is ascribed to God himself and his legislation; another is ascribed to Moses, not meaning that God gave the law through him, but that Moses legislated starting from his own understanding; and the third is ascribed to the elders of the people, who are themselves found from the beginning introducing ordinances of their own. *How this came about you may learn from the words of the Savior.* When the Savior was talk-ing somewhere to those arguing with him about divorce, which was allowed by the Law, he said to them, Moses because of the

hardness of your hearts permitted a man to put away his wife; from the beginning it was not so. For God joined them together, and what God has joined, let not a man, he said, put asunder. Here he shows that the law of God is one thing —it forbids a woman to be divorced by her husband—and the law of Moses is another—it permits this bond to be sundered because of hardness of heart. So in this way Moses ordains a law contrary to God, for divorce is contrary to no divorce. (Trans. Stevenson, ANE 92–93. Adapted and emphasis added)

For both Clement of Rome and Ptolemy, the words of Jesus undoubtedly functioned authoritatively as sacred scripture even when they were not quoted from a written text nor were there specific scriptural formulae designations ("the scriptures says," etc.) used in these passages. With the recognition of the authority of the words of Jesus and the value of the teachings of Paul, the emergence of a Christian scripture had its beginning. Undoubtedly, the teachings of Jesus as well as his deeds and his fate were at the heart of the emergence of a *Christian* scripture.

THE AUTHORITY OF THE APOSTLES AND THEIR WRITINGS

There are numerous citations and quotations of or allusions to various New Testament writings in the Apostolic Fathers (roughly 90–150 CE), the earliest Christian writings following the New Testament writings, and most of these church father references are from the canonical Gospels, especially the Gospel of Matthew and to a lesser extent the Gospel of John, but some are from writings attributed to the Apostle Paul. These references are most often citing Jesus (from the Gospels) and occasionally the Apostle Paul, but initially and generally they do not mention the apostolic names that were attached to this literature. That begins to take place around the middle of the second century. The early church writers and teachers began to cite the specific literature of the New Testament by name (after the apostles) and subsequently they began to refer to it as "scripture" in the last third of the second century. When these writings began to be introduced with the words "the scripture says," "it is written" and comparable formulae that were commonly used in reference to the Old Testament scriptures, then we have evidence of their recognition as sacred scripture.

As in the case of the emergence of the Old Testament scriptures, the New Testament writings began to attain something like a "canon 1" status earlier than the time when they were cited by name and identified as sacred scripture. When these writings and others began to be listed in catalogues of sacred scriptures ("canon 2" status), we have moved into the fourth century CE.

Citations of and allusions to the Gospels were common in the second century. The practice of citing Christian writings in a scriptural manner, that is, authoritatively, however, indicates some recognition of the esteem and authority these writings had in the Christian community. They are generally cited in an authoritative manner before they are more formally called "scripture." In other words, the New Testament writings functioned as scripture before they were called scripture. There is, however, an important qualification that needs to be observed, namely the distinction between the authoritative words or commands of Jesus, and the Gospels that contained them.

It was initially only the words of Jesus in written and oral traditions that were cited and had a scripture-like status in the churches from the beginning of their circulation in the churches, but this does not mean that the Gospel containing these words or the Apostle to whom the book was attributed had reached canonical status—at least not at first. It was a word from Jesus that, when written down, became scripture-like. The source for this written word of Jesus was of secondary importance to the early churches and that is why there is no reference to the authors of the Gospels until the last third of the second century. Around the middle of the second century, the Gospels were beginning to be called the "memoirs of the apostles" as we will see below, but the names of those apostles were seldom mentioned before the last third of the second century.

The lack of prominence given to a gospel writer or writing began to change by the end of the second century when those closest to Jesus were deemed more trustworthy than those who were not. In this context, a number of second century gospels and other literature paralleling the genres of the New Testament writings (gospel, acts, epistles, apocalypses) began to appear in apostolic names. It was rather the

sayings of Jesus located in these documents that were given prominence and recognition in the churches. Also, even though the Gospels
may have been intended from the outset to be used (or read) in the
churches, they did not initially attain the authority that they later
acquired. The freedom with which the early copiers of these documents made changes in the text of these Gospels in the first three
centuries suggests this. The numerous variants and intentional changes
in the manuscripts of these writings support this conclusion.

So when did the Gospels attain their scripture-like position in
the churches? Certainly no later than when they began to be read
alongside of, and sometimes instead of, the Old Testament scriptures
in the churches. When that happened, their recognition as sacred
scripture was certainly well on its way. The authority ascribed
to Jesus in the New Testament writings was eventually transferred to
some extent to the apostles who wrote the New Testament literature.
This does not mean that the apostles were ever viewed in the same
light as Jesus, but rather that they faithfully transmitted his teachings
and the story of his life, death, and resurrection. This confidence was
subsequently given to the apostolic community and the apostolic
writings that the churches believed they wrote. (See examples 7–10 in
the next section.)

EARLY RECOGNITION OF THE AUTHORITY
OF APOSTOLIC WRITINGS

Several late second century references to the New Testament literature are more explicit with regard to the authority and sacredness
of those writings, while earlier references are more ambiguous or
subdued. The following examples reflect some of the early first and
second century attitudes toward the locus of authority in the second
century churches. One can detect in them the early stages of extending
some of the authority of Jesus to the apostles and those in the apostolic community (Mark and Luke) as faithful witnesses to the Christ
event that gave birth to the church. By the middle to end of the second
century, apostolic authority is widely recognized in the churches and
as a result, pseudonymous writings in the names of apostles are much
more common. We will list a number of the examples of this gradual
extension of authority from Jesus to apostles testified to by faithful

witnesses in the apostolic community. We begin with Paul around 52 to 55 CE who shows the authority of Jesus over his own authority in matters facing the churches. This takes place some 20–25 years after the death of Jesus.

(1) **Paul**. In 1 Cor. 7.10–12 affirms the value of the words of the Lord (Jesus) over his own.

> To the married *I give this command—not I but the Lord*—that the wife should not separate from her husband (but if she does separate, let her remain unmarried or else be reconciled to her husband), and that the husband should not divorce his wife. *To the rest I say—I and not the Lord*—that if any believer has a wife who is an unbeliever, and she consents to live with him, he should not divorce her. (NRSV. Emphasis added.)

So also in 1 Cor. 11.23–26 in regard to problems at Corinth when Christians shared in the table fellowship, Paul cites the authority of Jesus himself to settle the issue.

> For I received *from the Lord* what I also handed on to you, that the Lord Jesus on the night when he was betrayed took a loaf of bread, and when he had given thanks, he broke it and said, "This is my body that is for you. Do this in remembrance of me." In the same way he took the cup also, after supper, saying, "This cup is the new covenant in my blood. Do this, as often as you drink it, in remembrance of me." For as often as you eat this bread and drink the cup, you proclaim the Lord's death until he comes.

Paul's authority for his Gospel came first from his special revelation from the risen Christ (Gal. 1.11–12, 15–16), but also from the words of Jesus that were passed on to him as we see also in his words in the following:

> For I received from the Lord what I also handed on to you, that *the Lord Jesus on the night that he was betrayed took a loaf of bread, and when he had given thanks, he broke it and said,* "This is my body that is for you. Do this in remembrance of me." In the same way he took the cup also, after supper, saying, "This cup is

the new covenant in my blood. Do this, as often as you drink it, in remembrance of me." (1 Cor. 11.23–25. Emphasis added)

Also,

For I passed on to you as of first importance *what I in turn had received*: that Christ died for our sins in accordance with the scriptures, and that he was buried, and that he was raised on the third day according to the scriptures. (1 Cor. 15.3–4. Emphasis added)

The authority for Paul's mission comes first from his encounter with the risen Christ (1 Cor. 9.1 and Gal. 1.15–16), which according to the Book of Acts came to him on the Damascus Road (9.1–19; 22.6–16; 12–18), but secondly, he acknowledges that he also learned what Jesus taught from others in the church (1 Cor. 15.1–3). This teaching, as we have seen above, was the primary source of authority for Paul.

(2) **2 Clement**. The unknown author of *2 Clement* (ca. 120–140, but no later than 170) acknowledges that the authoritative basis for his comments were the "scriptures" (no doubt the Jewish scriptures) and subsequently the "books and the Apostles."

Now I imagine that you are not ignorant that the living "Church is the body of Christ." For the scripture says, "God made man male and female;" the male is Christ, the female is the church. And moreover *the books and the Apostles* declare that the Church belongs not to the present, but has existed from the beginning; for she was spiritual, as was also our Jesus, but he was made manifest in the last days that he might save us. (14.2, LCL. Emphasis added)

In this passage, it is almost certain that the appeal to "the books" is a reference to the Old Testament scriptures (see also 2 Tim. 4.13) and "the Apostles" in the same text is probably a reference to the New Testament tradition common in the churches in both oral and probably also in written form. If this is so, then this text is an early indication that the New Testament tradition was placed in a parallel relationship to the Old Testament scriptures in that both are appealed to in an authoritative manner in support of the author's teaching about the preexistent Church. The apostles appear at this early date to function as the "guarantors" of the New Testament tradition, but their authority is a derived authority from Jesus. This is not unlike the "commands of the Lord" handed down to the apostles as one finds in 2 Pet. 3.2.

Again, in *2 Clement* 2.4, the author quotes Mk 2.17 (or Mt. 9.13b) introducing Jesus' words as an appeal to scripture. The author writes: "And another Scripture also says, 'I came not to call righteous, but sinners;' He means that those who are perishing must be saved, for it is great and wonderful to give strength to those which are falling" (*2 Clement* 2.4–6, LCL). Here, as in 14.2 above, it appears that the sayings of Jesus, which had not yet found a universally acknowledged fixed form, were recognized early on as on par with and closely related to the authority of the Old Testament scriptures. The words of Jesus were used to support theological arguments and moral behavior in the early church. For the author, if Jesus said it, the words had the authority of scripture.

(3) **Epistle of Barnabas** (ca. 90–130). This is a pseudonymous theological treatise produced by a Gentile Christian concerned about the death of Christ as a sacrifice in the Old Testament sense, introduced one of two gospel quotations (Mt. 22.14) in a scripture-like manner. "Let us take heed lest *as it is written* we be found 'many called but few chosen'" (*Barn.* 4.14, LCL. Emphasis added). The use of the phrase "as it is written" implies that the words of Jesus were equal in authority to the Old Testament,—that is, the words of Jesus, when written down, were equivalent to scripture. This passage may also indicate that an individual gospel text—the whole gospel itself—was beginning to be given equal authority with the Old Testament scriptures, but especially if the source in the text in question was Jesus.

(4) **Ignatius** (ca. 110–117). A frequently quoted passage from Ignatius' *Letter to the Philadelphians* showed his preference for the "Gospel" (probably the *kerygma* or preaching of and about Jesus in the oral and/or written tradition of the church) over the authority of the Old Testament scriptures. He writes:

But I beseech you to do nothing in factiousness, but after the teaching of Christ. For I heard some men saying, "If I find it not in the charters,[1] I do not believe in the Gospel." And when I said to them that it is in the Scripture, they answered me, "That is exactly the question." But *to me the charters are Jesus Christ, the inviolable charter is his cross, and death, and resurrection, and the faith which is through him;*—in these I desire to be justified by your prayers. (Ignatius, *Phld.* 8.2, LCL. Emphasis added)

It appears that Ignatius viewed Jesus' teaching as superior to the authority of the Old Testament scriptures ("charters"). More especially this text shows that for Ignatius the primary locus of authority for Christian faith was in the *event* of Jesus Christ, and more specifically, in early Christian preaching about "his cross, and death, and resurrection." The full extent of that tradition is not clear in Ignatius, but it appears that the oral and/or written traditions concerning Jesus the Christ were the superior authority for him. See, for instance, his threefold focus of authority (the Lord—or Jesus, the Apostles, and the Prophets) and the place of priority given to Jesus in the citation of the letter to the Philadelphians above. Also observe how the "Apostles" begin to take their place behind "the Lord" (Jesus).

> Brethren, I am overflowing with love to you and exceedingly joyful in watching over your safety. Yet not I, but Jesus Christ, whose bonds I bear, but am the more fearful in that I am not yet perfected; but your prayer will make me perfect for God, that I may attain the lot wherein I found mercy, *making the Gospel my refuge as the flesh of Jesus, and the Apostles as the presbytery of the Church. And the prophets also do we love because they also have announced the Gospel,* and are hoping in him and waiting for him, by faith in whom they also obtain salvation, being united with Jesus Christ, for they are worthy of love and saints worthy of admiration, approved by Jesus Christ, and numbered together in the Gospel of the common hope. (Ignatius, *Phld.* 5.1–2, LCL. Emphasis added)

Ignatius had familiarity with several New Testament writings, mostly the Gospels of Matthew and John and several of the epistles of Paul, but while he did not call this literature "scripture," the obvious parallels noted show Ignatius' knowledge and acceptance of the authority in these traditions. What Jesus said in these documents express for him what Christian attitudes and conduct ought to be. For Ignatius also, Jesus' words functioned as scripture.

(5) **Polycarp**. In his *Letter to the Philippians* (ca. 140–155), Polycarp wrote a couple of relevant passages recognizing the authority of Jesus in the church and he appears to extend that authority to the apostles. He recognized the authority of Jesus' teaching and example and admonished his hearers to obey and imitate it. Notice the following examples.

> Now "he who raised him" from the dead "will also raise us up" if we do his will, and *walk in his commandments* and love the things which he loved, refraining from all unrighteousness, covetousness, love of money, evil speaking, false witness, "rendering not evil for evil, or railing for railing," or blow for blow, or curse for curse, *but remembering what the Lord taught* when he said, "Judge not that you be not judged, forgive and it shall be forgiven unto you, be merciful that you may obtain mercy, with what measure you mete, it shall be measured to you again," and, "Blessed are the poor, and they who are persecuted for righteousness' sake, for theirs is the Kingdom of God." (Pol. *Phil.* 2.2, 3, LCL. Emphasis added.)

Next we see the authority of the words of Jesus coupled with the authority of the words of the New Testament writings (the Apostles?) in the early Christian communities in which Polycarp was ministering and also his advice on the danger of tampering with them. Clearly, one cannot tamper with the authority of Jesus nor with the writings of those who faithfully followed him and reflected his teachings. This is close to the warning given in Rev. 22.18–19 (compare to Deut. 4.2; 12.32) that is equivalent to a scripture-like status, that is, it is unchangeable. Polycarp writes:

> "For everyone who does not confess that Jesus Christ has come in the flesh is an anti-Christ" [compare 1 Jn 4.2]; and whosoever does not confess the testimony of the Cross is of the devil: *and whosoever perverts the oracles of the Lord for his own lusts*, and

says that there is neither resurrection nor judgment–this man is the first-born of Satan. Wherefore, leaving the foolishness of the crowd, and their false teaching, let us turn back to the word which was delivered to us in the beginning, "watching unto prayer" and persevering in fasting, beseeching the all-seeing God in our supplications "to lead us not into temptation," even as the Lord said, "The spirit is willing, but the flesh is weak." (*Pol. Phil.* 7.1, 2, LCL. Emphasis added)

Recognizing the example of Jesus as a rule or guide to the Christian community, his following comment is also instructive: "*Let us then be imitators of his endurance,* and if we suffer for his name's sake let us glorify him. *For this is the example which he gave us in himself,* and this is what we have believed" (Pol. *Phil.* 8.2, LCL. Emphasis added). He also cites portions of both Ps. 4.5 and Eph. 4.26 and calls them both "Scriptures." Although the original Greek portion of this passage has been lost, the Latin is still quite instructive. Polycarp writes:

For I am confident that you are well versed *in the Scriptures (in sacris literis),* and from you nothing is hid; but to me this is not granted. Only, *as it is said in these Scriptures (Modo, ut his scripturis dictum est),* "Be ye angry and sin not," and "Let not the sun go down upon your wrath." Blessed is the man who remembers this, and I believe that it is so with you. (Pol. *Phil.* 12.1, LCL. Emphasis added)

Polycarp appears to have consciously placed an Old Testament scripture and a Christian writing on an equal authoritative footing.[2] The least one could say about these two texts is that we find an authoritative appeal to texts found in both the Old Testament and the New Testament with the promise that persons following this advice will be blessed. These passages suggest a scripture-like status in the words and example of Jesus, and Polycarp assumes that his readers draw the same conclusion. Polycarp also gives evidence of a threefold focus of authority in the early churches (Jesus, the Apostles, and the Prophets [= Old Testament scriptures]) in the following comment: "So then 'let us serve *him* with fear and all reverence,' as he himself commanded us, and as did the *Apostles*, who brought us the Gospel, and the *Prophets* who foretold the coming of our Lord" (Pol. *Phil.* 6.3, LCL. Emphasis added). Evidently, the words of Jesus, when written down as in this case, take on the function of scripture even if they were not yet specifically called scripture. What is abundantly clear from the above examples is that *Jesus himself was the authoritative canon of the Church* for Polycarp.

(6) **Ptolemy**. In the *Letter of Ptolemy to Flora* (ca. 160), Ptolemy, while seeking to define the Jewish scriptures (the Old Testament) and add their correct interpretation, appealed throughout to the "words of the Savior" (3.5, 8; 4.1, 4) as well as to the command of the Savior (5.9) and his teachings (7.9) as the primary authority for the followers of Jesus. He also cites "the apostle" (John, in 3.6 citing Jn 1.3) as one would quote scripture. These references are especially meaningful, since Ptolemy comes from outside of what later was known as mainstream or "orthodox" Christianity. Nonetheless, they show quite clearly his acceptance of the authority of the words of Jesus, some of which he took from the Gospel of Matthew and some from John. Along with the authority of a properly interpreted Old Testament, Ptolemy also presents his understanding of the authority of the Law of Moses with an acknowledgment of the authority of the words of the Savior. A longer portion of this text is given above, but notice again that the priority here is given to the words of the Savior.

> First, you must learn that the entire Law contained in the Pentateuch of Moses was not ordained by one legislator—I mean, not by God alone; some commandments are Moses', and some were given by men. *The words of the Savior teach us this triple division.* The first part must be attributed to God himself and his legislating; the second to Moses—not in the sense that God legislates through him, but in the sense that Moses gave some legislation under the influence of his own ideas; and the third to the elders of the people, who seem to have ordained some commandments of their own at the beginning. You will now learn how *the truth of this theory is proved by the words of the Savior.* (*Letter to Flora* 3.5–8, Barnstone, *The Other Bible* 622. Emphasis added)

Although Jesus is clearly his primary authority, notice how he also cites Paul as one would scripture.

> *The disciples of the Savior and the apostle Paul showed that this theory is true,* speaking of the part dealing with images, as we have already said, in mentioning "the Passover for us" and the "unleavened bread"; of the law interwoven with injustice when he says that "the law of commandments in ordinances was destroyed" [Eph. 2.15]; and of that not mixed with anything inferior when he says that "the law is holy, and the commandment is holy and just and good" [Rom. 7.12]. (Barnstone, *The Other Bible* 624. Emphasis added)

(7) **2 Peter.** The author of 2 Peter (ca. 150 but possibly as late as ca. 180) referred to Paul's writings as being twisted by the "ignorant and unstable [that is, the heretics—Marcionites or Gnostics?] *as they do the other scriptures*" (3.15–16). It appears that this author placed Paul's epistles on an equal footing with the Old Testament scriptures (or, less likely perhaps, equal to other Christian writings) that were recognized as authoritative or normative at the time of writing 2 Peter. He is also aware of the "heretical" use of Paul's letters, a possible veiled reference to Marcion.

Why did the early churches in the middle to late second century extend the authority of Jesus to the Apostles as his faithful witnesses? There is no single factor that can be isolated, but recognition of the usefulness of the New Testament writings for instruction and preaching as well as the practice of reading them regularly in the churches during worship ensured the acknowledgment of their scriptural status in a matter of time. And that is an important question: how much time? Once their scriptural status was accepted, their eventual inclusion into an authoritative collection of Christian scriptures and placement alongside the Old Testament scriptures in Christian worship was only a matter of time.

The recognition of some Christian literature as sacred scripture was present in the middle of the second century and the processes of canonization of Christian literature likely began in the first century with the recognition of the authority of Jesus' words and deeds, but this process was not finalized until the fourth century and later in the churches.

(8) **Justin Martyr** (ca. 150–160). Justin offers two further strands of evidence for the recognition of the scriptural status of the canonical Gospel writings. First, he refers to Jesus' words in Mt. 11.27 with a scripture-like designation in the following comment: "In the Gospel *it is written* that He said: 'All things are delivered unto me by My Father;' and, 'no man knows the Father but the Son; nor the Son but the Father, and they to whom the Son will reveal Him'" (*Trypho* 100.1-ff., see also 101.3, ANF. Emphasis added).

Also, Justin identifies the Gospels as the "memoirs of the Apostles" (*1 Apology* 64), and used them to establish and argue for Christian doctrine (*Trypho* 100.1) as well as to relate the story of Jesus' passion. When introducing quotations from Lk. 22.42 and 44, Justin writes, "For *in the memoirs* which I say were drawn up by His apostles and those who followed them, [it is recorded] His sweat fell down like drops of blood" (*Trypho* 103.8, ANF. Emphasis added). He also appeals to the canonical gospels when explaining the apostolic testimony regarding the Eucharist, claiming that "the Apostles commanded them: that Jesus, taking bread and having given thanks he said" (*1 Apology* 66.3, ECF). After these opening words, Justin cites Mark 14:22–24 and 1 Corinthians 11:23–25 as descriptions of what was said in the Eucharist. He also describes the use of the Gospels as reading materials in church worship, either alongside of *or instead of* the Old Testament writings ("prophets"). In his description of a Christian worship service he says that "on the day called Sunday there is a meeting in one place of those who live in cities or the country, and *the memoirs of the apostles or the writings of the prophets are read as long as time permits*" (*1 Apology* 67.3, ECF. Emphasis added).

For Justin, the canonical gospels had a scriptural function and were equal in authority to the Old Testament scriptures ("prophets"), even though they are not yet called "scripture" by him. Strangely, however, he makes no clear reference to Paul's writings that were surely known in Rome well before Justin's time. On the other hand, Justin refers to Revelation with favor (*Trypho* 81.4) giving us one of the earliest expositions of a text from that document. This is evidence of an early welcome of Revelation in the Western churches. In *1 Apology* 28.1, Justin calls this book (Revelation) one of "our writings."

(9) *Martyrs of Lyons and Vienna*. In the letter known as *The Martyrs of Lyons and Vienna* (ca. 175–177)—cited and partially preserved in Eusebius' *Ecclesiastical History* (5.1.3–63), there are a number of references, allusions to, and quotations of the New Testament literature, including some references to noncanonical literature. One of the more interesting references for our purposes is the reference to Rev. 22.11 as scripture. While describing the terrible local persecutions of the Christians, the letter states in part: ". . . the governor and the people showed the like unrighteous hatred against us that the Scripture might be fulfilled. 'Let him that is unlawful be unlawful still, and he that is righteous, be righteous still'" (5.1.58, LCL). Not only does this text show a high regard for the Book of Revelation in the Western churches, but it is also one of the earliest references to the book as "Scripture." This is an unusual reference to the Book of Revelation at the end of the second century.

(10) **Irenaeus** (ca. 170–180). Expressing a threefold authority (Jesus, Apostles, and Prophets) in the early churches, Irenaeus says: "the *Lord* testifies, as the *apostles* confess, and as the *prophets* announce" (*Against Heresies* 3.17.4, adapted from ANF. Emphasis added). It is interesting that he put these three authorities in the order that he did ("prophets" last). However, this ordering is still very much like the triple sacred authorities found elsewhere and earlier in the second century as we saw above. Irenaeus acknowledged the authority of "the Lord" (the sayings or words of Jesus) the apostles (primarily Paul), and the prophets (Old Testament writings known at that time). I will return to Irenaeus later.

(11) **Tatian** (ca. 160–170). Tatian, a disciple of Justin, valued the four canonical Gospels, but did not deem them inviolable. His creation of the church's first harmony of the four evangelists, likely with other gospel traditions as well, is known as the *Diatessaron* (also the "Gospel of the Mixed"). It was used in the Syrian churches up through most of the fifth century. Tatian saw the conflicts in the Gospels and wanted to bring them into one harmonious volume. It appears that he also included in his production the *Gospel of Peter*.

Eusebius, speaking of heretical groups that originated with Tatian, wrote the following concerning this work:

> Their former leader Tatian composed in some way a combination and collection of the gospels, and gave this the name of *The Diatessaron,* and this is still extant in some places. And they say that he ventured to paraphrase words of the apostle, *as though correcting their style.* He has left a great number of writings, of which the most famous, quoted by many, is his discourse *Against the Greeks.* In it he deals with primitive history, and all those who are celebrated among the Greeks. This seems to be the best and most helpful of all his writings. Such are the facts of this period. (*Ecclesiastical History* 4.29.6–7, LCL. Emphasis added except the titles of works)

Tatian's willingness to harmonize the four canonical Gospels is important in that this not only shows his perception of their inspired and sacred status in the churches, but also his willingness to change them to make them harmonize. In the above passage, Eusebius indicates that Tatian "paraphrased some words of the apostle." After Tatian, both Athanagoras (ca. 180) and Theophilus of Antioch (ca. 190–200) made use of Paul's writings alongside the Gospels as normative Christian literature. Athanagoras, for instance, appeals to Paul to argue his case about life after death.

> The result of all of this is very plain to everyone,—namely, that, in the language of the apostle, "This corruptible (and dissoluble) must put on incorruption, in order that those who were dead . . . may, in accordance with justice, receive what he has done by the body, whether it be good or bad." (*The Resurrection of the Dead* 18, ANF; cf. 1 Cor. 15.54.)

Theophilus also shows heavy dependence upon the writings of Paul, especially Rom. 2.7–9 and 1 Cor. 2.9, in his calling upon Autolycus to hear and reverence the Word of God.

> But you also, please *give reverential attention to the prophetic Scriptures,* for they will make it plain to you how to escape the

eternal punishments and obtain the eternal prizes of God. For He who gave the mouth for speech, and formed the ear to hear and made the eye to see will examine all things and will judge [with] righteous judgment. [He will also] render merited awards for those who seek immortality, and He will give life everlasting, joy, peace, rest, and abundance of good things, which *neither has the eye seen nor ear heard nor has it entered into the heart of man to conceive.* But to the unbelieving and despisers, who do not obey the truth but are obedient to adulteries and fornications, and filthiness, and covetousness, and unlawful idolatries, there shall be anger and wrath, tribulation and anguish, and at the last an everlasting fire shall possess them. (Adapted from Theophilus, *To Autolycus* 1.14, ANF. Emphasis added)

The significance of these references is that they show a growing tendency on the part of the Church not only to recognize the authority Jesus preserved in the Gospels, but also to extend that authority to the documents themselves. This is seen for the first time in the writings of Justin and after him, Paul's epistles gained a greater scripture-like authority in the churches, especially in the writings of Irenaeus, Theophilus of Antioch, and Athenagoras.

By the year 200, it is almost certain that the collection of Christian writings that had achieved the status of scripture in the church at large had as its core the four canonical Gospels and the writings of Paul. This was by no means a closed canon of New Testament writings, even though Irenaeus accepted only the four canonical gospels among the literature of that genre and subsequently they obtained a widely recognized scriptural status in the majority of churches. The authority of Jesus was always the most important authority in the church, even though most of his teachings that survived to that time were found only in the written Gospels. The growth of authoritative writings for the church now included the Old Testament scriptures, the teachings of Jesus—located primarily in the canonical gospels—and the epistles of Paul. However, a number of other New Testament writings were circulating in the churches with growing appreciation and they were also achieving in some cases (Revelation), a scripture-like status like that earlier given to the Gospels and some letters of Paul.

In the earliest known description of Christian worship, Justin indicates that the "memoirs of the Apostles" (or Gospels) were read along with the Prophets as time allowed. The more complete text of this passage that we mentioned above is as follows:

> After these [services] we constantly remind each other of these things. Those who have more come to the aid of those who lack, and we are constantly together. Over all that we receive we bless the Maker of all things through his Son Jesus Christ and through the Holy Spirit. And on the day called Sunday there is a meeting in one place of those who live in cities or the country, and the *memoirs of the apostles* or the writings of the prophets are read as long as time permits. When the reader has finished, *the president in a discourse urges and invites [us] to the imitation of these noble things.* Then we all stand up together and offer prayers. And, as said before, when we have finished the prayer, bread is brought, and wine and water, and the president similarly sends up prayers and thanksgivings to the best of his ability, and the congregation assents, saying the Amen; the distribution, and reception of the consecrated [elements] by each one, takes place and they are sent to the absent by the deacons. Those who prosper, and who so wish, contribute, each one as much as he chooses to. What is collected is deposited with the president, and he takes care of orphans and widows, and those who are in bonds, and the strangers who are sojourners among [us], and, briefly, he is the protector of all those in need. We all hold this common gathering on Sunday, since it is the first day, on which God transforming darkness and matter made the universe, and Jesus Christ our Savior rose from the dead on the same day. For they crucified him on the day before Saturday, and on the day after Saturday, he appeared to his apostles and disciples and taught them these things that I have passed on to you also for your serious consideration. (*1 Apology.* 67, ECF. Emphasis added)

Those early Christian texts that were believed to have apostolic authorship were regularly cited in arguments against heresies, as we see in the case of Irenaeus at the end of the second century (170–180) who wrote against the Gnostics whom he believed threatened the church and he employed several New Testament writings in his arguments.

While some second century writers acknowledged the value of first century Christian writings and made use of them as scripture, this practice was not universal at the time. Even where there was considerable agreement at the end of the second century that Christian writings were employed as scripture, there was no agreement on precisely which writings had attained that status. By the end of the second century, some churches were using a number of New Testament writings in worship and instruction, as well as in their theological disputations with heretics and polemical arguments against those who posed threats to the peace and stability of the church. There was no widespread agreement in the second century on which writings should be used in such matters, although the Gospels and several letters of Paul were frequently cited. At that time there were also nodiscussions about forming these writings into a fixed collection of sacred New Testament books.

THE AGRAPHA: NONCANONICAL SAYINGS OF JESUS

A large number of sayings of Jesus circulated in the early Christian churches, some of them in what we now call noncanonical literature. Some 266 of these sayings have been discovered in nonbiblical literature but scholars disagree on how many of them actually are authentic sayings of the historical Jesus. These sayings, often called *agrapha*, are found in the New Testament apocryphal sources such as the *Gospel of Thomas* and the *Gospel of Peter*. The *agrapha* were also found in writings from the early church fathers as well as in copies of ancient manuscripts of the New Testament writings. These were made popular more recently through Joachim Jeremias' work, *The Unknown Sayings of Jesus*, a small but important source that both lists and discusses these sayings. Jeremias argued that of the much larger list of these sayings, only 18 of them are authentic to Jesus. After Jeremias, other scholars thought that he was perhaps too generous and reduced the number of authentic sayings of Jesus to somewhere between four and ten of the *agrapha*. The following more conservative selection of ten *agrapha* sayings have received more attention than the others and are worth noting but the ones that have received the most support are those marked with a star (*). These are as follows:

1. "As you are found, so will you be led away [sc. to judgment]." (*Syriac Liber Graduum, Serm.* III. 3; 15. 4)
2. "Ask for the great things, And God will add to you what is small." (Clem. Alex. *Strom.* 1.24.158)
3. "Be competent [approved] money-changers!" (*Ps. Clem. Hom.* 2. 51. 1; 3.50.2; 18.20.4)
*4. "On the same day he [Jesus] saw a man working on the sabbath. He said to him: 'Man, if you know what you are doing, you are blessed; but if you do not know, you are accursed and a transgressor of the law!'" (See Lk. 6.5 in Codex D)
*5. "He who is near me is near the fire; he who is far from me is far from the kingdom." (*GThom.* §82; Origen, *In Jer. hom.* lat. 3.3; Didymus, *In Psalm.* 88.8)
*6. "(He who today) stands far off will tomorrow be (near to you)." (POxy 1224)
*7. "And only then shall you be glad, when you look on your brother with love." (*Gospel of the Hebrews*, according to Jerome, *In Eph.* 5.4)
8. "The kingdom is like a wise fisherman who cast his net into the sea; he drew it up from the sea full of small fish; among them he found a large (and) good fish; that wise fisherman threw all the small fish down into the sea; he chose the large fish without regret." (*GThom* §8)
9. "How is it then with you? For you are here in the temple. Are you then clean? . . . Woe to you blind who see not! You have washed yourself in water that is poured forth, in which dogs and swine lie night and day, and washed and scoured your outer skin, which harlots and flute girls also anoint, bathe, scour, and beautify to arouse desire in men, but inwardly they are filled with scorpions and with [all manner of ev]il. But I and [my disciples], of whom you say that we have not [bathed, have bath]ed ourselves in the liv[ing and clean] water, which comes down from [the father in heaven]" (POxy840 §2).
*10. "And never be joyful, save when you look upon your brother in love." (*GHeb* §5; compare Jerome, *In Eph.* 3 [on Eph. 5.4])

These extra canonical sayings of Jesus no doubt functioned as "canon 1" (see discussion of this term in Chapter 2), or as an authority, in the communities in which they were discovered and circulated even though they never became a part of a fixed canonical collection ("canon 2") in the developing Christian communities.

The question today is not so much whether there may have been authentic sayings of Jesus found here or there in noncanonical sources, but rather what to do with them! Should we add them to the canonical scriptures of the Christian community if they are determined to be authentic sayings of Jesus? Should they also inform either the theology of the church today, as they did in ancient times, and more importantly, should they be read in church worship or form a part of the authoritative base for constructing the church's doctrinal teachings? There is no agreement among the scholars on these questions, but more and more, there is an acknowledgment that some authentic sayings of Jesus do exit in the noncanonical sources. While there is no agreement on which extra canonical sayings of Jesus are authentic, if the list of authentic sayings is only the four or five of these sayings noted above, there is not much advantage in making a big case for including them in the church's scriptural canon. That notwithstanding, a number of scholars agree that they may be a resource for historical Jesus research.

APOCRYPHAL AND NONCANONICAL CHRISTIAN WRITINGS

As most scholars of the canonical process know, evidence of apostolic authorship was a central factor in determining the scriptures and canon of the church. Besides the writings that actually made it into the New Testament, there are numerous other specifically Christian pseudepigraphal writings attributed to an apostle that were not included in the Christian biblical canon. These include gospels, various Acts, epistles, and apocalypses. This literature is mostly sectarian, and appears to appeal to an apostle's name in order to find acceptance in segments of the Christian community. Most of this literature is described in detail elsewhere (Schneemelcher's *New Testament Apocrypha*), but for the reader we will simply list in the following table some of the most important representatives of this collection, some of which currently exist only in fragments. This literature was listed above in Chapter 2, pp. 34–37. That list provides the reader with a list of writings that at one time were considered sacred literature in one or more churches in antiquity, but were eventually rejected by the majority of churches.

Doubts about the authorship of these writings existed in antiquity and perhaps that led to the decline in their usefulness to the church an eventually to their exclusion from the New Testament canon.

CONCLUSION

We have seen a progression in the acceptance and recognition of the authority and sacredness of the New Testament writings in early Christianity. This acceptance did not take place at the same time or in the same places or in a vacuum. The situation was fluid for a considerable period of time and acceptance was uneven at best, but there were other factors that contributed to the selection process. Eventually, the majority of the churches accepted the 27 books of the New Testament, but not initially. Over time the writings that best addressed the continuing needs and mission of the churches are the ones that were accepted into the church's New Testament canon. For now, however, it is clear that the process took a considerable amount of time and unanimity was seldom found in the churches. That is not unlike what churches today face. The most favored books in one congregation are often neglected in another, even though both churches subscribe to the authority of the same Bible. The emerging biblical canon of the churches reflected especially what they believed was true of Jesus, their first and most important authority. The second authority is a derived one and that came from the apostles whom churches believed faithfully transmitted the story of Jesus and its implications for Christian living. The books that garnered the greatest approval in the churches did so not because of any power the churches, especially in Rome, had to impose their will on other churches, or even about their financial resources such as those at Rome, but rather because they were the ones believed to best communicate the story of Jesus and its implications for church life and that they were the earliest and most reliable witnesses to that story.

One factor alleged in the canonical process is more controversial than the others, namely, the role of heresy in the canonical processes that will be our focus in the next chapter, but there are a number of the social-historical factors that need to be considered as factors leading to the canonization of the New Testament along with the basic criteria that led the ancient churches to adopt the writings of the New Testament. These factors will be discussed in Chapter 7. For now, however, we conclude by acknowledging that the above references and data show the complexity and a few of the important steps involved in the canonization of the New Testament writings.

We will now explore the role or supposed role that the "heretics" of the second century played in helping the church determine which writings constituted its sacred scriptures.

FURTHER READING

Allert, Craig D. *Revelation, Truth, Canon and Interpretation: Studies in Justin martyr's Dialogue with Trypho*. Supplements to Vigiliae Christianae. Leiden/Boston, MA/Köln: E. J. Brill, 2002.

Balla, Peter. "Evidence for an Early Christian Canon (Second and Third Century)," in *The Canon Debate*, ed. Lee McDonald and James A. Sanders. Peabody, MA: Hendrickson Publishers, 2002, pp. 372–385.

Bartholomew, Craig G., Scott Hahn, Robin Parry, Christopher Seitz, and Al Wolters, eds. *Canon and Biblical Interpretation*. Vol. 7 Scripture and Hermeneutics Series. Grand Rapids, MI: Zondervan, 2006.

Charlesworth, James A. and Craig A. Evans. "Jesus in the Agrapha and Apocryphal Gospels," *Studying the Historical Jesus: Evaluations of the State of Current Research*, ed. Bruce Chilton and C. A. Evans, NTTS 19. Leiden: E. J. Brill, 1994.

Childs, Brevard S. *The New Testament as Canon: An Introduction*. Philadelphia, PA: Fortress Press, 1984.

Comfort, Philip Wesley, ed. *The Origin of the Bible*. Wheaton, IL: Tyndale House Publishers, 1992.

Farkasfalvy, Denis M. and William R. Farmer. *The Formation of the New Testament Canon: An Ecumenical Approach*. Theological Inquiries. New York: Paulist Press, 1983.

Finkelberg, Margalit and Guy G. Stroumsa, eds. *Homer, the Bible, and Beyond: Literary and Religious Canons in the Ancient World*. Jerusalem Studies in Religion and Culture 2. Leiden/Boston, MA: E. J. Brill, 2003.

Grant, R. M. *The Formation of the New Testament*. New York: Harper & Row, 1965.

Gregory, Caspar Rene. *Canon and Text of the New Testament.* New York: Charles Scribner's Sons, 1907. Reprinted in Northville, MI: Biblical Viewpoints Publications, 1997.

Hahneman, Geoffrey M. *The Muratorian Fragment and the Development of the Canon.* Oxford Theological Monographs. Oxford: Clarendon Press, 1992.

Harnack, Adolf von. *The Origin of the New Testament and the Most Important Consequences of the New Creation.* Trans. J. R. Wilkinson. New York: Macmillan, 1925.

Hofius, Otfried. "Isolated Sayings of Jesus," in *New Testament Apocrypha*, 2nd edn., ed. Wilhelm Schneemelcher. Louisville, KY: Westminster John Knox Press, 1991, Vol. 1, pp. 88–91.

Hurtado, Larry W. *The Earliest Christian Artifacts: Manuscripts and Christian Origins.* Grand Rapids, MI/Cambridge: Eerdmans, 2006.

Hurtado, Larry W. "Unknown Sayings of Jesus," in *The Gospel and the Gospels*, ed. Peter Stuhlmacher. Grand Rapids, MI: Eerdmans, 1991, pp. 336–360.

Jeremias, Joachim. *Unbekannte Jesuworte.* Zürich: Zwingli, 1947; 2nd edn. Gütersloh: Bertelsmann, 1951; 3rd edn., 1961; ET: *The Unknown Sayings of Jesus.* London: SPCK, 1957; 2nd edn., 1964.

McDonald, Lee M. *The Biblical Canon: Its Origin, Transmission, and Authority.* Peabody, MA: Hendrickson Publishers, 2006.

Metzger, Bruce M. *The Canon of the New Testament: Its Origin, Development, and Significance.* Oxford: The Clarendon Press, 1987.

Morrice, William. *Hidden Sayings of Jesus: Words Attributed to Jesus outside the Four Gospels.* Peabody, MA: Hendrickson Publishers, 1997.

Patzia, Arthur G. *The Making of the New Testament: Origin, Collection, Text, and Canon.* Downers Grove, IL: InterVarsity Press, 1995.

Schneemelcher, Wilhelm, ed. *New Testament Apocrypha.* Trans. R. M. Wilson. 2nd edn. 2 vols. Louisville, KY: Westminster John Knox Press, 1991–1992.

Souter, Alexander. *The Text and Canon of the New Testament.* Studies in Theology. 2nd edn. Revised by C. S. C. Williams. London: Duckworth, 1913, 1954.

Stroker, W. D. *Extracanonical Sayings of Jesus.* SBLRBS 18. Atlanta, GA: Scholars Press, 1989.

Theron, Daniel J. *Evidence of Tradition.* Grand Rapids, MI: Baker Book House, 1957, reprinted in 1980.

Wyrick, Jed. *The Ascension of Authorship: Attribution and Canon Formation in Jewish, Hellenistic, and Christian Traditions.* Cambridge, MA and London: Harvard University Press, 2004.

Zahn, Theodore. *Forschungen zur Geschichte des neutestamentlichen Kanons und der altkirchlichen Literatur.* 10 vols. Leipzig: S Deichert, 1881–1929.

CHAPTER SIX

THE INFLUENCE OF "HERESY" AND "ORTHODOXY" ON CANON FORMATION

What role did heresy or orthodoxy play in the formation of the Christian biblical canon? Two conflicting arguments have emerged on these matters and both begin with the premise that one of these factors played a determinative role in the final scope of the Bible for the Christian Church. In the first of these, several canon scholars have argued at length that the formation of the New Testament canon was essentially the church's reaction to three dominating heresies in the second century. The second view is that the church responded to these challenges by strengthening the office of bishop and constructing creeds, called the *regula fidei* (Latin, "rule of faith"), but eventually also constructed a canon of scriptures (4th century) that reflected their theological perspective.

The first view, as we will argue below, will not stand up under historical scrutiny and the second may not go far enough. The formation of the New Testament canon most likely has its roots in the recognition and use of Christian writings as authoritative texts in the worship and instruction in the churches and subsequently in recognizing these writings as scripture, both of which took place in the second century. In other words, the processes of canon formation *began* at the latest in the second century, but the *fixed* collection of Jewish and Christian books that comprise the Christian Bible came to *completion* only in the fourth and fifth centuries. The writings that were included in the Bible generally were those that were more adaptable to the churches' worship, catechetical, and missional needs, and they remained in the emerging biblical canon.

Because the needs and circumstances facing the Christians varied from location to location and from time to time, it took much longer for Christians to come to an agreement on the scope of their New Testament. This variety of expressions in second century Christianity is evidenced by the variety of theological perspectives present in the ancient manuscripts that survived antiquity and by the many references in the writings of the church fathers to sectarian activity in the second and third centuries.

At the end of the first century and beginning of the second, the apostles had all died, Jesus had not returned as Christians had hoped, and several heresies, especially the Docetic heresy that emerged at the end of the first century, were affecting the life of a number of churches. Persecution of various churches was also appearing in several parts of the Roman Empire as a result of Christians losing their *religio licita* status (authorized and protected religion) when Roman authorities no longer saw them as a Jewish sect. As a result, when Christians refused to offer sacrifices to the emperor, they often faced loss of property and other more severe penalties imposed by Rome. These circumstances, along with the fact that there was little organized control over the theological thinking and development of the churches during this time, led to a number challenges for the church as it moved into the second century.

One consequence of these difficulties was the emergence of a stronger episcopate with more power vested in the office of bishop. Tough times often call for strong leaders, and Ignatius is a primary example of one who had to deal not only with persecution and facing his own martyrdom, but also the Docetic (from the Greek, *dokeo* = "I seem" or "appear") heresy in the church that claimed that Jesus only *appeared* or seemed to have a physical body. Jesus' full humanity was denied. Ignatius' letters reflect both the persecutions and also the heresy affecting the churches, and he vested more power in the office of bishop to deal with them. The emergence of a more powerful episcopate in the church remained and expanded in time.

In may be called a vacuum of authority in the churches following the death of the apostles, considerable theological diversity (from what later came to be known as orthodoxy) emerged and posed new challenges for the church. The church responded to these challenges by strengthening the office of bishop, creating creeds that they believed reflected the earliest and most authentic witness to the Christian faith, and eventually (4th century) forming a canon of scriptures that reflected this perspective. In the following discussion we will examine the influence of heresy in the churches, how they responded to it, and three major examples of it that gained prominence in the second century churches. We will begin with a discussion of sectarian views mentioned above and offer some perspective on how the churches dealt with them. We should also say that what we now called heresy was not initially viewed as such by all second churches and initially it had very little means of dealing with such diversity. At the beginning of the second century, churches had not yet come to any widespread agreement on all issues related to their beliefs and teachings. Consequently, it was not unusual to find many diverse voices in the churches at that time. How did the churches deal with such challenges?

THE ROLE OF "HERESY" IN FORMING
THE BIBLICAL CANON

A number of scholars contend that three primary second-century heresies (Marcionites, Gnostics, and the Montanists), and the church's response to them, are the most important factors in leading the church to formulate its own New Testament canon of Scriptures. We will now examine these movements through the activities and writings of leaders of these movements in the second century churches.

Marcion

It was Marcion (ca. 140–150), a native of Sinope in Pontus and a wealthy ship owner who made significant financial contributions to the church, but who also rejected the Jewish influences on early Christianity and saw the value of anchoring his faith and teachings in a limited collection of authoritative Christian writings that he employed in worship and teaching in his community of churches. His anti-Jewish sentiment was demonstrated by his rejection of the God of the Old Testament who he saw as cruel and not the God of Jesus who was loving and gracious. As a result, he also rejected the Jewish scriptures, the church's first scriptures. Marcion believed that the Christian Gospel was about unconditional or absolute love and that it was fundamentally contrary to the Law.

At that time the relevance of the Old Testament scriptures were made relevant for the church by allegorizing or spiritualizing them, but Marcion rejected all forms of spiritual or allegorical methods of interpretation. The church commonly employed this interpretive methodology to make the Old Testament a relevant scripture for Christian faith. Marcion, however, believed that Christianity was something completely new and he stressed that the God of the Law (Old Testament) was a *Demiurge*,[1] or the creator god. He argued that the god of the Old Testament could not be the same as the unknown God of the gospel and of Jesus. He therefore focused considerable attention on separating Christianity from its Jewish heritage. Although it has often been argued that Marcion was one of the Gnostics who will be discussed in the next section, or was heavily influenced by them, he would have had little sympathy with their mythological speculations or strange means of interpretation of the biblical literature.

Marcion is the first *known* person to set forth a clearly defined collection of what *later* were determined to be Christian scriptures. Since we have no independent Marcionite sources or documents, however, we depend completely on his critics, especially Irenaeus and Tertullian, for our information about his actions and scripture collection. Fortunately, their reports are extensive and generally considered reliable. Marcion accepted only an edited form of the Gospel of Luke and ten of Paul's epistles for reading in his churches. He did not include the Pastoral Epistles, but possibly he did not know of them. They may also have been written after the time of Marcion, as some scholars suggest, and perhaps in response to him (see 1 Tim. 6.20).

One support for this view is that these books are not found in the late second or early third century papyrus manuscript, P^{46}, the oldest extant manuscript containing the largest collection of Pauline Epistles. Further, the Pastorals Epistles are not cited elsewhere before the end of the second century. In another papyrus manuscript identified as P^{32} (ca. 200), only a small portion of Titus is found in it.

There are some verbal parallels between the Pastorals and the Apostolic Fathers, but those could be accounted for by the presence of a common oral tradition circulating in the churches in the second century or a mutual dependence upon earlier documents that are unnamed. A clear case can be made later for Irenaeus' citing Tit. 3.10 in his *Against Heresies* (*Adv. Haer.* 1.16.3) where he cites Paul by name. Other clear examples of Irenaeus' acceptance and citation of the Pastoral Epistles are found in citing 1 Tim. 6.20; 3.3.3 (*Adv. Haer.* 2.14.7) and referring to 2 Tim. 4.21 (3.3.3); and 3.14.1 citing 2 Tim. 4.10 (3.14.1). The Pastoral Epistles were not *widely* cited in the second century and allusions or "echoes" of this literature only begin to appear in the latter half of the second century and most clearly with Irenaeus. While there are parallels in language with the Apostolic Fathers, clear dependence cannot be established.

Tertullian specifically claimed that Marcion rejected the Pastoral letters, noting that he was clearly aware of them as we see in the following:

> I wonder, however, when he received this letter [Philemon] which was written but to one man, that he rejected the two epistles to Timothy and the one to Titus, which all treat of ecclesiastical discipline. His aim, was, I suppose, to carry out his interpolating process even to the number of epistles [of Paul]. (*Against Marcion* 5.21, ANF)

Returning to our point above, several scholars, beginning with Adolf von Harnack in 1921, claim that Marcion was the first to produce a canonical list of Christian Scriptures and that the churches responded to his action by producing a more inclusive scripture canon that contained an Old Testament and a wider collection of Christian writings that they believed represented their life and faith more precisely. If Marcion actually produced a biblical canon, as these scholars contend, this would have set a precedent for the existence of other such canons in the second century. Recently, scholars of the Bible have been moving away from this position as a better understanding of the time and influence of Marcion becomes clearer.

Marcion was no doubt aware of other gospels besides Luke, since Origen, in his *Commentary on Matthew* 15.3, cites Marcion's interpretation of Mt. 19.12. It is fairly certain, however, that he initially adopted only Luke and the Pauline letters in his collection. He does not mention the Ephesian letter, but includes rather a letter to the Laodiceans that may have been the Ephesian letter by a different name. Whether Marcion specifically rejected other Christian writings is not clear, since our current knowledge of his situation does not allow us to make that conclusion. The argument that he produced the first closed biblical canon and thereby set a precedent for the greater church doing so later, however, is more than what the available evidence allows. There is no evidence in the writings in the early church fathers that supports the popular view that Marcion created a biblical canon, nor does it show that he simply substituted one collection of the church's sacred scriptures (the Old Testament) for another one (Paul and Luke). That conclusion takes us beyond what the current evidence supports and it makes Marcion say more than his contemporaries claimed regarding the scriptural status of Paul and Luke.

There is evidence that various church fathers cited authoritatively the Gospels and Paul in their writings well before Marcion did as we see in the *Letters of Ignatius*, the *Didache*, and Clement of Rome in his *1 Clement*. All of these authors knew and cited the Gospels (mostly Matthew) and the writings of Paul along with several Old Testament writings before Marcion came to his influence. Marcion was not the first to refer to Paul or Luke and the church writers who wrote against Marcion later never argue that Marcion's collection was so limited that the rest of the churches felt the need to expand their collections of early Christian writings. They concluded that Marcion's understanding of the Christian faith was defective and his rejection of the Jewish scriptures and the church's historical roots in Judaism was wrong. This is a far cry, however, from the claim that Marcion invented the first closed Christian canon of scriptures.

Perhaps Marcion's rejection of the Old Testament scriptures was a result of scattered Jew persecutions of Christians that were growing in intensity during his time. As previously noted, in the early to middle second century, the Jews outnumbered the Christians by more than 60 or 70 to one. Jewish opposition to Christians can be seen in their reporting Christians to the authorities that led to the martyrdom of Polycarp in the middle of the second century (see *The Martyrdom of Polycarp*, chapters 13, 17 and 18) when Christians no longer had a "licensed religion" (or *religio licita*). Because Christians were not practicing an authorized religion, their meetings were illegal and when arrested, many were tortured to make them deny their faith and many died as a result.[2]

Marcion's rejection of the Jewish influences on early Christianity may also have been due to a significant decline in Jewish popularity in the second century following their failed rebellion against Rome initiated by the Bar Cochba messianic movement in Palestine (132–135 CE). Whatever the case may be, Marcion's prejudice against Judaism and what he called the vengeful god of the Jewish scriptures led him to reject the Jewish roots of Christianity and to use only the writings that he believed were important for the church to read. At this time, however, the New Testament writings were not *generally* called Scripture, but as early as the middle of the second century, as we saw in the previous chapter, several of the New Testament writings, namely the canonical Gospels (mostly Matthew) and letters of Paul (mostly 1, 2 Corinthians and Romans), began to be used along with the Old Testament Scriptures in worship and catechetical instruction in the churches.

By the mid-second century, various Christian communities/churches were coming to recognize the usefulness of a body of *Christian* literature for their life and worship. It is difficult to establish both the scriptural status of the Christian writings at this time since they are not generally called "scripture" until the latter part of the second century. Because of this, each citation or quotation must be considered in its own right before conclusions can be drawn about its use or function in the early churches. This does not preclude the use of Christian writings in the early churches, but the practice of calling them scripture was not yet widespread. At that time there was no notion of a fixed normative Christian collection of New Testament writings to which one could appeal. Marcion, like others of his time, saw the importance of using authoritative Christian writings in the worship, teaching, and mission of his community of churches, but his design was not so much his insight into establishing a fixed and normative collection of New Testament writings (an edited Paul and an abbreviated Luke) as it was his aim at effecting a separation between Judaism and Christianity. His anti-Jewish bias led him to reject the God of the Old Testament, the Old Testament Scriptures themselves, and all other Jewish influences on early Christianity.

Marcion recognized, perhaps more clearly than others of his day, the difficulty of accepting the Old Testament writings as normative sacred writings for the church when vast amounts of that literature was no longer deemed relevant or binding upon the Christians. This was especially so in regard to keeping the legal and moral codes, as well as other traditions associated with the Law. Believing that he was following a correct understanding of Paul's teaching, he argued that Christians were free from the Law and, therefore had no reason to give token allegiance to those traditions that had been rendered obsolete by faith in Christ. He rejected the use of the most arbitrary means of interpreting the Old Testament, that is, using allegory or typology that many Christians commonly employed to find meaning and guidance from that literature. His rejection of the Old Testament, together with the allegorical interpretation of it, stripped the church not only of its Scriptures, but also its prized claim to the heritage of Israel's antiquity and to being the religion of historical fulfillment.

The church responded to Marcion's challenge by returning his generous gifts and by excommunicating him. Tertullian later wrote of Marcion that he had "interpolated" Paul's epistles, and also, "as our heretic is so fond of his pruning knife, I do not wonder when syllables are expunged by his hand, seeing that entire pages are usually the matter on which he practices his effacing process" (*Against Marcion* 5.18.1, ANF).

There is no early church evidence that Marcion specifically called his collection of writings either "Scripture," though they functioned that way, nor yet a scripture "canon." It appears rather that the New Testament writings that he adopted functioned as sacred scripture in his churches, and his collection of Scriptures was available to him only because churches before him had also made use of Paul's writings and circulated them to other churches. It is safe to assume that several of Paul's writings were circulating in Asia Minor at the end of the first century, even in Rome. Paul himself may have instigated this circulation (see Col. 4.16). Clement of Rome (ca. 95–96 CE), for example, shows familiarity with four of Paul's epistles.

Finally, no second century literature suggests that the churches addressed the challenges presented by Marcion's teachings by producing a larger fixed collection of Christian Scriptures. There was a strong reaction to Marcion's actions (see Irenaeus, *Against Heresies* 4.29–34; Tertullian, *Against Marcion.* 4.2), but it did not include the creation of a canon of New Testament scriptures. The second century churches responded to him with their *regula fidei*, or "rule of faith," that was supported by a number of references to both the Old Testament and New Testament scriptures, and teachings passed on in the churches.

We do not know for sure how many other Christian writings were familiar to Marcion, but his followers felt free to edit his work and even welcome scripture verses from the other canonical Gospels. Ephraem Syrus of Syria (ca. 306–373 CE), for example, claimed that the followers of Marcion had *not* rejected Mt. 23.8 (*Song* 24.1). Likewise, both Jn 13.34 and 15.19 are authoritatively quoted by Marcus, a Marcionite, in a text by Adamantius (*Dialogue* 2.16, 20 ca. 310–320). We cannot demonstrate that Marcion was aware of all four canonical Gospels or other New Testament writings besides those in his list, but it is likely that he was at least aware of the Gospel of Matthew because of its widespread popularity in the second century and his followers were clearly aware of other Christian writings. When we observe that Marcion's followers also added a collection of psalms to his writings that were later rejected by the author of the Muratorian Fragment (see lines 83–84), and that the Armenian Marcionites appear to have accepted Tatian's *Diatessaron*, it appears that with Marcion we are not yet talking about a closed biblical canon or even about a biblical canon at all.

Valentinus (ca. 135–160)

As we noted above, it is likely that collections of Christian writings were present and circulating in churches earlier than the time of Marcion. Tertullian (ca. 200 CE), for instance, compared Valentinus (living in Rome ca. 136–165 CE) with Marcion and claimed that the former used *all* the scriptures and perverted them, while Marcion used the knife on what he did not like. The famous text reads as follows:

> One man perverts the Scriptures with his hand, another their meaning by his exposition. For although Valentinus seems to use *the entire volume,* he has none the less laid violent hands on the truth only with a more cunning mind and skill than Marcion. Marcion expressly and openly used the knife, not the pen, since he made such an excision of the Scriptures as suited his own subject-matter. Valentinus, however, abstained from such excision, because he did not invent Scriptures to square with his own subject-matter, but adapted his matter to the Scriptures; and yet he took away more, and added more, by removing the proper meaning of every particular word, and adding fantastic arrangements of things which had no real existence. (*On Prescriptions Against Heresies* 38.4-ff., ANF. Emphasis added)

The words "entire volume" (Latin, *integro instrumento*) appear to be a reference to a collection of scriptures, possibly New Testament writings, but possibly also a reference to the Old Testament scriptures. The context favors the former since Tertullian asks both Marcion and Valentinus what right they have to use the scriptures they received from the Apostles in the way that they did (*On Prescriptions* 32). The reference here, of course, probably does not refer to Old Testament writings since in Tertullian's time the use of the term "scripture" for New Testament writings was more common in his day than earlier. He sometimes uses the term in reference to the Old Testament as "one volume" (*On Prescriptions Against Heresies* 36), but the context seems to favor a New Testament collection. Tertullian evidently believed that Valentinus, unlike Marcion, used a collection of New Testament writings similar to his own, but gave them a different meaning.

The recent discovery of *Evangelium Veritatis* (*The Gospel of Truth*), believed by some scholars to have been written by Valentinus, shows acquaintance with the four Gospels, several of Paul's epistles, Hebrews, and Revelation. If an early dating of this work is credible, this would be the earliest and largest gathering of references to the

New Testament writings that we possess from that period. The Book of Revelation, for example, that was more widely accepted in the Western churches than in the East in the second and third centuries, is a part of that collection. However, it is possible that Tertullian's condemnation of both Marcion and Valentinus was based in part on a general awareness of the status or understanding of the New Testament scriptures from his own time (ca. 200 CE) and not necessarily theirs. When they wrote their treatises, the status of both the Old and New Testaments, and those writings that did not eventually become canonical literature, was still uncertain and in a state of flux.

The Gnostics

One of the more influential Christian sects in the second century, the Gnostics, had an enormous impact on many Christian communities. Until 1945, when a sizeable collection of some 40 Gnostic writings were found in Egypt at Nag Hammadi near the upper Nile, all that was known of this group was reported in the orthodox tradition championed by second century orthodox writers such as Justin, Irenaeus, Clement of Alexandria, Tertullian, and Hippolytus of Rome. Following the discovery of these Gnostic documents in Egypt, it became possible for the first time to examine their beliefs *from their perspective*. The roots of Gnostic thought are obscure and many scholars today believe that there was a pre-Christian form of Gnostic thought that owes much of its perspectives to Hellenistic views about immortality and the evil essence of matter and physicality. Some think that it was entertained in some churches as a result of the failed Jewish notions of the future coming of the Son of Man. Jesus did not return and that had an important impact on the emerging second century churches.

Some of the keys to this complex system of thought were rooted in prevalent Hellenistic views that had to do with the duality of spirit and matter; the spirit is divine and matter was considered evil. Such notions of duality in Jewish and Christian thought manifested themselves in the conflict between good and evil with good eventually triumphing over evil, as we see in the book of Revelation. The widespread notion that the body (matter) was the captor of the soul (spirit) and that the soul needed to be freed from the body is reflected in second century Gnostic thought. Similarly, for Christian Gnosticism, the creator god (a demiurge or craftsman) was inferior to the unknown God of Jesus.

The Gnostic idea of salvation came through a special knowledge that revealed the nature of the soul's heavenly origin and its subsequent imprisonment in a body or the world of matter, with its possible ascension to its original abode (the heavens). The focus on knowledge in antiquity is not unique to Gnosticism, but the emphasis on self-knowledge is more typical of Gnostic thought. The Gospel of John regularly refers to knowing (some 60 times), but the Gospel is not Gnostic and neither does it teach that creation is evil or that it started with some evil god or *demiurge*. The emphasis in John is on knowledge of God that brings persons into a right relationship with God and not on the self, self-fulfillment, or self-actualization (see Jn 14.7–14, 17; 17.3). Gnosticism and its several sects also conflicted with early Christian preaching about the resurrection body as when, for example, Paul spoke of the resurrection of Jesus in Athens (Acts 17.30–34). The Gnostic notion of salvation with its emphasis on self-knowledge can be seen in a quote from a Valentinian follower in the mid-second century CE cited by Clement of Alexandria's *Excerpta ex Theodoto:* "What liberates is the knowledge of who we were, what we became; where we were, whereinto we have been thrown; whereto we speed, wherefrom we are redeemed; what birth is, and what rebirth [is]" (*Exc. Theod.* 78.2, trans. Hans Jonas, 45).

The Christian notion of a God who became a part of the human race ran counter to the most widely held views among the Greeks and Romans. Whatever else the gods were, they were always remote and unconcerned (*apatheia*) with human affairs. These views normally ran counter to Jewish and Christian thought, even though some Jews (generally the wealthier and more educated ones) had learned to accommodate themselves to the Hellenistic perspectives of the Greeks. Judaism, like early Christianity, focused on the activity of God in human history. For both early Christianity and first century Judaism, God was a benevolent creator, but for the Christians, one who also raised Jesus bodily from the grave. The primary difference between Jews of the Pharisaic tradition and later the rabbinic tradition and the early Christians on this matter had to do with the bodily resurrection *of Jesus*, not the notion of resurrection of the body *from the grave*. These notions were both opposed and rejected by Gnostic thinkers.

No doubt some of the Christian Gnostic views (*not* those of the full blown Christian Gnosticism of the second century) found in the second century were probably also present in Palestine in the century before the birth of Jesus, when some of the Greek ideas were assimilated by wealthy and influential Jews of Palestine as well as by many Jews of the Dispersion (who outnumbered the Jews in Palestine by some three or four to one).

More recently, scholars have differentiated between gnosis and Gnosticism. The former is knowledge of divine mysteries reserved for an elite group whereas "Gnosticism" denotes a fully developed Gnostic system in the second century. The Gnostic expression of Christianity had a wide influence not only in the west, but also to the east of Palestine and was a forerunner of second and third century Mandaeism and Manichaeism. The Gnostic sect known as the Mandaeans began east of Jordan in the late first or second century CE. They taught that the body imprisoned the soul, but that the soul would be set free by the redeemer, *Manda da Hayye*, who personified knowledge of life and defeated the powers of darkness on earth. Frequent baptisms and the laying on of hands by the priest were practiced to help in this struggle for freedom. Both knowledge and ritual were the vehicles for salvation. Some Mandaean Christians still exist in modern Iraq near Baghdad.

The Manicheans, another Gnostic sect that originated with Manes (ca. 216–276 CE) who was born near the Persian capital, transformed the views of the Jewish-Christian sect in which he was raised into a complete Gnostic scheme of salvation through asceticism and knowledge. The Manicheans' influence was felt especially in North Africa, but they were also known in Rome and even in southeast China. St. Augustine himself was converted to orthodox Christianity out of this sect.

Since many of the figures within the Christian expressions of Gnosticism derive from the biblical images of the Old Testament, its roots may also be connected with the Jewish Palestinian context. Gnosticism had a considerable influence in many churches in the second and third centuries and Marcion may have been influenced to some extent by it in the sense that he, like they, eventually rejected the god of the Old Testament in favor of the unknown and more gracious God of Jesus.

The most developed systems of Gnostic thought in the second century churches were from Basilides and Valentinus. Irenaeus was a severe and detailed critic of this movement and, in his refutation of the Valentinian form of Gnostic thought, he claimed that its views derived from Simon Magus mentioned in Acts 8 (*Against Heresies* 1.23.1). Irenaeus may have received much of his information about Gnostic thought from a now lost work from Justin Martyr called *Against All Heresies*.

At the core of this Gnostic movement was a belief that the world (and all matter) came into being, through sin, negligence, and ignorance of spiritual beings. Salvation from sin comes through a divine spark that came to earth and awakened some to the knowledge (gnosis) of their kinship with God and their potential of being restored to him. The Redeemer, who first appears in Christian Gnosticism, removed the ignorance and brought self-knowledge to those spiritual individuals who could receive it. Among the many important views generally characteristic of Christian Gnosticism is its fixation on astrology where the moving stars were viewed as evil. The "aeons," which earlier were understood as periods of time in the present evil age as opposed to the future good age, were now understood as the astral spirits themselves. Jewish dualistic apocalyptic thought focused on the evil time now and the triumphant good time later with good but with evil coexisting with good for a time. However, Gnostic thought focused on the spirit above that was good now and the evil flesh and matter that are here below now. Most of these systems reject the God of the Jews, probably as a result of their failed hopes, and distanced themselves from the Jews. Some of them were even anti-Jewish. Again, the various systems of Gnostic thought were highly complex and essentially an amalgamation of various systems of thought including Hellenistic, Jewish, Christian, Zoroastrian, Mesopotamian, and Indian.

The reader wanting to become more familiar with this system of thought should consult the standard works on the subject listed at the end of this chapter in the Further Reading section. This brief description of a few of the characteristics of Gnosticism may only confuse those unacquainted with the general outlines of Gnostic belief. Indeed, the novice who tries to hold in his or her mind all the Ogdoads, Decads, Tetrads, other Aeons, and emanations from the *Pleroma*, described in meticulous detail in Irenaeus, will likely become lost in the detail and worse discouraged in the pursuit of it as well!

The relevance of the Gnostic Christians, for our purposes, has to do with a common view among some canon scholars that the so-called orthodox Christian community responded to the challenges posed by the Gnostic Christians by defining more precisely their sacred collection of scriptures. They excluded the Gnostic writings, so the argument goes, and limited the Christian scriptures to their own collection that eventually became our New Testament. The problem with this view, however, is that Irenaeus and the other church fathers argued against the Gnostic Christians not by limiting a collection of sacred scriptures (a biblical canon) or by arguments for limiting the number of Christian writings, but they answered rather with the truth of the "rule of faith" (the *regula fidei*). The Christian argument was that the rule of faith was passed on in the church by apostolic succession through the bishops and this apostolic deposit was used to distinguish between the church's earliest traditions and those that emerged in the second century. Notice, for example, Irenaeus' famous line of reasoning:

> For if the apostles had known hidden mysteries, which they were in the habit of imparting to "the perfect" apart and privately from the rest, they would have delivered them especially to those to whom they were also committing the leadership of the churches themselves. (Adapted from *Against Heresies* 3.3.1, ANF)

And again,

> Since therefore we have such proofs [of the truth], which is easily obtained from the Church, it is not necessary to seek the truth among others [heretics]. [This is so] because, the apostles, like a rich man who [deposited his money] in a bank, placed in her [the Church's] hands most copiously an abundance of all things pertaining to the truth: so that every man, whosoever will, can

draw from her the water of life. For she is the entrance to life and all others are thieves and robbers. Because of this are we are obligated to avoid them [the heretics], and to choose of the things pertaining to the Church with the utmost diligence laying hold of the tradition of the truth. Now how do we decide the issue? Suppose there arose a dispute relative to some important question among us. Should we not be obliged to turn to the most ancient Churches with which the apostles had dialogue and learn from them what is certain and clear in regard to the present question? *And what should we do if the apostles themselves had not left us writings?* Would it not be necessary, [in that case,] to follow the course of the tradition that they handed down to those to whom they entrusted the leadership of the Churches? (Adapted from *Against Heresies* 3.4.1, ANF. Emphasis added)

One can scarcely deny the force of Irenaeus' logic here, even if it is difficult to validate it in the surviving traditions. The apostles would surely have passed on the church's sacred teachings to their successors, the leaders or bishops of churches. As in the case of Marcion and his followers, the presence of Gnostic writings at the end of the second century did not lead the "orthodox" churches to define more precisely the boundaries of their New Testament scriptures, as some have argued, though they did reaffirm their adoption of the Jewish scriptures as their own. They addressed their concerns about Gnostic ideas by appealing to their *regula fidei* or "rule of faith" which is a canon of truth that was believed to go back to Jesus himself and transmitted faithfully through those closest to him, the apostles.

This "canon" or "rule of faith" was also a distinguishing feature in later canonical decisions that incorporated or excluded certain Christian writings from the biblical canon. From Irenaeus' perspective, this canon of faith included the following:

The Church, though dispersed throughout the whole world, even to the ends of the earth, has received from the apostles and their disciples this faith: It believes in one God, the Father Almighty, Maker of heaven, and earth and the sea and all things that are in them and in one Christ Jesus, the Son of God, who became incarnate for our salvation and in the Holy Spirit, who proclaimed through the prophets the dispensations of God, the advents, the birth from a virgin, the passion, the resurrection from the dead, and the ascension into heaven in the flesh of the beloved Christ Jesus, our Lord. He also proclaimed through the prophets his future manifestation from heaven in the glory of the Father "to gather all things in one," and to raise up anew all flesh of the whole human race, in order that to Christ Jesus, our Lord, God, Savior, and King, according to the will of the invisible Father, "every knee should bow, of things in heaven, and things in earth, and things under the earth, and that every tongue should confess" to him, and that he should execute just judgment towards all sending into everlasting fire "spiritual wickednesses," and the angels who transgressed and became apostates, together with the ungodly, and unrighteous, and wicked, and profane among men. But that he may, in the exercise of his grace, confer immortality on the righteous and holy, and those who have kept his commandments, and have persevered in his love, some from the beginning of their Christian course, and others from the time of their repentance. He will surround them with everlasting glory. (Adapted from *Against Heresies* 1.10.1, ANF; compare with 3.4.2.)

Evidence in the second century writings for a direct relationship between the church's dealing with Gnostic heresy and the development of a canon of orthodox Scriptures is unconvincing. Indirectly, however, it is certainly possible that eventually the Gnostic writings were evaluated in terms of what was commonly taught in the churches about Jesus the Christ and other related concerns. As that happened, these writings were rejected because the Gnostic writings did not cohere with the "apostolic deposit" that Irenaeus and others referred to and taught. This deposit is sometimes called the "proto-orthodox" position of the church that appeared before the more complete orthodox positions advocated in the fourth century.

While it is easy for the "winners" of church history to rewrite history in a way that reflects favorably on them, the second century evidence shows that the orthodox Christians, either the majority or most capable representatives or defenders of that position, argued their positions strongly enough to set in motion the triumph of orthodoxy that emerges in the fourth century. It is not at all certain that the majority of Christians at the end of the second century were "orthodox" in the sense that the term "orthodox" has come to mean. Exactly why the Gnostic Christians eventually lost the power play within orthodox Christianity is not always clear, but because it did, much of the history of the movement has been lost and undoubtedly some of the important ideas it proposed have also been lost. This, of course, could be said of all Christian sects that did not garner the acceptance of the majority of the church. What we have today is but a small amount of the literary activity that was produced by the Gnostic community.

To return to our major point, the second century churches did not respond to the threat of Gnostic Christianity by producing a fixed canon of Christian scriptures, but rather by promoting a rule (canon) of faith that was passed on in the churches. This rule of faith, it was cogently argued, reflected an early understanding of the Christian faith (proto-orthodoxy) that was handed down in the churches from the apostles through the bishops.

The Montanists

Finally, Montanus, possibly a former priest of Cybele, was joined by two women, Prisca and Maximilla, and came to Phrygia in Asia Minor claiming to be inspired by the Paraclete (Spirit) with an announcement of the *parousia* or coming of the Lord. Together they had a major impact upon the people of Phrygia and the rest of Asia Minor. Many Christians received the Montanist teaching with enthusiasm throughout the Mediterranean world, especially in North Africa where even the famed teacher Tertullian became a convert to this new charismatic movement. Their message focused on the end times when Jesus would come again, the role of the Spirit, and they had their own special interpretation of the message of the book of Revelation.

The Montanists focused on the need for a "New Prophecy," rigid asceticism, martyrdom, and the presence and power of the Holy Spirit. It was reported by Eusebius that the Montanists produced a large number of prophetic documents (*Ecclesiastical History* 5.16.3–4). Those who most vigorously opposed the Montanists and their new prophecy in Asia Minor, the so-called *Alogi* (the name comes from their rejection of the divine "logos" or "word" in John's prologue), also rejected the Gospel of John and the book of Revelation which were heavily used by the Montanists. The greater Church also rejected the Montanist movement, and was hesitant about the Gospel of John because of its focus on the Paraclete as well as the book of Revelation because of its apocalyptic character. Even the Book of Hebrews was called into question by the Alogi because it was linked with the Montanist crisis, probably due to its view of the hopeless condition of the apostate Christian (see Heb. 6.4–6 and 10.26–31), a view that coincided with the Montanists' harsh penitential practice. By around the year 200, they had expanded their influence to Rome and North Africa, though their most significant influence was among rural communities.

In their enthusiasm, the Montanists generated numerous "prophetic" books that they claimed were divinely inspired. Some canon scholars, especially Hans von Campenhausen and Bruce M. Metzger following him, argued that the Montanists produced a large amount of literature and that this new literature was influential in spurring the church into defining more precisely the limits of its sacred Scriptures.

But did the Montanists produce any "scriptural" literature? Scholarly opinion is divided on this question. According to Hippolytus, the Montanists produced "innumerable books" (*Elench.* 8.19.10), and Tertullian defended the practice of producing inspired literature, since it is, he said, mere prejudice to heed and value only past demonstrations of power and grace and that "those people who condemn the one power of the one Holy Spirit in accordance with chronological eras should beware" (*Pass. Perp.* 1.1–2). He argued that these new writings were from God who "in accordance with the testimony of Scripture, has destined [them] for precisely this period of time" (*Pass. Perp.* 1.1). It is important that Tertullian was not willing to close off the possibility of new inspired literature to inform his Christian faith. The fact that Tertullian joined the Montanists no doubt had an influence on his thoughts in this regard, but he also perceived that there were no historical or theological arguments in support of limiting the scope of Christian sacred texts to those of an earlier generation.

Scholars following von Campenhausen argue that the majority of churches rejected the Montanist prophecies essentially on the grounds that their prophecies were contrary to the earlier Christian writings (New Testament writings). In a polemic against the Montanists, recorded by Eusebius, a certain Apolinarius wrote:

> For a long and protracted time, my dear Abercius Marcellus, I have been urged by you to compose a treatise against the sect of those called after Miltiades, but until now I was somewhat reluctant, not from any lack of ability to refute the lie and testify to the truth, but from timidity and scruples *lest I might seem to some to be adding to the writings or injunctions of the word of the new covenant of the gospel,* to which no one who has chosen to live according to the gospel itself can add and from which he cannot take away. But when I have just come to Ancyra in Galatia and perceived that the church in that place was torn in two by this new movement [the Montanists] which is not, as they call it, prophecy but much rather, as will be shown, false prophecy, I disputed concerning these people themselves and their propositions so far as I could, with the Lord's help, for many days continuously in the church. Thus the church rejoiced and was strengthened in the truth, but our opponents were crushed for the moment and our adversaries were distressed (*Ecclesiastical History* 5.16.3–4, LCL. Emphasis added).

Von Campenhausen and others concluded that the Montanists and their production of numerous books were among the *primary* (not the only) factors that spurred the church into defining more precisely which books belonged to the New Testament. Several scholars continue to argue that it was at this point that the last phase of the canonical process began. Again, however, there is no evidence to conclude that the church brought the canonical process to a close as a result of its interaction with the Montanists. If the greater number of churches was interested in closing the New Testament canon at that time, one would expect to find several lists of canonical literature in this period such as we find in the fourth century, but that is missing in the second century along with any discussions of these developments in the church. As with Marcion and the Gnostics, the second century Church responded to the Montanists and all such heretical movements with an understanding of Christian truth. They did not respond by offering a closed or fixed collection of scriptures. It was their understanding of the Christian faith that the church believed had been handed on in the churches through its bishops that they employed in their defense of this faith. They also freely and generously used the writings of the early Christian community, especially the Gospels and writings of Paul, to support their criticisms of such movements.

THE "ORTHODOX" INFLUENCE: PAVING THE WAY

While there is no evidence that heretical movements in the second century forced the hand of the church to determine the limits of its scriptures, it is nonetheless fair to say that the church's engaging conversations with and about the heretical elements in the churches no doubt led them to reject the heretical writings and to consider what sacred or religious teachings and literature best reflected the church's identity and proclamation. When theological views emerged that did *not* reflect the long accepted positions of the church about Jesus, proto-orthodox teachers rejected them and made strong arguments against them that were widely accepted by the majority of churches. As a result the writings of these heretical communities were eventually discarded and left behind. Why would a church continue to copy and preserve writings that it no longer believed reflected its core beliefs?

It is not likely that decisions about the scope of the church's Bible could be made until the majority of Christians finally agreed on the identity of Jesus. That broad agreement took some three centuries. Was Jesus God, a man, an angel, a Spirit, or a God-man? Church teachers debated such matters at length through the fourth century and even later in the Arian controversies. As more agreement was found on this issue, it became possible to identify the sacred texts that reflected this perspective as the processes of canon formation were in their final stages of development. This does not mean that the churches in the second century had no idea what they believed about

Jesus, but only that there were many other voices flourishing in churches in the second and third centuries that reflected several diverse perspectives.

At the beginning of the third century church, there is evidence of the influence of this "rule of faith" in some churches. For example, when Bishop Serapion of Antioch (ca. 200) was asked by the Christians in Rhossus, one of the churches in his charge, for permission to read the *Gospel of Peter* in their church, he initially agreed to let it be read. Later, however, after he had the opportunity to read it, he believed that it rejected the humanity of Jesus. Consequently, Serapion reversed himself and denied the reading of this gospel in the churches. His decision was based on a rule of faith and not a fixed collection of books in a New Testament canon. Had it been the latter and based on a limited collection of Gospels, as Irenaeus had argued some 30 years earlier, he would have rejected the writing initially, but that was not the case. His letter to that effect is preserved by Eusebius as follows:

> For our part, brethren, we receive both Peter and the other apostles as Christ, but the writings which falsely bear their names we reject, as men of experience, knowing that such were not handed down to us. For I myself, when I came among you, imagined that all of you clung to the true faith, and, without going through the Gospel put forward by them in the name of Peter, I said, "If this is the only thing that seemingly causes captious feelings among you, let it be read." But since I have now learned from what has been told me that their mind was lurking in some hold of heresy, I shall give diligence to come again to you. Wherefore, brethren, expect me quickly. But we, brethren, having gathered an understanding of the kind of heresy to which Marcianus [Marcion] belonged (who used to contradict himself, not knowing what he was saying, as you will learn from what has been written to you), were enabled to understand by others who studied this very Gospel. By this we mean the successors of those who began it, whom we call Docetae [Docetics] (for most of the ideas belong to their teaching). Using the material supplied by them, we have discovered that the Gospel of Peter was, for the most part, *in accordance with the true teaching of the Savior,* but that

some things were added, which also we place below for your benefit. (Adapted from Eusebius, *Ecclesiastical History* 12.3–6, LCL. Emphasis added)

Serapion acknowledged that this writing was pseudonymous and could therefore not be read, but this conclusion came as he read the document and saw the Docetic and Gnostic thought in it. As a result, his concern for the truth—the widespread understanding of the truth of and about Jesus—that was the primary emphasis of the churches in the last half of the second century led him to reject the document. This focus, orthodoxy, eventually became one of the chief concerns of churches in the mid-to-late fourth century when the parameters of the Christian scriptures were established and *canon* came to mean a fairly precise collection of sacred writings. Four important "proto-orthodox" leaders at the end of the second century and first part of the third figured into the broad and lengthy processes that led the churches to define and identify their biblical canon. In the following discussion we will briefly examine their contributions to the emergence of a fixed collection (canon) of Christian scriptures.

Irenaeus

Irenaeus of Lyons (writing ca. 170–180) made a significant transition in the formation of the New Testament canon. Unlike Justin, he did not defend just the Old Testament scriptures alone, but he also explicitly named and defended the scriptural authority of Christian writings, especially the four canonical Gospels. His aim was not so much to establish a biblical canon or a closed collection of sacred writings since he never discusses that and has no fitting language for a fixed biblical tradition, but rather to establish and defend the truth of the Christian message. His contribution to canon formation was the first major step of several processes that led to the formation of the New Testament canon of scriptures. As we noted above, the "canon" of Irenaeus was not a list of inspired books, but rather the canon of faith of and about Jesus the Christ that he believed had been passed on in the church from the apostles to the bishops in the churches. This was his apostolic "deposit" that he set forth in his *Against Heresies* (3.2.2). Irenaeus' summary of "the faith" or "canon" on which the church depended for its life and witness merits careful attention. The major tenets of his canon became the foundation pillars of "orthodoxy" in the church and were a significant part of most of the ancient creedal formulations.

Irenaeus made use of the Old Testament scriptures familiar to him, as well as selected Christian writings to demonstrate the authenticity and authority of his teachings. He was the first, so far as our present knowledge shows and as we said earlier, to use the terms *Old Testament* and *New Testament,* claiming that both Testaments are the scriptures of the church and both are authoritative bodies of scripture for Christian faith. Irenaeus introduces the premise for his arguments with the words, "Inasmuch, then, as in both testaments there is the same righteousness of God [displayed] . . ." (*Against Heresies* 4.28.1, ANF). This is also found in his brief comment at the end of Book II of *Against Heresies* in which he claims:

> the preaching of the apostles, the authoritative teaching of the Lord, the announcements of the prophets, the dictated utterances of the apostles, and the ministration of the law—all of which praise one and the same Being, the God and Father of all, and not many diverse beings . . . are all in harmony with our statements. (2:35.4, ANF)

In another place he writes,

> If, therefore, even in the New Testament, the apostles are found granting certain precepts in consideration of human infirmity, . . . it ought not to be wondered at, if also in the Old Testament the same God permitted similar indulgences for the benefit of His people . . . so that they might obtain the gift of salvation through them (*Against Heresies* 4.15.2, ANF).

Establishing of a closed canon of inspired scriptures was not Irenaeus' idea or concern, but rather to defend the Christian message with all the tools at his disposal against the promoters of what he considered the heretical departures from the true apostolic faith. He anchored the church's knowledge of the apostolic faith in the teachings passed on in the succession of bishops as well as in the authority of the scriptures of both the Old and New Testaments. To our knowledge, he himself never listed the books that comprise either his Old or New Testament. In the fourth century, when Eusebius listed the sacred books acknowledged by Irenaeus, he likely created that list by simply listing the Christian texts that Irenaeus cited. Irenaeus emphasized the notion of apostolic succession repeatedly, but nowhere more clearly than in the following passage:

> The blessed apostles, then, having founded and built up the Church, committed into the hands of Linus the office of episcopate. Paul makes mention of this Linus in the Epistles to Timothy. Anacletus succeeded him, and Clement was allotted the bishopric. Clement, since he had seen the blessed apostles and had been conversant with them, might be said to have the preaching of the apostles still echoing in his ears, and their traditions before his eyes. . . . Evaristus succeeded Clement, and he was succeeded by Sixtus, the sixth from the apostles. After him came Telephorus, who was gloriously martyred, then Hyginus, after him Pius, and then after him Anicetus was appointed. Anicetus was succeeded by Soter and Eleutherius, who is the twelfth from the apostles and now holds the inheritance of the episcopate. *In this order, and by this succession, the ecclesiastical tradition from the apostles and the preaching of the truth have come down to us. And this is the most abundant proof that there is one and the same vivifying faith, which has been preserved in the Church from the apostles until now, and handed down in truth.* (*Against Heresies* 3.3.3, ANF. Emphasis added)

For Irenaeus, the apostolic witness was the primary determining principle for the recognition of the authority of New Testament scriptures (*Against Heresies* 3.2.2). It should also be noted that he did not limit that succession of the apostolic witness to the bishops at Rome (*Against Heresies* 3.3.2).

For Irenaeus, if questions are not clearly dealt with in the "apostolic deposit," or if no teaching had been left by the apostles, where does one turn for the answer? For him, the obvious answer lies with those to whom the apostolic deposit was given: the bishops of the churches. See his argument in *Against Heresies* 3.4.1 cited on p. 168 above.

The effect of Irenaeus' concern to preserve the truth of the gospel was that the church began to recognize Christian writings (the Gospels especially, but also Paul) as scripture in the churches. Apart from his affirmation that the Gospels could be no more than four (Matthew, Mark, Luke, and John), there is no indication in his surviving writings that his collection was closed in his day, though given the literature that he cited most and his argument about the apostolic deposit, it is likely that he would have selected the earliest writings that were produced by the apostles or those in the apostolic community.

In the fourth century, Eusebius (*Ecclesiastical History* 5.8.2–8) reported that Irenaeus had recognized a canon of Scriptures, but this may not necessarily be the case. There is no question that Irenaeus had a rule of faith to which he regularly appealed (see *Against Heresies* 1.10.1; cf. 3.4.2), and he frequently supported his teaching with references to the apostolic community to whom Christ had committed this "apostolic deposit," namely, the apostolic community and its writings (*Against Heresies* 4.15.2).

Irenaeus clearly accepted New Testament writings as scripture on par with Old Testament scriptures. If references or citations are any indication of what Irenaeus considered authoritative, he did not mention or favor Hebrews, James, Jude, Jude, or 2 Peter, but did acknowledge the authority of the *Shepherd of Hermas.* The scriptures, for Irenaeus, were evidently made up of the still fluid collection of Old Testament scriptures as well as the four Gospels, and several letters of Paul. Because our information from Irenaeus is limited to *ad hoc* writings, that is, writings addressing specific concerns facing the church, we cannot say with confidence that we know all of the books that he reckoned as scripture. Interestingly, in an overly optimistic statement about the interpretation of scripture he claims that, "*the entire Scriptures, the prophets and the Gospels*, can be clearly, unambiguously understood by all" (*Against Heresies* 2.27.2, ANF. Emphasis added). Is he suggesting that in his day only the Old Testament writings, whatever their scope, and the Gospels were scripture? He is not clear on this, though he clearly included letters from Paul in his collection of authoritative apostolic writings.

The *ad hoc* nature of Irenaeus' writings no doubt affected what literature he selected to support his arguments. The sources that he would have found helpful in his defense of orthodoxy do not necessarily include *all* of the writings that he thought were either scriptural or authoritative in the churches. Interestingly, his references to the Old Testament literature are fewer in number than his references to the New Testament books.

Irenaeus recognizes "apostles" as a collection of writings apparently distinct from the Gospel writers, but there are no clear statements on what other writings make up the "apostles" (see *Against Heresies* 1.3.6). Apart from his closed Gospel canon, nothing in his writings suggests that he carried out a "canonizing" procedure on other Christian writings. Since he often cited literature that was not later canonized by the Church—*1 Enoch*, the *Shepherd of Hermas* and *1 Clement*, it is not easy to discover the contours of his sacred scriptures.

Clement of Alexandria (ca. 150–215)

Titus Flavius Clemens, probably born in Athens of pagan parents around 150 CE, was converted to the Christian faith and came eventually to study under Pantaenus, the director of the Catechetical School in Alexandria. He succeeded Pantaenus as director of the school (ca. 190–200) and expanded the original catechetical aims of the school from educating new converts to becoming a training center "for the cultivation of theologians." During the persecutions of Septimus Severus (193–211), Clement fled Egypt and finally settled in Cappadocia. Like others before him, Clement referred to or cited as scripture many of the writings of the New Testament, for example, the four canonical Gospels, Acts, *fourteen* epistles of Paul (Hebrews was attributed to Paul), 1, 2 John, 1 Peter, Jude and Revelation, but he made no mention of James, 2 Peter, or 3 John. What is also interesting is that he also quoted various noncanonical texts to support his ideas such as the *Epistle of Barnabas, 1 Clement, Shepherd of Hermas, Preaching of Peter, Sibylline Writings*, and the *Didache*. Again, he does not make a list of all of the writings that he deemed inspired by God. Eusebius' description of the writings that informed Clement's theology is interesting and shows Clement's interest and use of many diverse religious texts.

Now in the *Stromateis* he [Clement] has composed a patchwork, not only of the divine Scripture, but of the writings of the Greeks as well, if he thought that they also had said anything useful, and he mentions opinions from many sources, explaining Greek and barbarian alike, and moreover sifts the false opinions of the heresiarchs; and unfolding much history he gives us a work of great erudition. With all these he mingles also the opinions of philosophers, and so he has suitably made the title of the *Stromateis* to correspond to the work itself. *And in them he has also made use of testimonies from the disputed writings, the book known as the Wisdom of Solomon, the Wisdom of Jesus the Son of Sirach, and the Epistle to the Hebrews, and those of Barnabas, and Clement, and Jude; and he mentions Tatian's book Against the Greeks,* and Cassian, since he also had composed a chronography, and moreover Philo and Aristobulus and Josephus and Demetrius and Eupolemus, Jewish writers, in that they would show, all of them, in writing, that Moses and the Jewish race went back further in their origins than the Greeks. And the books of Clement, of which we are speaking, are full of much other useful learning. In the first of these he shows with reference to himself that he came very near to the successors of the Apostles; and he promises in them also to write a commentary on Genesis. (*Ecclesiastical History* 6.13.4–8, LCL. Emphasis added)

And in the *Hypotyposeis,* to speak briefly, he has given concise explanations of all the Canonical Scriptures, not passing over even the disputed writings, I mean the Epistle of Jude and the remaining Catholic Epistles, and the Epistle of Barnabas, and the Apocalypse known as Peter's. And as for the Epistle to the Hebrews, he says indeed that it is Paul's, but that it was written for Hebrews in the Hebrew tongue, and that Luke, having carefully translated it, published it for the Greeks; hence, as a result of this translation, the same complexion of style is found in this Epistle and in the Acts: but that the [words] "Paul the apostle" were naturally not prefixed. For, says he, "in writing to Hebrews who had conceived a prejudice against him and were suspicious of him, he very wisely did not repel them at the beginning by putting his name." (*Ecclesiastical History* 6.14.1–3, LCL)

And again in the same books Clement has inserted a tradition of the primitive elders with regard to the order of the Gospels, as follows:

> He said that those Gospels were first written which include the genealogies, but that the Gospel according to Mark came into being in this manner: When Peter had publicly preached the word at Rome, and by the Spirit had proclaimed the Gospel, that those present, who were many, exhorted Mark, as one who had followed him for a long time and remembered what had been spoken, to make a record of what was said; and that he did this, and distributed the Gospel among those that asked him. And that when the matter came to Peter's knowledge he neither strongly forbade it nor urged it forward. But that John, last of all, conscious that the outward facts had been set forth in the Gospels, was urged on by his disciples, and, divinely moved by the Spirit, composed a spiritual Gospel. This is Clement's account. (*Ecclesiastical History* 6.14.5–7, LCL)

Even though Clement knew of and apparently did not reject the *Gospel of the Hebrews, The Gospel of the Egyptians*, and *The Tradition of Matthias*, he may not have acknowledged them as scripture (i.e., normative), but that is not clear. What is most surprising about Clement of Alexandria is his high regard for Greek philosophy as a means of preparing one to receive the Christian message. He writes:

> Even if Greek philosophy does not comprehend the truth in its entirety and, in addition, lacks the strength to fulfill the Lord's command, yet at least it prepares the way for the teaching which is royal in the highest sense of the word, by making a man self-controlled, by molding his character, and by making him ready to receive the truth. (*Stromateis* 7.20, ANF)

If Clement of Alexandria had a closed canon of Christian scripture, it is nowhere apparent. In his pursuit of the knowledge of God, he was informed by a broad selection of literature. He drew on

many different sources and appealed to apocryphal writings including those writers who were "Greek and barbarian alike" (Eusebius,
Ecclesiastical History 6.13.5), including those writings that Eusebius
later referred to as the "disputed writings," namely, Hebrews and
Jude, but also the *Epistle of Barnabas* and the *Apocalypse of Peter*
(*Ecclesiastical History* 6.13.4–7). Although Eusebius called this literature "disputed" (6.14.1), the *Muratorian Fragment* (lines 68–69)
reported that Jude and the Epistles of John are recognized "in the
catholic church," a feature that is found elsewhere only at the end
of the fourth century. Their undisputed appearance in such a list is
evidence of a late origin of the *Muratorian Fragment*.

Tertullian (ca. 160–225)

Tertullian, was a well-educated native of Carthage in Africa and
often was called the "Father of Latin Theology." Like Irenaeus before
him he also acknowledged all four canonical Gospels, but writing
around 200 CE he distinguished between them giving priority to
Mathew and John over Mark and Luke. He writes: "Of the apostles,
therefore, *John and Matthew first instill faith into us; whilst of apostolic men, Luke and Mark renew it afterwards.* These all start with the
same principles of faith" (Tertullian, *Against Marcion.* 4.2.2, ANF.
Emphasis added). Both here and elsewhere he seems to have relegated
Luke and Mark to a lower status than Matthew and John and chided
Marcion for choosing Luke instead of Matthew or John. He writes:

> Now of the authors whom we possess, Marcion seems to have
> singled out Luke for his mutilating process. Luke, however, was
> not an apostle, but only an apostolic man; *not a master, but a dis-
> ciple, and so inferior to a master*—at least as far subsequent to him
> as the apostle whom he followed . . . was subsequent to the others.
> (*Against Marcion* 4.2.5, ANF. Emphasis added)

For Tertullian, apostolicity was the chief criterion for recognizing
the authority of the Gospels. This same apostolic authority, which
was passed on by the apostles through the succession of bishops,
guaranteed the truthfulness of the Gospel. The apostolic writings

formed for him the *Novum Testamentum* (New Testament), though it is not clear the full extent of the writings that he considered apostolic. Again, he explains:

> If I fail in resolving this article (of our faith) by passages which may admit of dispute out of the Old Testament, I will take out of the New Testament a confirmation of our view, that you may not straightway attribute to the Father every possible (relation and condition) which I ascribe to the Son. Behold, then, I find both in the Gospels and in the (writings of the) apostles a visible and an invisible God (revealed to us), under a manifest and personal distinction in the condition of both. (*Against Praxeas* 15, ANF)

For him, the New Testament writings apparently consisted of the four Gospels, thirteen epistles of Paul, Acts, 1 John, 1 Peter and Jude, and Revelation; however, he did not produce a *fixed* list of these works, even though he cited these books frequently in an authoritative or scripture-like manner. These are likely the books that he included in his reference to the "entire volume" cited earlier (*Prescriptions Against Heretics* 32). He also writes that Rome "mingles the Law and the prophets in one volume" (*Prescriptions Against Heretics* 36). Before Tertullian became a Montanist, he also included in his collection of sacred writings the *Shepherd of Hermas*, but later he dismissed the work with scorn and surprisingly treated Hebrews as marginal because he thought that Barnabas had written it. Nowhere in his extant writings, however, do we find any listing or identification of precisely what was in his Old or New Testament collections. None of the books that Tertullian appears to have accepted as authoritative Christian literature (scripture) by the end of his career was later rejected except, of course, the Montanist prophecies that he later embraced.

Origen (ca. 184–235)

The transition from the authority of *oral* tradition to the authority of *written* traditions, which began with Irenaeus, was complete by the time of Origen. Like Clement of Alexandria, Origen drew from the four canonical Gospels, thirteen epistles of Paul (he appears to have included Hebrews but did not believe that Paul wrote it), 1 Peter, 1 John and Revelation. Rufinus' (345–410 CE) translation of Origen's *Homily* (7.1) on Joshua provides a listing of the scriptures that Origen accepted, but his translation is clearly inferior to that of Eusebius and unreliable. Whenever he found difficult passages in Origen, he simply left them out of his translation, believing that they were interpolations by heretics. Again, Eusebius is our primary witness to what Origen considered to be scriptural.

In the first of his *[Commentaries] on the Gospel according to Matthew, defending the canon of the Church*, he gives his testimony that he knows only four Gospels, writing somewhat as follows: "As having learned by tradition concerning the four Gospels, which alone are unquestionable in the Church of God under heaven, that the first gospel was written by Matthew, who was once a tax-collector but afterwards an apostle of Jesus Christ. He published it for those who came to believe from Judaism and composed it in the Hebrew language. Second, Mark, who wrote his Gospel in accordance with Peter's instructions, whom also Peter acknowledged as his son in the catholic epistle [1 Pet. 5.13], spoke in these terms: 'She that is in Babylon, elect together with you, salutes you; and so does Mark my son.' And third, Luke wrote his Gospel for those who came to believe from among the Gentiles, and it was the Gospel that was praised by Paul. After these gospels came the Gospel according to John."

And in the fifth of his *Expositions on the Gospel according to John* the same person [Origen] says this with reference to the epistles of the apostles: "But he who was made sufficient to become a minister of the new covenant, not of the letter but of the spirit, even Paul, who fully preached the Gospel from Jerusalem and round about even unto Illyricum, did not so much as write to all the churches that he taught. Indeed, even those churches to whom he wrote, he sent but a few lines. And Peter, on whom the Church of Christ is built and against whom the gates of Hades shall not prevail, has left *one* acknowledged epistle, *and, it may be, a second, though it is doubted.* Why do I need to speak of him who leaned back on Jesus' breast, even John, who has left behind one Gospel? He confessed that he could write so many [books about Jesus] that even the world itself could not contain them. He also wrote the Apocalypse, being ordered to keep silence and not to write the voices of seven thunders. He has also left *an epistle* of a very few lines, *and it may be, a second and a third*, for not all say that these are genuine. Only, the two of them together are not a hundred lines long."

Furthermore, he thus discusses the Epistle to the Hebrews, in his *Homilies* upon it: "That the character of the diction of the epistle entitled *To the Hebrews* has not the apostle's [Paul's] rudeness in speech [2 Cor. 11.6], who confessed himself rude in speech, that is, in style, but the epistle is better Greek in the framing of its diction and this will be admitted by everyone who is able to discern differences of style. But again, on the other hand, everyone will agree, if they have given due consideration to reading the apostle, that the thoughts of the epistle are admirable, and not inferior to the acknowledged writings of the apostle."

Further on, he adds the following remarks: "But as for myself, if I were to state my own opinion, I should say that the thoughts are the apostle's, but that the style and composition belong to one who called to mind the apostle's teachings and, as it were, made short notes of what his master said. If any church, therefore, holds this epistle as Paul's, let it be commended for this also. For not without reason have the men of old time handed it down as Paul's. *But who wrote the epistle, in truth God knows.* Yet the account which has reached us is twofold: some saying that Clement, who was bishop of the Romans, wrote the epistle and others that it was Luke who wrote the Gospel and the Acts." (Adapted from Eusebius, *Ecclesiastical History* 6.25.3–14, LCL. Emphasis added)

It is most likely that Origen's New Testament "canonical list," as in the case of Irenaeus' list, is a creation of Eusebius and Rufinus in the late fourth century, more than a hundred years after the death of Origen. Eusebius' source may well have been his own collection of references to or citations of the New Testament literature in Origen's writings. It is all but certain that such canonical lists were produced in the fourth century and later and such references to earlier "canons" of the church are most likely anachronistically claimed. The second-century heresies in the churches were not addressed in the second and third centuries with a canon of *scripture*, but with a canon of *faith*, or a *regula fidei*. The churches addressed their concerns with the notion of truth or, more precisely, those confessional statements of the church about Jesus, his relationship to God, and his activity and ministry. There is no doubt, however, that they also made use of many of the books that eventually became the church's New Testament canon in order to argue their positions.

According to Eusebius, then, Origen accepted the four canonical Gospels and an unspecified number of Paul's epistles as well as 1 John, Revelation, Hebrews with some doubt, and evidently with some question also about 2 Peter, 2 and 3 John. Origen apparently also made use of James and Jude with some hesitation because they were not generally acknowledged at that time as scripture or "recognized" writings. He also refers more positively to *Barnabas, Shepherd of Hermas*, and the *Didache*, and it appears that he may have acknowledged them as scripture. In his treatise *Against Celsus*, Origen introduces the *Epistle of Barnabas* with the words, "*It is written* in the catholic epistle of Barnabas" (1.63. Emphasis added) and in his *On Principles* he establishes his argument on the basis of scripture and cites the *Shepherd of Hermas* (2.1.5). However, if one is prone to claim that Origen acknowledged James and Jude as canon because he made use of them, then we could also say the same thing about his use and acceptance of *Barnabas, Shepherd of Hermas*, and the *Didache*.

Those who say that Origen accepted as scripture only writings of the later canonized New Testament literature have frequently noted that Origen never wrote a commentary on a book *not* found in the later New Testament. We should add, however, that so far as our present information goes, Origen did not write a commentary on every book of the New Testament either. If that argument were carried to its logical conclusion, Origen's Bible canon would be much smaller than the current New Testament canon!

The main problem with the supposed closed biblical canon of Origen is that we have no solid evidence *from him* as to what that canon was. The evidence from Origen is not strong enough to conclude that he accepted all of the writings that now make up our New Testament canon and *no others*. He seems to have been ambivalent about the status of 2 Peter and 2 and 3 John, but he likely included both *Barnabas* and the *Shepherd* in his collection of sacred writings. Origen himself, however, probably never had a closed collection of New Testament scriptures.

Origen apparently also refused to reduce his collection of Old Testament Scriptures to the 22 or 24 books of the Hebrew biblical canon. He simply acknowledged the number of books in the Jewish biblical canon, of which he was quite familiar (see Eusebius, *Ecclesiastical History* 6.25.1–2), but he does not appear to have sharply defined either the Old or New Testament books for the church or himself (Eusebius, *Ecclesiastical History* 6.25.3–14). The New Testament canon attributed to him is probably no more than a select list produced by Eusebius of the writings that Origen cited or quoted.

The primary arguments for establishing a widely recognized and largely closed biblical canon at the end of the second century are not convincing. It is more likely that there was a general recognition of something like an "open" biblical canon (canon 1) at the end of the second century with many writings cited to support arguments presented by the primary teachers of the church. It is not clear how widespread this recognition was or exactly what the scope of such a collection might have been. There can be no doubt, however, about the acceptance of many Christian writings as sacred scripture, but there is no evidence for a closed biblical canon at that time. Also, at the end of the second century, apart from the term "scripture," there were no generally accepted terms to identify this collection of Christian writings. Even the terms "Old Testament" and "New Testament" were only *beginning* to be used in that century, but they had not yet gained sufficient recognition in the churches by that time to function as synonyms for *closed* canonical collections. They appear to reflect only that the writings were Jewish or Christian, not the scope or extent of those collections. These terms were still unfamiliar to large sections of the Christian community in the third and fourth centuries. For example, observe how Origen introduces these terms in the following two passages from the first half of the third century:

> We take in addition, for the proof of our statements, testimonies from what are believed by us to be divine writings, viz., *from that which is called the Old Testament, and that which is styled the New*, and endeavor by reason to confirm our faith. (Origen, *On Principles* 4.1, ANF. Emphasis added)

Again, in a different context where he is refuting the speculations of the Gnostic Christians, he writes:

> It appears to me, therefore, to be necessary that one who is able to represent in a genuine manner the doctrine of the Church, and to refute those dealers in knowledge, falsely so-called, should take his stand against historical fictions, and oppose to them the true and lofty agreement of the doctrines, found both in the *so-called Old Testament and in the so-called New*, appears so plainly and fully. (*Commentary on John* 5.4, ANF. Emphasis added)

Later Eusebius in the fourth century (ca. 320–330 CE), when praising Josephus for his opposition to Apion, refers to the passage cited in the previous chapter (*Against Apion* §137–143) and says: "In the first of these [treatises by Josephus] he gives the number of the canonical scriptures *of the so-called Old Testament*, and showed as follows which are undisputed among the Hebrews as belonging to ancient tradition." (*Ecclesiastical History* 3.9.5, LCL. Emphasis added). Josephus, of course, would never have referred to the Jewish scriptures as "Old Testament" and this shows that Eusebius occasionally spoke anachronistically using these terms and imposing them backwards on earlier writers.

These examples show the lack of popularity of these terms in the churches in the mid third century and later in the fourth century.

Further, the fact that *Wisdom of Solomon* should appear in *New Testament* lists in the fourth century (those of Eusebius, the Muratorian Fragment, and Epiphanius) speaks against the widespread understanding of the meaning of these terms to identify a *fixed* collection of Scriptures in the second century. The most that can be said here is that there was a general recognition of the scriptural status of the four Gospels, Acts, some of the Epistles of Paul (not the Pastorals), and 1 Peter and 1 John at the end of the second century.

FURTHER READING

Gnosticism

Alastair, A. H. B. *Gnostic Truth and Christian Heresy: A Study in the History of Gnosticism*. Peabody, MA: Hendrickson Publishers, 1996.

Baaren, Th. P. van "Towards a Definition of Gnosticism," in *Le Origini dello Gnosticismo*. Acts of Messina Colloquium, 1966, ed. U. Bianchi. Leiden: E. J. Brill, 1967, pp. 178–180.

Filoramo, Giovanni. *A History of Gnosticism*. Trans. Anthony Alcock. Cambridge, MA/Oxford: Blackwell, 1990.

Grant, Robert M., ed. *Gnosticism: A Source Book of Heretical Writings from the Early Christian Period*. New York: Harper & Brothers, 1961.

Hedrick, C. W. and R. Hodgson, Jr., eds. *Nag Hammadi, Gnosticism, and Early Christianity*. Peabody, MA: Hendrickson Publishers, 1986.

Jonas, Hans. *The Gnostic Religion: The Message of the Alien God and the Beginnings of Christianity*. 2nd edn, revised. Boston, MA: Beacon Press, 1963.

King, Karen. *Revelation of the Unknowable God*. Santa Rosa, CA: Polebridge Press, 1995.

King, Karen. *What is Gnosticism?* London/Cambridge: Belknap Press of Harvard University Press, 2003.

Layton, Bentley. *The Gnostic Scriptures: A New Translation with Annotations and Introductions*. Garden City, NY: Doubleday, 1987.

Logan. H. B. and A. J. M. Wedderburn, eds. *The New Testament and Gnosis: Essays in Honour of Robert McL. Wilson*. Edinburgh: T.&T. Clark, 1983.

Lupieri, Edmondo. *The Mandaeans: The Last Gnostics*. Trans. Charles Hindley. Grand Rapids, MI/Cambridge: Eerdmans, 2002.

MacRae, George W. "Why the Church Rejected Gnosticism," in *Jewish and Christian Self-Definition*. The Shaping of Christianity in the Second and Third Centuries, ed. E. P. Sanders. Philadelphia, PA: Fortress Press, 1980, Vol. 1, pp. 126–133.

Pearson, Birger A. *Gnosticism, Judaism, and Egyptian Christianity*. Studies in Antiquity & Christianity. Minneapolis, MN: Fortress Press, 1990.

Perkins, Pheme. "Gnosticism and the Christian Bible," in *The Canon Debate*, ed. Lee M. McDonald and J. A. Sanders. Peabody, MA: Hendrickson Publishers, 2002, pp. 355–371.

Perkins, Pheme . *Gnosticism and the New Testament.* Minneapolis, MN: Fortress Press, 1993.

Rudolph, Kurt. *Gnosis: The Nature and History of Gnosticism.* Trans. and ed. Robert McLachlan Wilson. San Francisco, CA: Harper & Row Publishers, 1987.

Walker, Benjamin. *Gnosticism: Its History and Influence.* Wellingborough: The Aquarian Press, 1989.

Wink, Walter. *Cracking the Gnostic Code: The Powers in Gnosticism.* SBLMS 46. Atlanta, GA: Scholars Press, 1993.

Other second century heresies

Bauer, Walter. *Orthodoxy and Heresy in Earliest Christianity.* 2nd edn., ed. Robert Kraft and Gerhard Krodel. Philadelphia, PA: Fortress Press, 1971.

Blackman, E. C. *Marcion and His Influence.* London: SPCK, 1948.

Casey, R. "The Armenian Marcionites and the *Diatessaron*," *JBL* 57 (1938), 185–194.

Campenhausen, Hans von. *The Formation of the Christian Bible.* Trans. J. A. Baker. Philadelphia, PA: Fortress, 1972.

Clabeaux, John J. "Marcion," *ABD*.(1992) 4:514–516.

Clabeaux, John J. "Marcionite Prologues to Paul," *ABD*.(1992) 4:520–521.

Dahl, Nils A. "The Origin of the Earliest Prologues to the Pauline Letters," *Semeia* 12 (1978), 233–277.

Ehrman, Bart D. *Lost Christianities: The Battles for Scripture and the Faiths we Never Knew.* New York/Oxford: Oxford University Press, 2003.

Ehrman, Bart D. *Lost Scriptures: Books that Did Not Make It into the New Testament.* New York/Oxford: Oxford University Press, 2003.

Ellens, J. H. "The Ancient Library of Alexandria and Early Theological Development," *Occasional Papers of the Institute for Antiquity and Christianity* 27 (1993), 1–51.

Heine, Ronald E. *The Montanist Oracles and Testimonia.* Patristic Monograph Series 14. Macon, GA: Mercer University Press, 1989.

Heine, Ronald E. "Montanus, Montanism," *ABD*. (1992) 4:898–902.

Hultgren, Arland J. and Steven A. Haggmark, eds. *The Earliest Christian Heretics: Readings from Their Opponents.* Minneapolis, MN: Fortress Press, 1996.

McDonald, Lee M. "Anti-Judaism in the Early Church Fathers," in *Anti-Semitism and Early Christianity: Issues of Polemic and Faith*, ed. Craig A. Evans and Donald A. Hagner. Minneapolis, MN: Fortress Press, 1993, pp. 215–252.

McDonald, Lee M. "Anti-Marcionite (Gospel) Prologues," *ABD*. (1992) 1:262–263.

Robinson, James M. and Helmut Koester. *Trajectories through Early Christianity*. Philadelphia, PA: Fortress Press, 1971.

Tabberne, W. "Early Montanism and Voluntary Martyrdom," *Colloquim* 17 (1985), 33–43.

Theron, Daniel J. *Evidence of Tradition*. Grand Rapids, MI: Baker Book House, 1957, 1980.

CHAPTER SEVEN

FIXING THE NEW TESTAMENT CANON

Several historical factors contributed to the final decisions about the scope of the sacred Christian scriptures. Some of the most important factors that led the churches to adopt the final shape of the New Testament canon and why they are important will be explored below. We will also examine the most important ancient criteria employed by the early churches to determine the scope of their sacred scriptures.

PERSECUTION AND THE BURNING OF BOOKS

For some early Christians a likely termination point for the recognition of which books were sacred in individual Christian communities, we have to consider the persecution of the Roman Emperor Diocletian (303–313 CE) when Christians were asked to hand over their sacred books to the authorities to be burned. On February 23, in the year 303, Diocletian launched the last full empire-wide persecution of the Christians. The reasons for this attack are not fully clear, but it likely had to do with the growing influence of the Christians who did not support the religious system promoted by the majority population in the Roman Empire. The most notable acts of hostility against the Christians in this persecution are well known and included arrest, imprisonment, torture, and even death if Christians failed to turn over their sacred writings. Christian properties were also confiscated during these times. Problems of loyalty to the emperor and threats of the disintegration of the empire loomed large, especially in Britain, Persia, and North Africa. Diocletian, in an almost paranoid state of mind, significantly increased the size of his military and initiated a large number of building programs, hoping to return the empire to its former years of glory.

More significant for our purposes, however, were Diocletian's actions aimed at restoring the Roman virtues, whose religious roots were in earlier acts of devotion to the Roman deities. His edict (ca. 295) regarding marriages (On Marriage) focuses again and again on the need to return to religious uniformity. Although he insisted that no blood be shed, he nevertheless demanded that Christian churches be destroyed and that Christian sacred scriptures be burned. Christians in public office were removed and those in the upper classes had privileges taken from them. Finally he insisted that Christian slaves could not be freed. The earlier first empire-wide persecution of Christians initiated by the Roman Emperor Decius in 250 CE required Christians to sacrifice to the emperor and sought to destroy the organization and life of the Church by eliminating their sacred books, buildings, and offices. Contrary to Diocletian's initial plan, however, deaths of Christians did occur in many locations where the Christians refused to turn over their scriptures. Within a short period of time, Christians in several locations were also being forced to offer sacrifices to the Emperor as well.

One such example of the Roman authorities attempting to destroy the Christian scriptures took place in Alexandria, Egypt, in May of 303 CE. The following text is helpful for understanding this discussion.

In the eighth and seventh consulships of Diocletian and Maximian, 19th May, from the records of Munatius Felix, high priest of the province for life, Mayor of the colony of Cirta, arrived at the house where the Christians used to meet. The Mayor said to Paul the bishop: "Bring out the writings of the law and anything else you have here, according to the order, so that you may obey the command."

The Bishop: The readers have the scriptures, but we will give what we have here.

The Mayor: Point out the readers or send for them.

The Bishop: You all know them.

The Mayor: We do not know them.

The Bishop: The municipal office knows them, that is, the clerks Edusius and Junius.

The Mayor: Leaving over the matter of the readers, whom the office will point out, produce what you have.

[Then follows an inventory of the church plate and other property, including large stores of male and female clothes and shoes, produced in the presence of the clergy, who included three priests, two deacons, and four subdeacons, all named, and a number of "diggers."]

The story resumes as follows:

The Mayor: Bring out what you have.

Silvanus and Carosus (two of the subdeacons): We have thrown out everything that was here.

The Mayor: Your answer is entered on the record.

After some empty cupboards have been found in the library, Silvanus then produced a silver box and a silver lamp, which he said he had found behind a barrel.

Victor (the mayor's clerk): You would have been a dead man if you hadn't found them.

The Mayor: Look more carefully, in case there is anything left here.

Silvanus: There is nothing left. We have thrown everything out.

And when the dining-room was opened, there were found there four bins and six barrels.

The Mayor: Bring out the scripture that you have so that we can obey the orders and command of the emperors.

Catullinus (another subdeacon) produced one very large volume.

The Mayor: Why have you given one volume only? Produce the scriptures that you have.

Marcuclius and Catullinus (two subdeacons): We haven't any more, because we are subdeacons; the readers have the books.

The Mayor: If you don't know where they live, tell me their names.

Marcuclius and Catullinus: We are not traitors: here we are, order us to be killed.

The Mayor: Put them under arrest.

They apparently weakened so far as to reveal one reader, for the Mayor now moved on to the house of Eugenius, who produced four books.

The Mayor now turned on the other two subdeacons, Silvanus and Carosus:

The Mayor: Show me the other readers.

Silvanus and Carosus: The bishop has already said that Edusius and Junius the clerks know them all: they will show you the way to their houses.

Edusius and Junius: We will show them, sir.

The Mayor went on to visit the six remaining readers. Four produced their books without demur. One declared he had none, and the Mayor was content with entering his statement of the record. The last was out, but his wife produced his books; the Mayor had the house searched by the public slave to make sure that none had been overlooked. This task over, he addressed the subdeacons: "If there has been any omission, the responsibility is yours." (*Gesta apud Zenophilum* XXVI in Stevenson, ANE, 287–289)

Eusebius describes this persecution in significant detail, emphasizing especially the martyrs at Nicomedia. His introduction to the Diocletian persecution specifically mentions the burning of the sacred scriptures.

All things in truth were fulfilled in our day, when we saw with our very eyes the houses of prayer cast down to their foundations from top to bottom, and the inspired and sacred Scriptures committed to the flames in the midst of the marketplaces, and the pastors of the churches, some shamefully hiding themselves here and there, while others were ignominiously captured and made a mockery by their enemies; when also, according to another prophetic word, He poureth contempt upon princes, and causeth them to wander in the waste, where there is no way. . . .

It was the nineteenth year of the reign of Diocletian, and the month Dystrus, or March, as the Romans would call it, in which, as the festival of the Savior's Passion was coming on, an imperial letter was everywhere promulgated, ordering the razing of the churches to the ground and the destruction by fire of the Scriptures, and proclaiming that those who held high positions would lose all civil rights, while those in households, if they persisted in their profession of Christianity, would be deprived of their liberty. Such was the first document against us. But not long afterwards we were further visited with other letters, and in them the order was given that the presidents of the churches should all, in every place, be first committed to prison, and then afterwards compelled by every kind of device to sacrifice. (*Ecclesiastical History* 8.2.1, 4–5, LCL.)

During this persecution, the Christians who gave into the persecution and handed over copies of their sacred scriptures to the Roman authorities were called the "traitors" (*traditores*). They were despised by the Christians, especially by the Donatists, who were not at all forgiving of those who had betrayed their sacred scriptures by turning them over to the authorities. These Donatists condemned all *traditor* clergy as those who had committed a sacrilegious act worthy of damnation in an everlasting fire because they sought "to destroy the testaments and divine commands of Almighty God and our Lord Jesus Christ" (*Acta Saturnini*, XVIII, col. 701). The Christians who did not deny their faith during the persecutions and tortures and survived their abuse were called "confessors." Those who died without giving up their scriptures and remaining faithful to their Christian beliefs were called "martyrs." A significant problem emerged in the fourth-century Church on how to deal with the "traitors" (*traditores*) or "lapsed" (*lapsi*), and the controversy eventually involved Constantine himself.

At any rate, the point in all of this is that the matter of knowing which books could be handed over to the authorities without one's attaining the charge of being a *traditor* was evidently settled by the time of the persecutions in *individual* churches. This does not say that all churches agreed on which religious writings were sacred and needed protection, but the handing over of scriptures to Roman authorities presupposes a knowledge on the part of the Christians at that time of what books in fact were acknowledged as sacred scripture. There was no complete agreement in all churches on these matters, but the decision of which books to hand over to the authorities would have been determined in *local* churches certainly by the time of the Diocletian persecution. Again, we cannot presume that all churches agreed on which books were sacred and could not be handed over to the authorities to be burned. Indeed, many churches disagreed on such matters.

Evidence of disagreement can be seen in the variations in the lists of scriptures that have survived from the fourth through the sixth centuries. Before the end of the fourth century, no church councils had dealt with the canonization of the Christian scriptures, and when they did (393 at Hippo and later in 397 at Carthage, also in North Africa), there is no evidence that all churches were willing to abide by those decisions. Individual churches or regions of churches appear to have decided these questions for themselves. There is no doubt that there was wide agreement on the majority of the New Testament scriptures in the fourth century, and this can be demonstrated by viewing the actions of the early church councils that met to deliberate which literature would serve the Church as its scriptures. Differences of opinion about the contents of the New Testament canon focused generally only on the "fringes" of the New Testament literature (Hebrews, James, 2 Peter, 2 and 3 John, Jude, and Revelation) and not the "core" books (Gospels, Acts, Pauline letters and 1 Peter and 1 John) that were already in widespread use in the churches.

The individual churches most likely had already made choices about which books were sacred and which could be handed over to the authorities by the time the persecutions got underway. There is no evidence that larger churches or regional organizations of churches made decisions about the scope or limits of their Christian Scriptures before the end of the fourth century. Eusebius (ca. 320–330 CE) set forth the first listing of the books considered sacred by the early churches, but even then we cannot say with certainty what the church at large was thinking on these matters. The variations in the catalogues or lists of sacred scriptures at the end of the fourth century and later demonstrate the fluidity of sacred scripture canons at that time. This is especially so in regard to the peripheral books that were later either included (Revelation, Hebrews, and others) or excluded (*Shepherd of Hermas, Epistle of Barnabas*, and others) from the church's scriptures.

The traditions that have survived about the book burning in the early fourth century do not tell us specifically which books were handed over to the authorities to be burned. Decisions on which books could be turned over to the authorities were undoubtedly made before or no later than the time when persecution broke out. This aspect of the Diocletian persecution had to be a strong incentive for the churches to come to grips with the issue of which writings they considered sacred. Clearly, those books that no longer functioned in a sacred fashion or were less popular in the churches were more likely to be turned over to the authorities than those that were still useful and highly valued in the churches and would more likely be protected by the Christians when possible. Still some books deemed sacred by churches were also destroyed at this time.

CONSTANTINE AND EUSEBIUS

It was noted earlier that a move toward unity and conformity in the churches was taking place by the time of Irenaeus (ca. 170–180 CE). Also, the move on the part of Diocletian to bring religious unity and conformity to pagan Roman worship was a characteristic trait of Roman society and likely had an affect on the church's decisions about the scope of its Bible. Several examples of this same tendency toward uniformity in Roman society took place in the reign of Constantine (306–337 CE). The significance of this is that during Constantine's reign and thereafter many moves toward religious conformity in the churches was also initiated. The clearest and most precise catalogues of authoritative Christian scriptures are products of this and the immediately following periods of history and there is evidence that Constantine pushed the churches toward greater uniformity that was not present before.

It is indisputable that the reign of Constantine marked the church's highly significant transition from the role of a persecuted community by a pagan government to a long time relationship with the state.

At first, it was an especially beneficial marriage for the churches, but later this union made profound and lasting changes in the make up and mission of the Church itself.

The so-called conversion of Constantine came as a result of his most famous vision of the cross (Eusebius, *Life of Constantine* 2.45; 3.2, 3) and led him to provide many significant benefits for the Christians. The most important of these benefits was, of course, the cessation of hostilities toward the church and the resultant freedom for Christians to worship without fear of persecution (2.14). This was accomplished first through the Edict of Milan in 313 that gave religious freedom to all Roman subjects, not just the Christians. The benefits for the Christians even increased later when Constantine ordered, at Rome's expense, the repair or replacement of the church buildings that were damaged or destroyed in the severe persecutions of the years 303–313. He not only replaced damaged or destroyed structures, but also ordered the bestowal of extravagant gifts upon the church (2.46; 3.1) and its leaders (3.16), including the making of extra copies of the church's "inspired records" (scriptures) which had earlier been destroyed. Finally, he "took vengeance" upon those who were involved in persecuting the Christians (3.1).

These events obviously had benefits for the church as one sees in the euphoric manner that Eusebius describes these events. Eusebius and the whole Church were understandably delighted by their reception of the new honors and blessings bestowed on them. It is understandable that Christians then had only praise for Constantine who is referred to by Eusebius as one "like a powerful herald of God" (2.61), a "pious emperor" (2.73), "the divinely favored emperor" (3.1), and one who "thus made it his constant aim to glorify his Savior God" (3.54).

Although Eusebius finds no fault in Constantine, early church historians have not universally accepted the widespread belief in the Roman Emperor's "conversion" to Christianity. This is because of his continued brutality in the treatment of his opponents following his conversion experience and also his practice of coercing the church to conform to his policies. Constantine appears to have been benignly disposed toward Christianity at first and only later came to a more complete acceptance of its teachings. He was not baptized until shortly before his death. Following his conversion, he continued to revere the pagan god of his father and tended toward a syncretistic Christianity, in which he identified the Christian God with the sun. He made the first day of the week (the Lord's Day) a holiday and called it "the venerable day of the sun" (*Sun*day). Eusebius seems to have ignored many of Constantine inconsistencies with Christian teaching, even passing over his breaking of his pledge not to murder the Caesar Licinius (a rival to Constantine) or his wife Faust, and their son, Crispus.

The impact of Constantine's conversion was nonetheless a most important historical event for Christians, bringing the church to an altogether new era. Eusebius proudly claims that with Constantine, "a new and fresh era of existence had begun to appear, and a light heretofore unknown suddenly [brought forth the Church] to the dawn from the midst of darkness on the human race" (3.1).

Constantine's involvement in the affairs of the Church was extensive. Although he was initially invited by the Christians to become involved in settling church disputes, almost from the beginning he saw it as his duty to become involved in numerous decisions of the churches. This involved not only the calling/ordering of the bishops and other church leaders to gather at various church councils (3.6, 4.41–43), but also the resolving of *theological* disputes (for instance, the one between Alexander and Arius, 2.61 that resulted in the Nicene Creed in 325 CE). He also settled disputes concerning a bishop (whether Eusebius was to go to Antioch or remain in Caesarea, see 3.59–61). He was even involved in settling the time for the celebration of Easter (3.6–18) and made decisions on whether and how to punish heretics (3.20, 64–65) and when, where, and how to build churches (3.29–43).

He not only arbitrated in such matters, but also reconvened a council when its decision went contrary to his own wishes as in the case of the Donatist controversy in North Africa in 321 (the controversy began in 311 and continued for roughly a hundred years). Constantine threatened bishops under penalty of banishment if they did not obey his orders to convene at Tyre (4.41, 42), and he even sent his representative of "consular rank" (Dionysus) to ensure order at the church council as well as to remind bishops of their duty (4.42). Finally, he ordered the same church leaders to go to Jerusalem to help him celebrate the dedication of a new church building there!

It is ironic that on one occasion he even wrote that while the bishops were overseers of the internal affairs of the Church, he himself was a "bishop, ordained by God to overlook whatever is external to the church" (4.24). One is hard pressed, however, to find the "internal" issues in which he did not involve himself!

No one would deny the involvement of Constantine in church activities and decisions, and it is clear from Eusebius that he would tolerate no rivals to the rule of peace and harmony either in his empire or in the churches. Although he can in no way be considered to be as cruel as his predecessors were toward the Christians, he still wanted "harmony" (uniformity) in the churches at all costs. Those whose doctrines were not in keeping with the "orthodoxy" of the day were banished into exile, their writings burned, and their meeting places confiscated (3.66).

At times Constantine was gracious, generous, and even humble, but he did not easily tolerate differences of opinion or challenges to his authority in church matters (4.42). His understanding of "harmony" was not so much about peaceful coexistence, as it was uniform thinking—that is, to bring about a consensus and harmony among the people. On the one hand he destroyed certain temples and banned the practices of sacrificing to pagan deities and idol worship (2.44; 3.54–58) and on the other he intimidated the dissident bishops into conformity to his wishes or to those of the majority of the bishops (3.13).

As with earlier emperors, Constantine seems to have viewed anything out of step as a threat to be dealt with. Several of the previous Roman rulers considered any opposition to or rejection of Roman deities as a threat to the Empire. Constantine, at times, appears only to have changed the favored religion, not the example of his predecessors. His overriding concern appears at times not to be the moral and inner transformation of the Christian faith so much as peace in its outward social influence and in the empire. Following his suppression of the Arian controversy regarding the divinity of Jesus, Eusebius wrote with pleasure: "Thus the members of the entire body became united and compacted in one harmonious whole . . . while no heretical or schismatic body anywhere continued to exist" (*Life of Constantine* 3.66, NPNF).

Constantine took action to unify the churches under the all powerful state and exercised power to convene councils of bishops and discipline dissident church members. He appears to have established also the authoritarian pattern for later popes to follow in dealing with ecclesiastical activities, heresies, and with the appointment of bishops in churches. Constantine's title Pontifex Maximus ("chief priest") that was kept throughout his rule is one that was also used earlier by the Roman emperors starting with Augustus (31 BCE–12 CE). He saw himself as the chief protector and high priest of the church and was actively involved in many church decisions. This was not so different from that of the kind of power that eventually was vested in the church's popes. Constantine even granted power to the bishop's council over decisions of local magistrates (3.20), a practice that continued in subsequent periods of church history and served to politicize the clergy.

The major consequences for Christians of Constantine's conversion included the "Christianizing" of the Roman Empire, the cessation of the persecution of the Christians, and guaranteed the triumph of Christian orthodoxy (primarily Western "orthodoxy") in the greater church. This does not suggest, as others claim, that the orthodox beliefs of the church were a minority position before Constantine and only later obtained priority. Orthodoxy was well on its way to dominance in the churches by the end of the second century at the latest when the church had no political power. Nevertheless, the major dissidents in the churches were all but silenced during this time, which shows that the major theological stance that took priority earlier and at this time was later called "orthodoxy." As a result, in terms of the subsequent identity of the Christian biblical canon, the theological views that obtained supremacy at this time also had a significant impact on which scriptures would receive priority in the churches. We should also note that the church could hardly arrive at a consensus on the scope of its sacred scriptures before it had agreement on the basic outlines of its core beliefs. In this sense, only after Constantine's actions toward the Church could the final stages of the formation of the Christian canon take place.

The role of Constantine in the closing of the Christian biblical canon is not inconsiderable when we also consider that he asked Eusebius to supervise the production of 50 copies of the scriptures (presumably both Old and New Testaments) for use in the new capital city ("New Rome") later called Constantinople. If the matter of which books belonged in the Christian Bible was not finalized before the copies of the scriptures were made, one can conclude that the influence of these copies had considerable affect on the churches not only in Constantinople, but also on the churches in that region. Earlier, Eusebius' listing of the Christian sacred books in the categories of "confessed" books (those acknowledged by the majority of churches to be sacred, namely, the Gospels, Acts, letters of Paul, 1 Peter and 1 John), the "doubted" books (namely, Hebrews, James, 2 Peter, 2 and 3 John, Jude and probably Revelation), and the "spurious" books (Gospel of Hebrews and other books deemed heretical) anticipated some agreement among the churches on much of its New Testament books (see his *Ecclesiastical History* 3.25.1–7). This clearly shows that the final issue of which books were selected had not yet been settled for the greater church earlier, at least not on the perimeters ("fringe" books) of the biblical canon (ca. 325 CE).

It is likely that much of the ambiguity was settled for Eusebius when Constantine asked him to produce the 50 copies of the Christian scriptures. Some decision had to be made by that time about what books to include and it is likely that Eusebius himself also played a significant role in what went into those copies. In Eusebius' words, the production of these copies of sacred scriptures went as follows:

> Ever careful for the welfare of the churches of God, the emperor addressed me personally in a letter on the means of providing copies of the inspired oracles [church's sacred scriptures], and also on the subject of the most holy feast of Easter. For I had myself dedicated to him an exposition of the mystical import of that feast; and the manner of which he honored me with a reply may be understood by anyone who reads the following letter. (chapter 34)

> VICTOR CONSTANTINUS, MAXIMUS AUGUSTUS, to Eusebius:
>
> It is indeed an arduous task, and beyond the power of language itself, worthily to treat of the mysteries of Christ, and to explain in a fitting manner the controversy respecting the feast

of Easter, its origin as well as its precious and toilsome accomplishment. For it is not within the power even of those who are able to apprehend them, adequately to describe the things of God. I am, notwithstanding, filled with admiration of your learning and zeal, and have not only myself read your work with pleasure, but have given directions, according to your own desire, that it be communicated to many sincere followers of our holy religion. Seeing, then, with what pleasure we receive favors of this kind from your sagacity, be pleased to gladden us more frequently with those compositions, to the practice of which, indeed, you confess yourself to have been trained from an early period, so that I am urging a willing man, as they say, in exhorting you to your customary pursuits. And certainly the high and confident judgment we entertain is a proof that the person who has translated your writings into the Latin tongue is in no respect incompetent to the task, impossible though it be that such version should fully equal the excellence of the works themselves. God preserve you, beloved brother." Such was his letter on this subject: and that which related to the providing of copies of the Scriptures for reading in the churches was to the following purport. (chapter 35)

VICTOR CONSTANTINUS, MAXIMUS AUGUSTUS, to Eusebius:

It happens, through the favoring providence of God our Saviour, that great numbers have united themselves to the most holy church in the city which is called by my name. It seems, therefore, highly requisite, since that city is rapidly advancing in prosperity in all other respects, that the number of churches should also be increased. Do you, therefore, receive with all readiness my determination on this behalf. I have thought it expedient to instruct your Prudence to order fifty copies of the sacred Scriptures, the provision and use of which you know to be most needful for the instruction of the Church, to be written on prepared parchment in a legible manner, and in a convenient, portable form, by professional transcribers thoroughly practiced in their art. The catholicus of the diocese has also received instructions by letter from our Clemency to be careful to furnish all things necessary for the preparation of such copies; and it will be for you to take special care that they be completed with as little delay as possible. You have authority also, in virtue of this letter, to use two of the public carriages for their conveyance, by which arrangement the copies when fairly written will most easily be forwarded for my personal inspection; and one of the deacons of your church may be entrusted with this service, who, on his arrival here, shall experience my liberality. God preserve you, beloved brother! (chapter 36)

Such were the emperor's commands, which were followed by the immediate execution of the work itself, which we sent him in magnificent and *elaborately bound volumes of a threefold and fourfold form.*[1] This fact is attested by another letter, which the emperor wrote in acknowledgment, in which, having heard that the city Constantia in our country, the inhabitants of which had been more than commonly devoted to superstition, had been impelled by a sense of religion to abandon their past idolatry, he testified his joy, and approval of their conduct. (chapter 37) (Eusebius, *The Life of Constantine*, Book 3, NPNF. Emphasis added)

By the time Constantine made his request of Eusebius (ca. 334–336 CE), we can assume that there was a fairly widespread acceptance of a broadly defined collection of books of both the Old and New Testament circulating and known in the churches. This does not settle the debate over the canonicity of all of the New Testament books for everyone for some time later. Evidence of this shows up in Christian manuscripts of scriptures circulating in the churches after Eusebius and the construction of many catalogues of New Testament books that were circulating in the empire. Before the year 1000 CE, there are only four manuscripts known that contain all of the books of the New Testament *and only those books.* Most of the 5740 known New Testament manuscripts have considerably fewer books, though some contain noncanonical books alongside the canonical ones. The most ignored books in the New Testament manuscripts are generally also the same ones that Eusebius considered doubtful (noted above) and this reveals a lack of agreement on the scope of the New Testament in churches for centuries to come. Also, the uses of lectionaries (selected texts for reading in the church worship) in antiquity allow us to see which biblical books informed the faith of the early Christians. Combined, these lectionaries seldom contain books outside of the core-accepted books of the canon and almost never make use of most of the so-called fringe books in the canon.

The copies of the sacred books ordered by Constantine may well have become the standard or model for the later expertly copied biblical books by professional scribes. Several scholars have suggested that one or more of our best surviving uncial manuscripts (capital-lettered manuscripts produced on parchment in the fourth century and later) came from this period. Codex Vaticanus (B) and possibly also Codex Sinaiticus (ℵ), both likely from approximately 350–375 CE, may be among the manuscripts produced by Eusebius at the request of Constantine or were modeled aft the them. Although they may be manuscripts stemming from that earlier tradition begun by Constantine, some scholars argue that only later manuscripts (e.g., the Washington Codex) actually fit this description.

Although Vaticanus has three columns per page (mostly), except in some sections of the Old Testament part of the volume, and Sinaiticus has four columns per page, the suggestion that one or the other of these manuscripts might be from the 50 copies sent to the emperor, however tempting, is still only a possibility. Manuscripts of the entire Bible from any time in antiquity are quite rare (only about 1 percent contain all of the books of the Bible and most are later than the Middle Ages), but it is likely that Eusebius intended to say that full copies of the Bible were copied (*Life of Constantine* 4.36 or 37 cited above). It is possible, however, that the *text* employed in the 50 copies may have been a forerunner to the later Byzantine or "majority" biblical text that influenced almost all subsequent copies of the New Testament writings.

More importantly, if Constantine's 50 copies of the church's sacred books included the current 27 books of the New Testament— or books of both Old and New Testaments since the technology of book making at that time would allow for that, that in itself would have had a powerful impact on the eventual acceptance of the 27 book New Testament canon. Even though Eusebius doubted the authority and receptivity of the Book of Revelation (*Ecclesiastical History* 3.25.4), Constantine himself was impressed with the book and possibly influenced Eusebius' inclusion of it in his collection. Eusebius himself had many doubts about the plausibility of accepting the book of Revelation (or Apocalypse of John) as we see in his *Ecclesiastical History* (3.25.2, 4). Who could have withstood the influence and preference of the emperor given what we know of his involvement in the churches? It is therefore likely that not only Eusebius but also the Roman emperor himself had an influenced on the scope of the New Testament canon.

Whether or not Constantine's call for unity in both the Roman Empire and in the churches had any significant influence upon the contents of the biblical canon of the church is difficult to determine. No church tradition says this, but the fact that Constantine was involved in most major decisions of the church in the second quarter of the fourth century in matters of doctrine, discipline, leadership, and ecclesiastical harmony strongly suggests that he may well have had some influence on the contours of the biblical canon. Whether coincidental or not, it is remarkable that during and immediately after this time Christians showed considerable interest in dealing with the diversity in their churches especially with regard to doctrine and the scope of their scriptures.

Constantine's personal request that Eusebius produce copies of the Scriptures for use in churches in Constantinople, the "New Rome" formerly known as Byzantium, would imply at the least a strong influence of Eusebius' decisions on the scope of the Christian scriptures on churches in that area, if not upon much of the empire. Whatever books were included in the collection of books that Eusebius sent to the emperor which the emperor accepted, would logically carry significant weight in the churches. That is probably especially true in the east in and around Constantinople, but likely elsewhere as well. As the later canonical lists show, there was never full agreement on the scope of the Christian scriptures in the fourth through the sixth centuries. If the copies produced by Eusebius included all 27 books of the New Testament Scriptures (rather than just the canonical Gospels, as a few scholars argue), then knowledge of their contents and their approval by the emperor would go a long way in commending them and their contents to other Christians throughout the empire.

Eusebius was the first to publish a list or catalogue of the church's canonical scriptures, which he called "encovenanted" (Greek = *endiatheke*) writings; his oversight of the production of the 50 copies of the "sacred Scriptures" requested by Constantine and these activities made him and Constantine pivotal players in the formation of the New Testament canon.

WHY THESE BOOKS? THE CRITERIA QUESTION

It is much easier to answer why the New Testament books were included in the Christian biblical canon than the Old Testament books. In the case of the Old Testament books, it is likely that the time of writing (before the time of Artaxerxes) and original languages of those writings (Hebrew and Aramaic) were contributing factors along with an emerging belief among some Jews (not all) that the Spirit had departed from Israel and that writings produced before that departure were sacred and inspired and those produced later were not.

Beyond arguing that the early Church was interested in preserving certain of its literature for use as sacred texts in its life and worship, the question must inevitably be raised about what criteria were used to distinguish this literature from all other literature. In the New Testament itself, there is a call to discern among those calling themselves prophets and claiming to speak in the power of the Spirit. Paul, for example, says that some Christians were given the ability to discern the spirits (1 Cor. 12.10) and John says that "every spirit confesses that Jesus Christ is come in the flesh, is from God, and every spirit that does not confess Jesus is not from God" (1 Jn 4.2–3). The presence of "false spirits" in early Christianity was cause for a number of cautions to be given to the Christian community. Besides having a correct theology or "orthodox" beliefs and practices regarding baptism, fasting, and the Eucharist, the author(s) of the *Didache* (ca. late first century CE) advised the readers to test the prophets against correct doctrine and personal conduct. If, for instance, a prophet or an apostle came to them and stayed for more than one or two days, that one was deemed to be a false prophet. Further, it was required that the prophet must also have the "behavior of the Lord" when speaking (*Did.* 11.3–10). If the prophet "shall say in a spirit, 'Give me money, or something else', you shall not listen to him; but if he tell you to give on behalf of others in want, let none judge him" (11.12, LCL).

In chapter 12 and 13 of the *Didache*, there are further guidelines on how to deal with the prophets who wish to settle among them, but these guidelines clearly indicate that some Christians had abused their office. Consequently, early Christian communities required the presence of some criteria to maintain the proper behaviors of their religious leaders. Even Paul placed his own peculiar signature on his letters to avoid others sending out writings in his name (see 1 Cor. 16.21; Gal. 6.11; Col. 4.18; 2 Thess. 3.17; and Phlm. 19).

In the case of Marcion, the criteria that he employed to establish a collection of sacred writings was his rejection of Judaism and its influence upon Christianity through the writings of the Old Testament and their influence in the writings of the Christian writings as well. He chose the writings that he thought best represented both a Christian perspective and an anti-Jewish bias and did not hesitate to "use the knife" to cut from those documents those things that he believed did not belong to the Christian message. His criteria for selection is clear, but what it was that separated the New Testament literature from all other ancient Christian literature from that period is not always as clear. His followers did not follow consistently his use of the Gospel of Luke and the letters of Paul alone. Early Christian literature affirms that Jesus had a special relationship with God and that God acted in him like no other on behalf of humanity in order to bring to humanity the salvation of God. This may be said of most early Christian literature, including the books that did not make it into the biblical canon. So what was it that led the churches of antiquity to choose the books that they did? The traditional criteria of apostolicity, orthodoxy, antiquity, inspiration, church use, and adaptability are often set forth to answer these questions, but there are limitations. No one in antiquity lists all of these criteria and those that employed some of them did not always do so with consistency. We will examine each of the criteria below and then raise several important questions that they pose for contemporary use of the Bible in churches, including the big question about whether the ancient churches "got it right!"

Apostolicity

The church's most readily available weapon against the heretical movements in early Christianity was its claim of apostolicity that guaranteed its sacred traditions and teachings by historical succession preserved in its oral and written traditions. In its basic form this meant that the apostles who received their faith and teachings from Jesus passed it on to the succeeding leaders of the church. This "apostolic deposit" became the core teaching that determined and shaped the scope of the acceptable writings that were included in the church's canon of scriptures. The earliest churches did not possess the critical ability to define their sacred canon of scriptures quickly, uniformly or exactly, but they eventually isolated those works that they believed embodied the general doctrinal tradition of the apostles and the early churches. The believed apostolic authority inherent in the books that later became the church's biblical canon were not obvious initially, but in time it became more clear to the leadership in the churches. For them, Christ spoke through these writings. It is not clear, however, how one can determine with precision what the apostolic authority was in an ancient work.

It is not too much to say that the early church sought to root its tradition in the apostles and Jesus. It was an insistence upon grounding its faith in Jesus, represented by the apostles' teaching that has historically led the Church to contend for the apostolic authorship of a given New Testament writing. This was done to promote the reliability of those documents and to maintain that the Church's tradition was not severed from its historical roots.

The problem the application of the criterion of apostolicity presents for canonical studies is most pronounced in an age in which historical-critical methods of assessment lead scholars to question whether *most* of the literature of the New Testament was written by any one of the "Twelve" Apostles. It is not certain that John the Apostle wrote all of the books attributed to him in the New Testament, especially the Book of Revelation. Although some biblical scholars have argued the case for apostolic authorship of 1 Peter, 1 John, and possibly Jude (*if* he was the brother of Jesus and James), the arguments are not conclusive, and there is no consensus among scholars on such matters. In antiquity the authorship of Hebrews was questioned openly in churches and today no one seriously argues that Paul wrote the book of Hebrews.

There are also many legitimate questions raised by scholars about Paul's authorship of Ephesians, Colossians, 2 Thessalonians, and especially the Pastoral Epistles, even though some authentic Pauline traditions may be carried on in them. For example, how Paul died may be accurately portrayed in 2 Tim. 4.6–17. Also, there is no reason to doubt that "all of the churches in Asia" had turned against Paul (2 Tim. 1.15). These are likely accurate reflections of Paul's words and what happened to him. James, even if he was the brother of Jesus and wrote the epistle that bears his name as some scholars claim, was not an apostle. Further, no credible Bible scholars today argue credibly that the Apostle Peter wrote 2 Peter. Further, the Gospels of Mark and Luke make no claim of apostolicity even though they *may* have been written during the apostolic period (ca. 30–65) or shortly thereafter. It is likely that the apostolic community significantly influenced both. A contemporary understanding of what comprises *apostolic* documents today is often different from the conclusions promoted by the early Church about the matter.

If apostolicity was an ancient criterion that determined the recognition of the authority of a work, as it most assuredly was for many churches, then it must be admitted that this criterion was not as carefully and consistently applied as it is today. However well intentioned the early Christians might have been in attributing apostolic authorship to most writers of the New Testament books, that position is difficult to maintain today. In the case of Hebrews, the attributing of it to Paul may have been more political than well intentioned in order to help the book gain acceptance among the churches since many in the ancient Church rejected its Pauline authorship. Its message was considered highly relevant to a church that was facing an uncertain future due to many challenges and threats against its existence. The testimony of Origen on this matter illustrates many of the doubts about Hebrews, at least in the Eastern Churches. Eusebius had doubts about the apostolic authorship of

2 Peter and in his initial comments questioned 2 Peter, but he accepted 1 Peter because he believed it was written by the Apostle Peter. He writes: "Of Peter, one epistle, that which is called his first, is admitted, and the ancient presbyters used this in their own writings as unquestioned, but the so-called second Epistle we have not received as canonical, but nevertheless it has appeared useful to many, and has been studied with other Scriptures" (*Hist. eccl.* 3.3.1, LCL). Those who doubted the apostolic authorship of various New Testament writings, as in the case of 2 and 3 John and the Book of Revelation, also tended to doubt their canonical status also.

It is interesting that various Christian movements that were later condemned as heretical also claimed genuine apostolic origin. For example, the Gnostic Christians of the second century and the Donatists of the fourth century claimed to have apostolic support for their teachings. Apostolic authorship was also attributed to the *Gospel of Thomas* by the end of the second century. Some biblical scholars today acknowledge that some of the sayings of Jesus in this ancient gospel may be genuine sayings of Jesus.

The apostolic criterion employed by the early churches had more to do with rooting or establishing the churches' sacred traditions in those who were closest in proximity to the apostles to Jesus historically and to their presumed better knowledge of him and his ministry. Tertullian, for example, placed Mark and Luke in secondary positions behind Matthew and John. The importance of apostolicity in early Christianity is seen especially in the tendency for some in the early churches to write pseudonymous writings in the name of apostles to insure their reception in the churches. Likewise, it is unlikely that any New Testament book would have been included in the Church's Bible if it were *known* to be pseudonymous.

Biblical scholars regularly challenge apostolic authorship of the several writings of the New Testament. The most common disputes about authorship of New Testament books are over the Gospels of Matthew and John (anonymously written), and the authorship of Ephesians, Colossians, 2 Thessalonians, 1 and 2 Timothy and Titus, and Hebrews (also anonymously written), 2 Peter, 2 and 3 John, and Revelation. Some scholars raise questions about several other writings as well, but the ones listed are the most commonly disputed.

This raises the question of whether an ancient Christian writing could have been rightly accepted into the biblical canon, but for the wrong reasons (attribution of apostolic authorship). For a discussion of these matters, readers need to consult more recent New Testament introductions.

Orthodoxy

While some scholars have argued that one of the unifying and distinguishing factors in the New Testament literature is the *truth,* or canon of faith that it presents, a careful examination of the New Testament literature shows that there are few aspects of "orthodoxy" that all early Christians equally welcomed. For example, it is difficult to harmonize the focus on the future coming of the Kingdom of God in the Synoptic Gospels (Matthew, Mark, Luke) with John's focus on eternal life in the present and its limited focus on the future. Also, how does Paul's emphasis on the death of Christ "for our sins" square with Luke's apparent lack of interest in that matter? Notice that in the speeches in Acts the death of Christ "for our sins" is never mentioned (see Acts 2.14–39; 3.11–26), but this is regularly emphasized in Paul's writings as in the case of 1 Cor. 15.3, 1 Cor. 1.17–2:2, Rom. 3.23–25, and Gal. 2.21, and elsewhere.

In Rom. 13.1–3, Paul admonishes Christians to be subject to the governing authorities (which are appointed by God) and claims that those who resist such authorities resist God. On the other hand, Peter and John appear to reject the authority of governing officials in favor of obedience to God (Acts 4.18–20 and 5.27–29). Apart from relativizing the message of Paul to a specific context, it is difficult to harmonize these two positions. Compare also the baptismal formulas in the book of Acts (2.38; 10.48; 19.5) with that in Mt. 28.19. Again, can the organizational structure of the early Church in Acts, Paul, John, the Pastorals, and Mt. 16.18–19 be easily harmonized? Many other examples could be listed here to show that there is a fair amount of diversity in the New Testament literature.

There is a popular assumption that the faith of the early apostolic churches was somehow unified, pure, the same in all of churches, and normative. That notion is, of course, uninformed by what we know of the New Testament and early church history. On the other hand, it is wrong to ignore the unity in the midst of all of the diversity. There were, of course, significant tensions in early Christianity that are difficult to ignore and attempts to harmonize them often dull or mute the very points intended by the original writers.

If the New Testament has a theological core everywhere acknowledged or reasonably assumed, it is at the least that the man called Jesus is now exalted in his resurrection and worthy of faithful obedience and that those who honor and follow him will receive the blessing of God. We can add to this the overwhelming belief that Jesus, a righteous man in a special relationship with God, died for the sins of humanity and was raised to a new life by God and will return one day to judge both the living and the dead. However, this brief confession is not confined to the New Testament literature alone, but is affirmed in many noncanonical Christian writings, such as the Apostolic Fathers (*1 Clement of Rome,* the *Letters of Ignatius,* the *Martyrdom of Polycarp,* the *Shepherd of Hermas, the Epistle of Barnabas,* and the *Didache*) written in the late first and early second centuries who certainly agree with this much, and perhaps also Marcion and the Montanists as well. The leaders in the ancient churches who deliberated the scope of the New Testament writings, nonetheless, *believed* that they reliably conveyed the message of and about Jesus the Christ. Apostolicity—the view that the writings of the New Testament were composed by apostolic individuals, was believed by second century and later Christians to preserve a more faithful witness to God's activity in Jesus. Orthodoxy reflects what many early Christians believed the core message of Jesus and his followers was.

The presence of creedal formulations in the early church, before and after the formation of a biblical canon within the Christian communities manifestly demonstrates that "orthodoxy" itself was based upon a "canon within the canon," namely, there was a core faith transmitted in the early church, but not everything was "core" in the transmission or many books produced by the early Christians. The scope of the biblical canon therefore suggests that the church accepted some diversity and may rightly be said to have canonized some diversity in its sacred canon. The above statements about Jesus, or something similar, may well be considered the core Christian teaching that was a "canon within the canon" in the early church. If, however, the New Testament literature alone, or the Bible as a whole, was believed by all followers of Jesus to be sufficient for faith and the church's catechetical and missional needs, many of the subsequent creedal formulations hammered out in lengthy debates (e.g., the Nicene creed) and often under great stress would not have been necessary.

I often ask in more conservative theological discussions over creedal formulations about the Bible and Christian faith, "What is wrong with the Bible?" The response, as usual, is that "there is nothing wrong with the Bible!" But the consequent question, "So why do we need another creedal statement? Why not just believe the Bible?" The point is not so easily dismissed. "Orthodoxy" as such appears to be another "canon within the canon." It does not answer all of the questions posed by the church, but it is sufficient for faith and lies at the core of Christian unity. The task of the interpreter of the New Testament should, therefore, be to find the true biblical priorities in that literature and allow them to take priority in the church's witness, worship, and instruction.

There were other voices (trajectories) in early Christianity that, even though they lost the battle against what later became known as "orthodoxy," may not have been considered as heretical until a later period. Some scholars have argued that in the post-New Testament era (after 95–100 CE) the so-called orthodox Christians were actually fewer in number than the so-called heretics. Other scholars have disputed this view claiming that proponents failed to recognize the force of the arguments against Christianity by Celsus in the second century, one of the church's most fierce opponents. His arguments against Christianity are essentially against the orthodox positions of Christians who were in the majority.

More Christian sects were present in the early churches than simply the orthodox in the second and third centuries. In the fourth century, uniformity and not diversity, was in vogue and many of the so-called heretical sects disappeared in the fourth century and following when orthodoxy gained a stronger position in the churches. It is interesting that most Gnostic literature is not polemical, like much of the "orthodox" literature that survived the second century, and this may be because Gnostic Christianity was both popular and widespread during that time and did not see the need to respond in kind. When such views were seen as a significant threat to the unity of the churches, they were marginalized, criticized, and eventually destroyed. Interestingly, many of the early Christian polemics against heresy were *ad hominem*, or directed against persons, rather than *ad doctrinam,* or directed against established doctrines because there were few accepted *ad doctrinam* standards by which to judge. Orthodoxy was generally more clearly stated, rationally argued, and conformed more to the church's acceptable sacred traditions. Heresy, on the other hand, was often incoherent, confusing, and contradictory. While some may contend that this is an overstatement, it is important to remember that there was considerable theological diversity in the early churches.

Recognition of this diversity does not say, however, that all theologies of the early churches equally represent the earliest Christian preaching and teaching. There were justifiable reasons why the majority of ancient churches rejected the Gnostic esoteric and unhistorical interpretation of the Christian faith. Now as then, interpreters of the New Testament must prioritize those elements that are essential to Christian faith and those that are not. It is far too easy to omit this more complex step of inquiry and conclude that all ancient theologies are essentially equal. They are not.

Antiquity

Some early Christians came to believe that only the tradition that comes closest to the time of Jesus could be accepted as authoritative sacred writings for the church. The author of the fourth century Muratorian Fragment, for example, argued against the acceptance of the *Shepherd of Hermas* as an authoritative sacred document of the church specifically because it was not written in the apostolic age but more recently, —namely, after the apostolic age. He writes:

> But Hermas wrote the Shepherd very recently, in our times, in the city of Rome, while bishop Pius, his brother, was occupying the [Episcopal] chair of the church of the city of Rome. And therefore

it ought indeed to be read; but it cannot be read publicly to the people in church either among the prophets, whose number is complete, or among the apostles, for it is after [their] time. (Metzger translation)

Antiquity, linked also with apostolicity and a "rule of faith" (ortho-doxy), appears to have been an important criterion for canonicity for some of the churches.

The more critical tools of biblical inquiry today have enabled scholars to show fairly convincingly that some literature of the New Testament—especially 2 Peter, probably the Pastorals, Revelation and possibly other books as well, may well have been written later than some noncanonical Christian books—later than the *Didache*, *1 Clement, the Letters (or Epistles) of Ignatius, The Martyrdom of Polycarp, Epistle of Barnabas*, and the *Shepherd of Hermas*. A strong argument has been made for an earlier dating of some of this literature than some of the canonical literature, which is enough to show that the criterion of antiquity was not as carefully applied in the patristic Church as is possible today. When one combines the orthodoxtraditions in the noncanonical books with an earlier known date, it is possible that these books that were considered as sacred texts earlier were wrongly excluded from inclusion in the biblical canon. They do appear variously in early ancient New Testament manuscripts. Codex Sinaiticus (350–375 CE) includes the *Epistle of Barnabas* and the *Shepherd of Hermas* in its collection of sacred Christian texts.

Some scholars have argued that if "antiquity" continues to be used as a criterion for canonicity, then special attention should be given to some of the second century apocryphal gospels that also represent some of the early strands of Christianity. Some of these writings have a rightful claim to as early a date of composition as some of the canonical writings and possibly even earlier. There may be evidence for an early dating (around the end of the first century or shortly thereafter) of about a dozen noncanonical gospels. Although a number of scholars argue that the Gospel of Thomas could be dated sometime around the end of the first century and that it contains some very authentic early sayings of Jesus, others place it in the early to late part of the second century. The same may be said for the so-called Egerton Papyrus (also called the *Unknown Gospel*) and the *Gospel of the Hebrews*. Modern scholars debate whether they depended on the canonical Gospels or were depended on by them. Similar claims have been made for the *Dialogue of the Savior*, the *Apocryphon of John*, and the *Gospel of Peter*. Regardless, they are significant witnesses for the development of the New Testament gospel literature in its formative stages.

Comparisons of the Gospel of John (other than just the one in Jn 8.12–59) to the apocryphal sayings sources sometimes demonstrate that there was an even broader "sayings" tradition than is found in the Synoptic Gospels (Matthew, Mark, and Luke). Such a comparison may give clues for understanding the often elusive process of the composition of the Johannine discourses as well as aid in the identification of the traditional sayings of Jesus used in them. Although there may be some "gall mixed with honey" (as Irenaeus puts it) in the Gnostic gospels, there is little doubt that a serious study of them will produce important results for our study of early Christianity and also some of the sayings of Jesus.

How useful is the criterion of antiquity for determining which books should be in the New Testament? If our previous comments have any importance here, the significance of antiquity as a criterion for determining the biblical canon may need some reconsideration. If the goal of the canonizing process is in part to anchor the church's faith in the earliest sayings and deeds of Jesus, then some attention should be given to the additional sources mentioned above.

In most discussions of canonicity, an implied value is put on antiquity, and to some extent we must agree. The older the document, the more reliable it is presumed to be, but this is not necessarily the case. If antiquity alone were the chief criterion for canonicity, a great deal of rethinking would need to be done regarding the present biblical canon; however, it is unwise to build a canon of scriptures on an ever-changing and imprecise criterion on which the best of New Testament scholars cannot agree. The earlier writings cannot by that fact alone be considered more reliable. Given that word of caution, the aim of recovering the earliest and most reliable tradition about Jesus has nevertheless always been one of the goals of the Christian Church, and especially of its teachers. This does not imply that the Christian biblical canon ought to be either broadened or even paired down based on the criterion of antiquity. The criteria of apostolicity and orthodoxy are far more important in this process and they, along with antiquity, should make a stronger case for disallowing traditions that are too far away theologically or historically from the traditional pictures of Jesus in the canonical Gospels. In some of the later writings (second and third century) the story of Jesus is not as clearly presented and often blurred.

We should also be aware that the same methods that are employed in a study of the canonical Gospels to determine the authentic sayings of Jesus may also be legitimately applied to the noncanonical Christian literature with significant value in our overall understanding of the origins of the Christian faith. The antiquity of some of the noncanonical documents is sufficient reason to examine them carefully to determine whether they may help in our quest to understand better the one who gave rise to the Christian faith. If in that examination it is determined with some sense of confidence that authentic sayings of Jesus are couched in one of the noncanonical texts, then it would be prudent to learn from those voices.

Inspiration

All of the ancient church fathers believed that their scriptures were inspired, but inspiration of the New Testament writings is not a criterion for acceptance of a book for canonicity so much as a corollary for canonicity. In other words, if the writing was accepted as sacred and authoritative in the church's Bible, it was also acknowledged as inspired literature. The New Testament writings generally do not commend themselves as inspired literature. The clearest exception to this is, of course, the author of the book of Revelation who claims prophetic inspiration as he warns:

> Everyone who hears *the words of the prophecy of this book:* if any one adds to them, God will add to him the plagues described in

this book, and if any one takes away from the words of *the book of this prophecy*, God will take away his share in the tree of life and in the holy city, which are described in this book. (Rev. 22.18–19, NRSV. Emphasis added)

Whether the author of the Revelation (or Apocalypse) was the author of the Gospel of John and 1 John or another John, as seems likely from the style and focus of the book, his claim for acceptance was not on the basis of apostleship, but inspiration. Also, in 1 Cor. 7.40 following Paul's advice regarding the freedom of widows to remarry, he is supported by his belief that this view was also prompted by the Holy Spirit. Apart from this text, however, Paul more frequently appeals to his apostleship as the primary reason for accepting his teaching and ministry (see Gal. 1.1; 1 Cor. 9.1; 2 Cor. 13.3, 10—compare 1 Cor. 9.1–12 where he appeals to his authority as an apostle).

There are no ancient voices that denied the inspiration of the church's scriptures, but to what extent did an awareness of their inspiration play a part in the canonizing process? Irenaeus makes it clear that the scriptures, even when the church's scriptures are not clearly understood, they were nevertheless "spoken by the Word of God and by His Spirit" (*Adv. Haer.* 2.28.2, ANF). Origen is quite explicit that the Scriptures were written or inspired by the Holy Spirit. Notice, for example, his stress that "the Scriptures were written by the Spirit of God, and have a meaning, not such only as is apparent at first sight, but also another which escapes the notice of most" (*De Prin.*, preface 8, ANF). Interestingly, Irenaeus was the first Christian writer to allegorize the various New Testament writings because he was among the first to treat them as unreservedly inspired. Origen after him, and very much like Philo earlier, felt free to allegorize the scriptures precisely because they were considered to be inspired by God. While seeking to discredit the authenticity of the treatise, *The Doctrine of Peter*, Origen writes in the same text, "we can show that it was not composed by Peter or by any other person inspired by the Spirit of God." The operating assumption here, of course, is that scripture is inspired by God and that heresy or falsehood is not. Later, in his discussion of the

Holy Spirit, he presented his best evidence for a son belonging to God and wrote:

> We however, in conformity with our belief in the doctrine, which we assuredly hold to be divinely inspired, believe that it is possible in no other way to explain and bring within the reach of human knowledge this higher and diviner reason as Son of God, than by means of those Scriptures alone which were inspired by the Holy Spirit, i.e., the Gospels and Epistles, and the Law and the Prophets, according to the declaration of Christ himself. (*De Prin.*, preface 8, ANF)

Theophilus of Antioch (ca. 180) also believed that the scriptures had their origins in God and held to the relationship between scripture ("holy writings") and inspiration expressing it as follows: "the holy writings teach us, and all the spirit bearing [inspired] men . . . showing that at first God was alone, and the Word [was] in Him" (*Ad Autolycum* 2.22, ANF).

There is no question that the early church believed that its scriptures were divinely inspired, but the biggest problem with using inspiration as a criterion for canonicity in the early Church is that *the canonical scriptures were not the only ancient literature that was believed by the early Christians to be inspired by God.* Hermas, for example, who has no definite reference to any Old Testament or New Testament literature, uses none of the traditional formula for introducing scripture when citing or alluding to biblical literature, but he quotes the noncanonical apocalypse of Eldad and Modat (now lost) using a familiar designation formula for a scriptural text. He writes, "The Lord is near those that turn to him, *as it is written* in the *Book of Eldad and Modat, who prophesied* to the people in the wilderness" (*Shepherd, Vis.,* 2.3.4, LCL. Emphasis added). This apocalypse is possibly also alluded to in *2 Clement* 11.2. The two names are mentioned in Num. 11.26.

The author of *2 Clement* quotes *1 Clement* 23.3, 4 with the introductory words, "For the prophetic word also says" (11.2), the usual words to designate works deemed inspired and authoritative. Again, the author of the *Epistle of Barnabas* in 16.5 introduces a passage from *2 Enoch* 89.56 with the words, "For the scripture says." Theophilus apparently also included Sibyl as an inspired document along with the prophets of God (2.9) and also makes clear what he means by inspiration. He writes: "But men of God carrying in them a holy spirit [= 'borne along by the spirit'] and becoming prophets, being inspired and made wise by God, became God-taught, and holy and righteous" (2.9 in ANF).

In a somewhat different light, Clement of Rome (ca. 95) recommended the teaching of the Apostle Paul saying that he wrote 1 Corinthians "with true inspiration" (*ep' alétheias pneumatikos*) (1 Clem. 47.3, LCL). On the other hand, he also said that his own epistle was "written by us through the Holy Spirit" (63.2, LCL). Similarly, Ignatius expressed his own awareness of speaking by the power of the Holy Spirit when he commented:

> I spoke with a great voice,—with God's own voice . . . But some suspected me of saying this because I had previous knowledge of the division of some persons: but he in whom I am bound is my witness that I had no knowledge of this from any human being, *but the Spirit was preaching and saying this.* (Ign. *Phld.*, 7.1b-2, LCL. Emphasis added)

There are many examples in the post-apostolic and early patristic communities where various authors either claimed, or were acknowledged by others to have been filled by the Spirit and inspired to talk or to write. Some scholars have argued, however, that the New Testament word for inspiration (*theopneustos*) in 2 Tim. 3.16 was only used in reference to the biblical scriptures. While that is normally the case, the term is also used of individuals in the early church and not just those who wrote scripture. Gregory of Nyssa (ca. 330–395), for example, when commenting on Basil's commentary on the creation story, claimed that Basil (ca. 330–379) was inspired by God and that his words even surpassed those of Moses in terms of beauty, complexity, and form (*Apologia hexaemeron* in Migne, *Patrologia Graeca* 44.61). The actual words in this praise are that the commentary is an "exposition given by inspiration of God . . . [admired] no less than the words composed by Moses himself." Likewise, the famous epitaph of Abercius, bishop of

Hierapolis in Phrygia of Asia Minor from the late second century (died ca. 200 CE), was called an "inspired inscription" (*Vita Abercii* 76), as well as a synodical epistle of the council of Ephesus (ca. 433) that describes the council's condemnation of Nestorious (d. ca. 451) as "their inspired [Greek = *theopneustou*] judgment" (or "decision").

The conclusion one is led to from this gathering of texts is that inspiration as such was not believed to have been limited to the Old Testament or New Testament literature alone, or even to literature alone. Justin Martyr, for example, who is certainly in harmony with the literature of the New Testament, believed that inspiration and the Holy Spirit's power were the possessions of the whole church. He writes: "For the prophetical gifts remain with us even to the present time. And hence you ought to understand that [the gifts] formerly among your nation [the Jewish nation] have been transferred to us" (*Trypho* 82, ANF. See other illustrations of this in *Trypho* 87–88). It is especially worth mentioning here that Justin believed that even the translators of the Septuagint were divinely inspired to do their work. This, he claims, was shown by the evidence from their work which not only agreed in meaning, but also that their separate translations from the Hebrew even had the very same Greek words! See also Justin's *Hortatory Address to the Greeks* in which he tells of King Ptolemy's approval of the translation of the LXX:

> And when he ascertained that the seventy men had not only given the same meaning, but had employed the same words, and had failed in agreement with one another not even to the extent of one word, but had written the same things, and concerning the same things, he was struck with amazement, and *believed that the translation had been written by divine power*, and perceived that the men were worthy of all honor, as beloved of God; and with many gifts ordered them to return to their own country. And having, as was natural, marveled at the books, and *concluded them to be divine*, he consecrated them in that library. (ANF. Emphasis added)

Even in the ancient fragments that dealt with the Montanist controversy there is no evidence from the early church that inspiration was confined to the apostolic age or apostolic literature (Eusebius, *Ecclesiastical History* 5.14–19 is helpful here), or even to a collection of sacred writings. Also, on the other hand, the broad consensus of the early church fathers, especially Irenaeus, Origen, Eusebius, is that the work of the false prophets and all heathen oracles and philosophy were uninspired. The traditional belief that *only* the canonical writings were deemed inspired by the early Christians is simply not the case. The ancient Jewish belief about the Old Testament scriptures that "When the last prophets, Haggai, Zechariah and Malachi, died, the Holy Spirit ceased out of Israel" (*Tosefta² Sotah* 13.2) was not a belief shared by the post-apostolic Church.

The primary distinction between "inspired" and "noninspired" writings was that the latter lay outside the whole life and belief structure of the Christian community; such as in the case of heretical writings. Scholars of the early church fathers up to 400 CE have shown that there are no examples where an orthodox writing outside of the New Testament was ever called uninspired. That designation was only for heretical authors. The early church fathers through the end of the fifth century never say that *only* the sacred scriptures were inspired by God. In the early churches, inspiration was applied not only to all scripture, but also to the Christian community as a whole as it bore "living witness of Jesus Christ." It appears that only heresy was deemed to be noninspired because it was contrary to this "living witness of Jesus Christ" in the churches.

Our earlier discussion of the prophetic literature produced by the Montanists, and believed by them to be born of or prompted by the Holy Spirit, is relevant to this discussion and shows that there was no belief at the end of the second century that inspiration was confined to first-century literature. For these reasons, the concept of inspiration apparently played almost no role in the later discussions of the biblical canon.

Inspiration and canonicity, however, cannot be completely separated, but inspiration is not a basis for canonicity. One cannot argue that if a text is inspired it must be canonical. That is, this view simply cannot be argued historically. The traditional view of inspiration that all books within the canon are fully inspired by the Holy Spirit, and no books outside it are inspired, cannot be argued historically.

It is like putting the cart before the horse and failing to see that inspiration is more of a corollary of canonicity than a criterion for it. Certainly, all books admitted to the biblical canon were considered inspired by God. One of the difficulties in the development of the biblical canon was the difficulty it had of distinguishing inspired and noninspired writings. The problem the early churches had in deciding what literature was or was not inspired demonstrates a lack of agreement on the meaning of inspiration, and is illustrated by the differences in which ancient sacred authoritative books are cited. For example, Clement of Alexandria cited the *Didache* as Scripture *(Strom.* 1.100.4) and regarded *1 Clement*, the *Epistle of Barnabas*, the *Shepherd of Hermas*, the *Preaching of Peter*, and the *Apocalypse Peter* as inspired.

Inspiration apparently was originally attached to prophetic utterances in the Old Testament (2 Tim. 3.16), but subsequently to the writings of the New Testament. It has been argued that Origen is the likely source for initiating a transition in the church that claimed that God inspired all scriptures of both Testaments. His application of inspiration to all of the books of the Bible was modified in time, and subsequently continued in the Church. Interestingly, throughout its history, the church has not developed a coherent and widely accepted definition of inspiration. Neither has it articulated clearly a distinction between the inspiration of a biblical writing and the inspiration present in the ongoing life of the church and in its acts of preaching.

The continuing prophetic ministry of the Holy Spirit of the first century, which called individuals through the proclamation of the Good News to faith in Christ, was believed by the church of the second and following centuries to be resident in *their* community of faith and in *their* ministry as well. The Christian community then believed that God continued to inspire individuals in their proclamation *just as God did* the writers of the New Testament literature. *The early church believed that the Holy Spirit and inspiration were gifts of God to the whole church and not simply the possession of the writers of sacred literature.* Does this conclusion then pose an affront to the uniqueness, inspiration, and authority of the biblical literature? That would be true if the only unique factor of that literature were its inspiration. Inspiration was never believed to be the distinguishing factor that separated either the apostles from subsequent generations of Christians or the Christian scriptures from all other Christian literature.

Inspiration is of course the divine presupposition for the New Testament writings, but the 27 books were not chosen because they, and only they, were recognized as inspired. The biblical authors were inspired by God, but a biblical writing was not deemed canonical because it was recognized that the author was inspired. Rather the biblical authors were deemed inspired because what they wrote was recognized as sacred and authoritative literature. What was true or not true concerning the message of and about Jesus—the church's canon of faith (*regula fidei*)—appears to have been more of a determining factor of what was authoritative in the life of the early church than a notion of what was and what was not inspired.

Use and adaptability

Whether a book should be regarded as scripture and placed within a fixed collection of sacred scriptures seems to have been determined ultimately by early church use. If use refers to the widespread use and recognition of an authoritative document in the ancient Church, then, of course, one of the earliest testimonies for this criterion is Eusebius. Notice, for example, how he shows acceptance of the Gospel of John and 1 John but has a reluctance to accept 2 and 3 John and Revelation. This is because the Gospel of John, 1 John have been:

> *accepted without controversy by ancients and moderns alike but the other two are disputed,* and as to the Revelation there have been many advocates of either opinion up to the present. This, too, shall be similarly illustrated by *quotations from the ancients* at the proper time. (Eusebius, *Ecclesiastical History* 3.24.18, LCL. Emphasis added)

Further, Eusebius held the "disputed" and "spurious" books (James, Jude, 2 Peter, 2 and 3 John, and possibly Revelation, as well as the *Acts of Paul, Shepherd of Hermas*, the *Apocalypse of Peter, Epistle of*

Barnabas, The Gospel of the Gospel according to the Hebrews, and the *Didache*) as different from those that were "recognized" based on the tradition of recognition in the Church (*Ecclesiastical History* 3.25.1–7). Notice what he says separates these writings:

> But we have nevertheless been obliged to make a list of them, distinguishing between those writings which, according to the tradition of the Church, are true, genuine, and recognized, and those which differ from them in that they are not canonical but disputed, yet nevertheless are known to most of the writers of the Church. (*Ecclesiastical History* 3.25.6, LCL)

Widespread use in the churches appears to be the best explanation of why some writings were recognized and preserved as authoritative in most churches but not in others; some writings met the worship and instructional needs of the churches, but others did not. The writings that did not survive in the majority of churches did not meet the needs of those churches. Although acknowledging a modified form of apostolicity—that is, authorship by the apostles or their disciples—the final criterion for accepting or rejecting a book as part of the church's biblical canon certainly involved how well that book represented the teachings of the churches from the earliest period, and had actually remained in use in the churches since that time.

Although use was undoubtedly one of the important factors in determining canonicity, this alone does not answer all of the questions concerning the selection process. More specifically, it is likely that use in major or *larger* churches—for example, Rome, Antioch of Syria, Ephesus, and Alexandria—was the controlling criterion. In that day as well as in our own, the smaller churches were strongly influenced by the larger ones.

However, some writings of the New Testament, for example, Philemon, 2 Peter, Jude, 2 and 3 John and possibly others—were not cited, referred to, or even used as frequently in the life of the ancient churches as were several nonbiblical sources such as *1 Clement,* the *Shepherd of Hermas,* the *Didache,* and possibly also the *Epistle of Barnabas, Letters of Ignatius,* and the *Martyrdom of Polycarp.*

One may ask, therefore, whether all of the teachings of the current New Testament canon are of equal value for informing Christian faith and its ministry. Some books are not necessarily more important or closer to that "canon of truth" than the several other ancient Christian writings that were not included in the biblical canon.

Another side of use in early Christianity is what may be "catholicity." By it we mean the unwillingness of a church to be out of step with other churches in regard to which documents were recognized as authoritative. Without question, the classic argument for this criterion is Augustine who admonishes the reader of Scripture to

> prefer those [writings] that are received by all Catholic Churches to those which some of them do not receive. Among those, again, which are not received by all, let him prefer those which the more numerous and the weightier churches receive to those which fewer and less authoritative churches hold. But if, however, he finds some held by the more numerous, and some held by the churches of more authority (though this is not very likely to happen), I think that in such a case they ought to be regarded as of equal authority. (*De. doct. chr.* ii. 12. Trans. Metzger, 237)

Although this concern no doubt had an important influence on many of the churches from time to time, especially the influence of the larger churches upon the smaller ones, still the variety in the canonical lists of scriptures of the fourth century and later shows that this criterion of catholicity was far from absolute.

Not only usage, but also other historical circumstances helped determine which books were included in the church's biblical canon. After the reaction to Montanism, prophetic literature was much more suspect and tended to be neglected, especially in the East. *The Apocalypse of Peter*, for instance, was not looked upon as authoritatively *after* the Montanist controversies than before, and even the book of Revelation had a stormy reception, especially through the fourth century and later in many Eastern churches. What the historical circumstances were that led to the canonization of the New Testament literature are still not altogether clear today, but probably all of the above criteria to a certain extent played a role in helping the ancient churches define their canon of scriptures, with the exception of the criterion of inspiration. These criteria were employed regardless of how carefully they were applied by the church leaders who were involved in the canonization process.

Ultimately, it appears that the writings that were believed to convey best and more faithfully the earliest Christian proclamation and that also best met the needs of local churches in the third and fourth centuries were the writings that were selected for inclusion among their sacred scriptures. Conversely, it appears that the literature that was no longer deemed relevant to the churches' needs, even though it may have been considered sacred at an earlier time, was simply eliminated from consideration. If that is the case, this would not be the first time the church focused on literature that was most relevant to its own historical situation. New Testament scholars have long recognized that the *Sitz im Leben* (social and historical circumstances) of the early church played a significant role in the selection, organization, and editing of the materials that form the New Testament Gospels.

The relevance of these and other materials for the life of the emerging churches no doubt also played a major role in either their preservation and canonization or in the forced and gradual disappearance of other contenders because they ceased to be relevant and useful to the majority of churches. This also reflects the continuing adaptability of these writings to the needs of the churches and best answers the question why there were differing lists of New Testament books in the ancient churches. Although leaders of the Church in the fourth century and later pushed for a unity in the recognition of which books were inspired, authoritative, and canonical, such unanimity could hardly have been achieved due to the variety of historical circumstances that the churches faced. Usage in this sense, as well as the sense of widespread use in the larger churches of the third through the fifth centuries, is probably the primary key to understanding the preservation and canonization of the books that make up our current New Testament by the early Church.

Writings that were adaptable to the changing circumstances of the churches were preserved and those that did not lend themselves to that were eventually dropped. Once the books were canonized, however, a series of hermeneutical (interpretive) procedures emerged to continue the adaptability of those ancient writings. Before then, some writings had a temporary or local authority within churches but their recognition as scripture ceased when their message was no longer considered relevant or adaptable.

Again, these criteria are not seen everywhere in antiquity and no ancient text identifies all of them as the criteria for canonicity, but, as we have shown, they do appear variously among many of the ancient church fathers and help account for the selection of many of the books that now comprise the New Testament.

FURTHER READING

Barton, John. *Holy Writings, Sacred Text: The Canon in Early Christianity*. Louisville, KY: Westminster John Knox Press, 1997.

Campenhausen, Hans von. *The Formation of the Christian Bible*. Trans. J. A. Baker. Philadelphia, PA: Fortress, 1972.

Grant, Robert M. "The New Testament Canon," in *The Cambridge History of the Bible: From the Beginnings to Jerome*, ed. P. R. Ackroyd and C. F. Evans. Cambridge: Cambridge University Press, 1970, Vol. 1, pp. 284–308.

Harry Y. Gamble. *Books and Readers in the Early Church: A History of Early Christian Texts*. New Haven, CT/London: Yale University Press, 1995.

Kalin, Everett R. *Argument from Inspiration in the Canonization of the New Testament*. Th.D. Diss., Harvard University, 1967.

Kalin, Everett R. "The Inspired Community: A Glance at Canon History," *CTM* 24 (1971), 541–549.

Koester, Helmut. "Apocryphal and Canonical Gospels," *HTR* 73 (1980), 105–130.

Koester, Helmut. "Gnostic Sayings and Controversy Traditions in John 8:12–59," in *Nag Hammadi, Gnosticism, and Early Christianity*, ed. Charles W. Hedrick and Robert Hodgson, Jr. Peabody, MA: Hendrickson Publishers, 1986, pp. 97–110.

MacMullen, Ramsay. *Christianizing the Roman Empire* [A.D. 100–400]. New Haven, CT: Yale University Press, 1984.

McDonald, Lee M. *The Biblical Canon: Its Origin, Transmission, and Authority*. Peabody, MA: Hendrickson Publishers, 2006.

McDonald, Lee M. *Forgotten Scriptures: The Selection and Rejection of Early Religious Writings*. Louisville, KY: Westminster John Knox Press, 2009.

McDonald, Lee M. "Identifying Scripture and Canon in the Early Church: The Criteria Question," in *The Canon Debate*, ed. Lee M. McDonald and J. A. Sanders. Peabody, MA: Hendrickson Publishers, 2002, pp. 416–439.

McDonald, Lee M. and Stanley E. Porter. *Early Christianity and Its Sacred Literature*. Peabody, MA: Hendrickson Publishers, 2000.

Metzger, Bruce M. *The Canon of the New Testament: Its Origin, Development, and Significance.* Oxford: The Clarendon Press, 1987.

Petersen, William L. *Tatian's Diatessaron: Its Creation, Dissemination, Significance, and History in Scholarship.* Supplements to Vigiliae Christianae, ed. J. Den Boeft, R. Van Den Broek, A. F. J. Klijn, G. Quispel, J. C. M. Van Winden, Vol. 25. Leiden/New York/Köln: E. J. Brill, 1994.

Robbins, G. A. "Fifty Copies of the Sacred Writings," *Studia Patristica* 19 (1989), 91–98.

Rutgers, L. V., P. W. van der Horst, H. W. Havelaar, and L. Teugels, eds. *The Use of Sacred Books in the Ancient World.* Biblical Exegesis and Theology 22. Leuven: Peeters, 1988.

Stendahl, Krister. *Meanings: The Bible as Document and Guide.* Philadelphia, PA: Fortress, 1984.

CHAPTER EIGHT

FINAL COMMENT

In the foregoing discussion, we have seen some of the complexity surrounding the origins and development of the Jewish and Christian biblical canons. Although the picture is obscured here and there due in part to the lack of any known ancient literature that explicitly tells this story, it is nonetheless clear that the literature that the Jews and Christians believed best identified their faith and hopes was the literature that was selected for inclusion in their sacred collection of scriptures and it continues to serve the synagogue and church.

The processes involved in this selection, as we have seen, began with the writing of the literature by those believed to be spirit-endowed messengers who wrote down the words that God spoke to them and who also believed that those words have considerable value for the people of God. As we have shown, the selection process in some instances (e.g., Song of Songs, Esther, Ecclesiastes, but also 2 Peter, Hebrews, 2 and 3 John, Jude and Revelation, and others) took considerably longer than it did with others (the Gospels and some letters of Paul). In some cases, the reason for their selection and inclusion in a closed biblical canon is more obvious than in other cases, but there were also considerable differences on the value of some of the literature that was included and also excluded. Several of the so-called fringe books took centuries longer to be included in sacred collections. Others that were initially included or recognized as sacred inspired literature were eventually excluded in some sacred canons (Sirach, Wisdom of Solomon, Shepherd of Hermas, Didache, Epistle of Barnabas). They had something of a temporary canonicity in some churches or synagogues, but not a lasting one.

There are still questions unanswered, but writings that no longer addressed the needs of most of the churches when decisions were being made on the scope of the Bible were eventually dropped from inclusion in sacred collections. *After* various church councils began making decisions about these matters, some of the excluded literature continued to show up in many biblical manuscripts circulating in the churches for centuries to come! Most of the early church councils that addressed the books that comprise the biblical canons of the church simply reflected the views of the communities that they served. Over time, the literature that had once been accepted by a large number of churches, but no longer reflected their concerns or needs that they had earlier, was either left behind (excluded) or reinterpreted in ways that made those books more relevant to the churches. This more creative interpretive process almost always follows notions of canonization and is the presupposition for it.

When books were reinterpreted for communities of faith, we have evidence of their earlier acceptance with canonical authority attached to them. In some cases, however, books that were earlier well established in the church but no longer seemed to have a relevant message for communities of faith were eventually marginalized in those communities. The phrase most scholars use to describe this marginalization practice is "a canon within a canon." In such cases, the books have not lost their place in sacred collections, but they no longer speak as strongly as they once did. For example, some churches almost never read the Book of Revelation in their worship nor include it in the books they study in their church school classes. Christians often ignore several books in the Bible and while they have not been dropped from the biblical canon, they essentially play no role in the life of the church. Several Old Testament books are like this (Leviticus, Ecclesiastes, Song of Songs, Nahum) and also a number of New Testament books as well (Hebrews, 2 and 3 John, Jude, Revelation). These books often get only scant attention in churches and the "canon within the canon" has effectively eliminated them. It may be that in time they will be rediscovered and play a more important role in communities of faith, but for the time being, they are ignored.

Christian lectionaries today reflect this highly selective use of biblical books in churches and they seldom include readings from all of the books of the Bible for Christian worship. Churches that do not use a lectionary also are quite selective in the books that they make use of in their worship and Bible teaching. One or more Gospels and the Letters of Paul generally get more priority in the churches, but occasionally attention is also given to the Psalms, the Book of Isaiah, and a few others. It is not uncommon in antiquity for churches to ignore large portions of the canonical literature. It may be appropriate that such books are preserved for the churches in their fixed collections of sacred literature since they may one day have a more powerful voice in the community's life when their circumstances change. In antiquity, before the canonization process was complete, some books were marginalized and often dropped from sacred collections.

On the other hand, there is a shortage of commentaries on some books of the Bible and some of them are essentially ignored (only brief introductions to that literature are given in a survey course) in formal theological training in church based schools. Because of time constraints in theological education curricula today, only a few biblical books get careful scrutiny in most theological seminaries and only a few books get special attention in elective courses. On what basis are such decisions made about what to include in ministry preparation? Relevance and adaptability of the biblical literature are not far from the conscious decisions made in such matters. In this sense, some things do not change much in the churches!

As we have shown, it is not always clear why some books that were fairly popular among Jews and Christians were left behind by large segments of those communities, and again, why some that were rather popular both in Judaism and early Christianity were dropped from some biblical collections (1 Enoch, Sirach, Didache and Shepherd of Hermas). Again, the ones that were eventually included in fixed sacred collections were believed to meet the particular needs of religious communities and they could be adapted by various interpretive means to meet the continuing worship, catechetical, and missional needs of Jewish and Christian communities. They obviously were believed to be able to address the current social context at the time they were included and did not meet those needs when decisions were made to exclude some of them.

Along with a fixed collection of books, the fixed or stabilized text of the Bible also seems important to us, but it was not *as* important in the ancient churches. As we have seen earlier, some of the early church fathers were concerned over the considerable variants in the sacred books, for the most part such matters were not addressed as often as one would think. While it seems logical to us today to seek a stabilized and reliable text of the Bible, this was apparently not as important in antiquity. Matters that concern us today were often of little concern in antiquity. This may have been because there are no two ancient biblical manuscripts exactly alike in its text and since most churches did not have multiple copies of their scriptures, they simply relied on the only texts that they had believing them to be reliable transmissions of the biblical text.

Modern comparisons of these manuscripts reveals that the earlier trust in the text of the Scriptures afforded the manuscripts (most if not all were received as sacred scripture) may not have been warranted. Considerable attention today is given to establishing the most reliable Hebrew, Aramaic and Greek texts of the Bible and these are the basis for all translations of biblical literature. Because of the significant variety of variants in the surviving biblical manuscripts, few scholars today hold out hopes of establishing the original text of these sacred books, but they are demonstrably much closer today than they have ever been in the past. While we are undoubtedly closer to the original text of both the Old and New Testament books today because of considerable advances in text critical analysis as well as the discovery of many ancient manuscripts in the nineteenth and twentieth centuries, no one today seriously argues that we have established the original text of the Bible. How significant is that for religious faith today? It is significant that most of the variants, intentional or otherwise, do not adversely or seriously affect the core teachings of the Bible or the core identity as a Christian community.

In some cases the most significant variants are clarified by appealing to the texts that are not in question and have long been well established. In a few instances, scholars are left with doubts about the text, but the essentials of the Christian faith do not rest on such matters. Most biblical scholars agree that we know the basic message of the biblical books and their various translations are generally reliable. As a result we have been able to establish the basic biblical message unusually well. Although some books may have been excluded later because they did not support the emerging orthodox positions of the majority of churches, many excluded books, as we noted above, were just as orthodox as those that were included. There was also considerable theological diversity in early Christianity, even more than there is today as we can see even in the New Testament, but this diversity has not seriously affected the core teachings and beliefs of the church.

Because of the recent scholarly attention given to canonical inquiry, we are now more capable of understanding some of the processes that were involved in the stabilization of the books and text of the Bible. This does not mean that all Christians will now agree on all matters of the Christian faith or even on issues related to canon formation, but we are closer now than was possible before in our understanding of the processes involved. Now that we have a better understanding of these processes, some Christians are asking whether we should reapply some of the ancient criteria employed by the churches in the selection of their sacred literature. That could lead to adding or dropping various books if, for instance, the criterion of authorship were more carefully applied today.

Any new application of the ancient criteria with consequences for the contents of the Bible is not likely to happen. It could be that an ancient text was rightly accepted but for the wrong reason! For instance, the value of the Book of Hebrews, especially in early Jewish Christianity was widely recognized, but it was most likely accepted into the biblical canon because it was attributed to Paul. Few biblical scholars think Paul wrote this book, but no one seems to be willing to take it out of the biblical canon. Discovering *why* some of the literature that was left behind, when we can discern the reasons, considerably enhances our understanding of early Christianity and also early Judaism as well. Some of the literature that was left behind is not heretical and much can be gleaned from it.

Do we need to change the scope of the Bible as a result of our investigations? Probably not, but we also do not need to fear being informed by the same literature that often informed various segments of early Christianity. That can be an enriching experience that will add to our understanding of the context of early Judaism and early Christianity! By examining carefully the various issues related to the origins of the Bible, we will also be able to acquire a greater understanding of the issues that divide the churches today and we can minimize some of the things that have led to earlier divisions. Knowing the context of early Christianity and why some decisions were made about the books of the Bible enables us to understand better the context of early Christianity and the core values and teachings that formed the churches that we know today. Such inquiries will hopefully bring a greater understanding among Christians and Jews and possibly more tolerance for those who disagree with us on these matters.

Since the beliefs, practices, and mission of Jewish and Christian communities of faith are rooted in the books that were included in their biblical canons, the questions that we have raised above and our historical examination of them have considerable importance and consequence today.

More importantly, making this information available to a wider audience than the academic community can initiate valuable dialogue and discussion in churches and synagogues. I continue to be invited not only to address academic conferences, but happily I also regularly receive invitations to address communities of faith that rely on the teaching and authority of the Bible. Not only have many pastors expressed an interest in canon formation, but also the laity in their churches. They often raise many very well thought out questions and appear eager to discuss related issues with me and others who take the time to share this untold story with them. On the other hand, and not infrequently, some clergy are fearful of sharing such matters with their congregations and even more insecure saying to their congregations that they simply do not have all of the answers to such questions.

As I said at the beginning of this volume, I believe, however, that the church is, or should be, capable of discussing all matters that impact our faith and conduct. It is also capable of being informed by many other ancient writings that informed the early Christians, but in time ceased doing so. We all can learn from a careful and rigorous biblical inquiry and that will provide an important opportunity of growth in our understanding. Hopefully, this volume will answer many important questions on the Bible for the nonspecialist in the churches, and also offer evidence to those outside of the church that we who are in it are not fearful of examining our faith and the significant issues that impact it.

The books of the Bible, whether in the Catholic, Orthodox, or Protestant Old Testaments and the shared New Testament that all receive, sufficiently inform us of the core of the ancient activities and beliefs that gave rise to the earliest Jewish and Christian communities. For the most part, the church rooted its biblical canon in the earliest surviving literature that reflects the earliest teachings passed on in the churches. Almost all biblical scholars (Protestant, Orthodox, and Catholic), agree today that there is little in the Old Testament apocryphal and pseudepigraphal literature that could be called "heresy" and consequently most agree that there is much that canbe learned about the context of Judaism and the emergence of early Christianity in this literature. Also, New Testament scholars generally agree that the literature that now comprises the New Testament sufficiently informs Christian faith and clarifies the essential teachings of the church. Is there some ambiguity here and there in our knowledge of the processes that established the current biblical canons? Yes, of course, but none of those ambiguities challenge the most essential areas of Christian faith. That faith is rooted in the activity of God in Jesus of Nazareth and the Bible sufficiently informs us of the identity of Jesus, the identity and essence of Christian faith, and the mission of the church today.

NOTES

1. INTRODUCTION AND PRELIMINARY OBSERVATIONS

1. The terms CE for "Common Era" and BCE for "Before the Common Era" are equivalent to AD and BC, respectively. These designations are frequently used in academic communities and academic publications because many participants in biblical discussions and readers are not Christians. These terms allow for a broader level of interaction between Christians, Jews, and non-Christians over biblical literature and biblical issues.

2. The Mishnah (Hebrew = "what is repeated" or "oral instruction"), a philosophical law code that pious Jews sometimes call the "Oral Torah," claiming that God gave to Moses not only written Laws, but also oral laws that built a fence about the written Law. By the mid-third century CE, similar additional materials were placed alongside the Mishnah called the "Tosefta" (Hebrew = "supplement"). The rabbinic teachers of the third to the sixth centuries used the Mishnah as a foundation text for the later Talmudic law. These interpretations, called *gemara* (Aramaic = "completion"), are known as the Talmud (Hebrew = "learning," pl. = *Talmudim*). There were two major Talmuds, one from Babylon (the *Bavli*) and one from the Land of Israel (*Yerushalmi*). Both follow the order of the Mishnah tractates. The rabbis distinguished the Mishnah, Tosefta, and the two Talmudim from their sacred scriptures, but they viewed these interpretations of the Jewish scriptures similar to their sacred writings. These additional writings present the implications of the Scriptures for religious conduct. The Mishnah reflects the teachings of Jewish teachers of the Law roughly from 10 CE to 200 CE and are known by the term "*Tanna'im*" (Aramaic *tanna'* = "one who studies" or "teaches" or "repeats"). Rabbi Judah the Prince gathered together and codified the 63 tractates that comprise the Mishnah in the early decades of the third century CE.

3. This document, likely written between 109–106 BCE during the reign of John Hyrcanus who was a Hasmonean king of the Jewish people in the land of Palestine, sheds light on the beliefs about Messianic expectations among the Jews at the close of the second century BCE. Christians interpolated the volume and it eventually fell into disuse because it was perceived to be a forgery.

4. Clement of Alexandria (*Miscellanies* 15.5.85) and Origen (*On First Principles* 4.11, 10.28) refer to sacred scriptures as "Old Testament" and "New Testaments."

2. AN OVERVIEW OF THE STORY

1. The "Hebrew Bible" (or HB) is a common designation given to the collection of books that comprise the sacred scriptures of the Jewish people. The HB is sometimes called the *Tanakh*, a composite word that depends on the first letters of each of the three parts of the Hebrew Bible, namely *Torah* (Law), *Nebiim* (Prophets), and *Ketubim* (Writings or *Hagiographa*).

2. Many of the Psalms, especially 19, 119, which focus on the meditation on the word, law, precepts, and statutes of God, are almost certainly pre-exilic in origin, but most of these do not pre-date the "Deuteronomistic history" of the Jews that flourished in Josiah's day (ca. 622–619 BCE) when the book of the Law (probably Deuteronomy) was found and became an important feature in the religious life of the Jews at that time. Before then, there is little focus on a written sacred tradition in the land of Israel. The reference in 2 Kgs 17.13–15 to the law commanded by God and sent among the Jews by the prophets was exceptional in those days and earlier. The Law and prophetic writings were largely neglected (if they were known) and perhaps even despised by some Jews. Apart from the reign of Josiah and until the time of Ezra (ca. 460–450 BCE) the law apparently did not play a significant role in the life of the nation of Israel. Compare 2 Kgs 18.6–12 with 22.3–13 where only Hezekiah and later Josiah seem to have followed the commandments of God. 1 and 2 Kings tell the story of Israel until its destruction by the Babylonians. They were likely written during Josiah's reign (ca. 619 BCE) and a second edition followed probably around 560 BCE after the last event described in the book had taken place (2 Kgs 25.27–30), and the final writing of 2 Kings came perhaps as late as 400 BCE.

3. A *baraita* (Aramaic = "external" [to the Mishnah]), that is, a writing from a "Tanna" (Aramaic = "one who studies or teaches," or "repeats" referring to Jewish teachers from the 1st and 2nd centuries CE) is a Jewish text that was *not* included in the Mishnah. A *baraita* may not have gained widespread approval among the Jews in the second century in the Land of Israel and so it was not included in the Mishnah. The *b.* in front of the *Baba Bathra* is the symbol that indicates that the writing is a part of the Babylonian Talmud (the *Bavli*), one of the two Jewish interpretations of the Mishnah (the other is the *Yerushalmi* with the *y* symbol or siglum). Because *b. Baba Bathra* 14b is a *baraita* it is likely that it was not well known or widely accepted among the Jews in the first or second centuries CE.

4. To the above list, we would add the following: *Apocryphon of James* (preserved in Nag Hammadi Codex I); *Dialogue of the Savior* (preserved

in Nag Hammadi Codex III); *Gospel of the Ebionites* (preserved in quotations by Epiphanius); Oxyrhynchus Papyrus 840; Oxyrhynchus Papyrus 1224; Papyrus Egerton (+ Papyrus Köln 255); Fayyum Fragment (= Papyrus Vindobonensis Greek 2325).

3. THE EMERGENCE OF AN OLD TESTAMENT CANON

1. Mishnah (Hebrew = "what is repeated" or "repetition"). For a definition of terms and information on this collection, see fn 1 in Chapter 1.
2. Talmud (Hebrew, pl., *Talmudim* = "learning."). See fn. 1 in Chapter 1 for a more complete definition and reference to the originators of the Talmudim.
3. *Tanakh* is an acronym of the combined *Torah* [= Law or Pentateuch], *Nebiim* [=Prophets], and *Ketubim* [=Writings] or TaNaKh) that comprises the 24 books of the Hebrew Bible. The origin of the term is somewhat obscure, but it began to be used in reference to the Jewish Scriptures in the medieval times.

4. THE COMPLETION OF THE OLD TESTAMENT CANON

1. "Peace" refers to the Temple of Peace that was dedicated by Vespasian in 75 CE after the capture and destruction of Jerusalem. The Forum of Pallas was also the Forum of Nerva, the Roman emperor, which was begun by Domitian (81–96 CE) and completed by Nerva (96–98 CE).
2. In this case, since Livy published 142 books, Martial writes: "Vast Livy, for whom my library does not have room, is compressed in tiny skins" (*Epigrams* 14.190, LCL).
3. The assumption or myth of the "oral Torah" was that God gave both written and oral laws to Moses at Sinai and the latter were passed on by word of mouth and eventually passed on in written form to the people of Israel.
4. Heb. = "lift up from." According to the Torah, a number of sacred gifts are said to be "lifted" up, that is, separated or set apart for God. At first it referred to any offering made to God and it was lifted up before God in the offering. It came to be used mostly for the offering of the tithes paid to the priests. It is also known as the heave or wave offerings.

5. THE EMERGENCE OF CHRISTIAN SCRIPTURES

1. "Charters" (Greek, *archeiois*) is generally considered to be a reference to the Old Testament scriptures. Some scholars translate it as "archives."
2. Since the Greek text for this passage is missing and it was supplied later in Latin, an argument could be made for a late dating of this reference, though that is generally considered unlikely.

6. THE INFLUENCE OF "HERESY" AND "ORTHODOXY" ON CANON FORMATION

1. The "Demiurge" or "Craftsman" (Greek, *demiourgos*) is Plato's term for the creator of the universe. Later in the second and third centuries CE, the creator god was also referred to by some Gnostics as "Ialdabaoth," a non-spiritual being. Ptolemy, of the Valentinian school of gnosticism in the second century, claimed that the Demiurge was an angel, the parent of all animate things, who was the God of Israel and *ordinary* Christians.
2. For more examples of early Jewish and Christian hostilities toward each other, see Lee M. McDonald, "Anti-Judaism in the Early Church Fathers," in *Anti-Semitism and Early Christianity: Issues of Polemic and Faith*, C. A. Evans and D. A. Hagner, eds. Minneapolis, MA: Fortress Press, 1993, pp. 215–252.

7. FIXING THE NEW TESTAMENT CANON

1. These are the most perplexing words in this passage. They can refer to making three or four copies at a time or to three or four columns per page. It is more likely the latter.
2. Tosefta (Heb. = "supplements" or "additions") is believed by many to be an alternative to the Mishnah that sometimes preserves independent parallels to the Mishnah.

BIBLIOGRAPHY

Ackroyd, P. R. and C. F. Evans, eds. *The Cambridge History of the Bible: From Beginnings to Jerome*. Vol. 1. Cambridge, England/New York: Cambridge University Press, 1970.

Alastair, A. H. B. *Gnostic Truth and Christian Heresy: A Study in the History of Gnosticism*. Peabody, MA: Hendrickson Publishers, 1996.

Allert, Craig D. *Revelation, Truth, Canon and Interpretation: Studies in Justin martyr's Dialogue with Trypho*. Supplements to Vigiliae Christianae. Leiden/Boston, MA/Köln: E. J. Brill, 2002.

Auwer, J.–M. and H. J. De Jonge, eds. *The Biblical Canons*. BETL clxiii. Leuven: Leuven University Press, 2003.

Baaren, Th. P. van "Towards a Definition of Gnosticism," in *Le Origini dello Gnosticismo*. Acts of Messina Colloquium, 1966, ed. U. Bianchi. Leiden: E. J. Brill, 1967, pp. 178–180.

Balla, Peter. "Evidence for an Early Christian Canon (Second and Third Century)," in *The Canon Debate*, ed. Lee McDonald and James A. Sanders. Peabody, MA: Hendrickson Publishers, 2002, pp. 372–385.

Barr, James. *Holy Scripture: Canon, Authority, Criticism*. Philadelphia, PA: The Westminster Press, 1983.

Barrera, Julio Trebolle. *The Jewish Bible and the Christian Bible: An Introduction to the History of the Bible*. Trans. Wilfred G. E. Watson. Leiden, New York and Köln: E. J. Brill; Grand Rapids, MI: Eerdmans, 1998.

Bartholomew, Craig G., Scott Hahn, Robin Parry, Christopher Seitz, and Al Wolters, eds. *Canon and Biblical Interpretation*. Vol. 7 Scripture and Hermeneutics Series. Grand Rapids, MI: Zondervan, 2006.

Barton, John. *Holy Writings, Sacred Text: The Canon in Early Christianity*. Louisville, KY: Westminster John Knox Press, 1997.

Barton, John. *How the Bible Came to Be*. Louisville, KY: Westminster John Knox Press, 1997.

Bauer, Walter. *Orthodoxy and Heresy in Earliest Christianity*. 2nd edn., ed. Robert Kraft and Gerhard Krodel. Philadelphia, PA: Fortress Press, 1971.

Beckwith, Roger. *The Old Testament of the New Testament Church and Its Background in Early Judaism*. Grand Rapids, MI: Eerdmans, 1985.

Blackman, E. C. *Marcion and His Influence*. London: SPCK, 1948.

Bruce, F. F. *The Canon of Scripture*. Downers Grove, IL: InterVarsity Press, 1988.

Campenhausen, Hans von. *The Formation of the Christian Bible.* Trans. J. A. Baker. Philadelphia, PA: Fortress, 1972.

Casey, R. "The Armenian Marcionites and the *Diatessaron*," *JBL* 57 (1938), 185–194.

Chapman, Stephen B. *The Law and the Prophets: A Study in Old Testament Canon Formation.* Forschungen zum Alten Testament 27. Tübingen: Mohr Siebeck, 2000.

Charlesworth, James A. and Craig A. Evans. "Jesus in the Agrapha and Apocryphal Gospels," *Studying the Historical Jesus: Evaluations of the State of Current Research*, ed. Bruce Chilton and C. A. Evans, NTTS 19. Leiden: E. J. Brill, 1994.

Childs, Brevard S. *Biblical Theology of the Old and New Testament: Theological Reflection on the Christian Bible.* Philadelphia, PA: Fortress Press, 1993.

Childs, Brevard S. *Introduction to the Old Testament as Scripture.* Philadelphia, PA: Fortress Press, 1979.

Childs, Brevard S. *The New Testament as Canon: An Introduction.* Philadelphia, PA: Fortress Press, 1984.

Clabeaux, John J. "Marcion," *ABD* (1992), 4:514–516.

Clabeaux, John J. "Marcionite Prologues to Paul," *ABD* (1992), 4:520–521.

Comfort, Philip Wesley, ed. *The Origin of the Bible.* Wheaton, IL: Tyndale House Publishers, 1992.

Cross, Frank Moore. *From Epic to Canon: History and Literature in Ancient Israel.* Baltimore, MD and London: Johns Hopkins University Press, 1998.

Dahl, Nils A. "The Origin of the Earliest Prologues to the Pauline Letters," *Semeia* 12 (1978), 233–277.

Davies, Philip R. "The Jewish Scriptural Canon in Cultural Perspective," in *Canon Debate*, ed. Lee M. McDonald and James A. Sanders. Peabody, MA: Hendrickson Publishers, 2002, pp. 42–44.

Davies, Philip R. *Scribes and Schools: The Canonization of the Hebrew Scriptures.* Library of Ancient Israel. Louisville, KY: Westminster John Knox Press, 1998.

Edrei, Arye and Doran Mendels. "A Split Jewish Diaspora: Its Dramatic Consequences," *JSP* 16 (2007), 2:91–137.

Ehrman, Bart D. *Lost Christianities: The Battles for Scripture and the Faiths we Never Knew.* New York/Oxford: Oxford University Press, 2003.

Ehrman, Bart D. *Lost Scriptures: Books that Did Not Make It into the New Testament.* New York/Oxford: Oxford University Press, 2003.

Ellens, J. H. "The Ancient Library of Alexandria and Early Theological Development," *Occasional Papers of the Institute for Antiquity and Christianity* 27 (1993), 1–51.

Ellis, Earle E. *The Old Testament in Early Christianity: Canon and Interpretation in the Light of Modern Research.* Grand Rapids, MI: Baker Book House, 1991.

Farkasfalvy, Denis M. and William R. Farmer. *The Formation of the New Testament Canon: An Ecumenical Approach.* Theological Inquiries. New York: Paulist Press, 1983.

Filoramo, Giovanni. *A History of Gnosticism.* Trans. Anthony Alcock. Cambridge, MA/Oxford: Blackwell, 1990.

Finkelberg, Margalit and Guy G. Stroumsa, eds. *Homer, the Bible, and Beyond: Literary and Religious Canons in the Ancient World.* Jerusalem Studies in Religion and Culture 2. Leiden/Boston, MA: E. J. Brill, 2003.

Grant, Robert M. *The Formation of the New Testament.* New York: Harper & Row, 1965.

Grant, Robert M., ed. *Gnosticism: A Source Book of Heretical Writings from the Early Christian Period.* New York: Harper & Brothers, 1961.

Grant, Robert M. "The New Testament Canon," in *The Cambridge History of the Bible: From the Beginnings to Jerome,* ed. P. R. Ackroyd and C. F. Evans. Cambridge: Cambridge University Press, 1970, Vol. 1, pp. 284–308.

Gregory, Caspar Rene. *Canon and Text of the New Testament.* New York: Charles Scribner's Sons, 1907. Reprinted in Northville, MI: Biblical Viewpoints Publications, 1997.

Guillory, John. *Cultural Capital: The Problem of Literary Canon Formation.* Chicago, IL: University of Chicago Press, 1995.

Hahneman, Geoffrey M. *The Muratorian Fragment and the Development of the Canon.* Oxford Theological Monographs. Oxford: Clarendon Press, 1992.

Hallberg, Robert von, ed. *Canons.* Chicago, IL: University of Chicago Press, 1985.

Harnack, Adolf von. *The Origin of the New Testament and the Most Important Consequences of the New Creation.* Trans. J. R. Wilkinson. New York: Macmillan, 1925.

Harry Y. Gamble. *Books and Readers in the Early Church: A History of Early Christian Texts.* New Haven, CT/London: Yale University Press, 1995.

Hedrick, C. W. and R. Hodgson, Jr., eds. *Nag Hammadi, Gnosticism, and Early Christianity.* Peabody, MA: Hendrickson Publishers, 1986.

Heine, Ronald E. *The Montanist Oracles and Testimonia.* Patristic Monograph Series 14. Macon, GA: Mercer University Press, 1989.

Heine, Ronald E. "Montanus, Montanism," *ABD* (1992), 4:898–902.

Hofius, Otfried. "Isolated Sayings of Jesus," in *New Testament Apocrypha,* 2nd edn., ed. Wilhelm Schneemelcher. Louisville, KY: Westminster John Knox Press, 1991, Vol. 1, pp. 88–91.

Hultgren, Arland J. and Steven A. Haggmark, eds. *The Earliest Christian Heretics: Readings from Their Opponents.* Minneapolis, MN: Fortress Press, 1996.

Hurtado, Larry W. *The Earliest Christian Artifacts: Manuscripts and Christian Origins.* Grand Rapids, MI/Cambridge: Eerdmans, 2006.

Hurtado, Larry W. "Unknown Sayings of Jesus," in *The Gospel and the Gospels,* ed. Peter Stuhlmacher. Grand Rapids, MI: Eerdmans, 1991, pp. 336–360.

Jeremias, Joachim. *Unbekannte Jesuworte*. Zürich: Zwingli, 1947; 2nd edn. Gütersloh: Bertelsmann, 1951; 3rd edn., 1961; ET: *The Unknown Sayings of Jesus*. London: SPCK, 1957; 2nd edn., 1964.

Jonas, Hans. *The Gnostic Religion: The Message of the Alien God and the Beginnings of Christianity*. 2nd edn, revised. Boston, MA: Beacon Press, 1963.

Jones, Barry Alan. *The Formation of the Book of the Twelve: A Study in Text and Canon*. SBL Dissertation series 149. Atlanta, GA: Scholars Press, 1995.

Kalin, Everett R. *Argument from Inspiration in the Canonization of the New Testament*. Th.D. Diss., Harvard University, 1967.

Kalin, Everett R. "The Inspired Community: A Glance at Canon History," *CTM* 24 (1971), 541–549.

King, Karen. *Revelation of the Unknowable God*. Santa Rosa, CA: Polebridge Press, 1995.

King, Karen. *What is Gnosticism?* London/Cambridge: Belknap Press of Harvard University Press, 2003.

Koester, Helmut. "Apocryphal and Canonical Gospels," *HTR* 73 (1980), 105–130.

Koester, Helmut. "Gnostic Sayings and Controversy Traditions in John 8:12–59," in *Nag Hammadi, Gnosticism, and Early Christianity*, ed. Charles W. Hedrick and Robert Hodgson, Jr. Peabody, MA: Hendrickson Publishers, 1986, pp. 97–110.

Kraemer, David. "The Formation of the Rabbinic Canon: Authority and Boundaries," *JBL* 110 (1991), 4:613–630.

Layton, Bentley. *The Gnostic Scriptures: A New Translation with Annotations and Introductions*. Garden City, NY: Doubleday, 1987.

Leiman, Sid. Z. *The Canon and Masorah of the Hebrew Bible: An Introductory Reader*. New York: Ktav, 1974.

Logan. H. B. and A. J. M. Wedderburn, eds. *The New Testament and Gnosis: Essays in Honour of Robert McL. Wilson*. Edinburgh: T.&T. Clark, 1983.

Lupieri, Edmondo. *The Mandaeans: The Last Gnostics*. Trans. Charles Hindley. Grand Rapids, MI/Cambridge: Eerdmans, 2002.

MacMullen, Ramsay. *Christianizing the Roman Empire* [A.D. 100–400]. New Haven, CT: Yale University Press, 1984.

MacRae, George W. "Why the Church Rejected Gnosticism," in *Jewish and Christian Self-Definition*. The Shaping of Christianity in the Second and Third Centuries, ed. E. P. Sanders. Philadelphia, PA: Fortress Press, 1980, Vol. 1, pp. 126–133.

McDonald, Lee M. "Ancient Biblical Manuscripts and the Biblical Canon," in *The Pseudepigrapha and Christian Origins: Essays from Studiorum Novi Testamentum Societas*. ed. Gerbern S. Oegema and James H. Charlesworth. T&T Clark Jewish and Christian Texts Series. New York and London: T&T Clark, 2008, pp. 255–281.

McDonald, Lee M. "Anti-Judaism in the Early Church Fathers," in *Anti-Semitism and Early Christianity: Issues of Polemic and Faith*, ed. Craig A. Evans and Donald A. Hagner. Minneapolis, MN: Fortress Press, 1993, pp. 215–252.

McDonald, Lee M. "Anti-Marcionite (Gospel) Prologues," *ABD* (1992), 1:262–263.

McDonald, Lee M. *The Biblical Canon: Its Origin, Transmission, and Authority*. Peabody, MA: Hendrickson Publishers, 2007 (3rd printing with corrections, March, 2008).

McDonald, Lee M. *Forgotten Scriptures: The Selection and Rejection of Early Religious Writings*. Louisville, KY: Westminster John Knox Press, 2009.

McDonald, Lee M. "Identifying Scripture and Canon in the Early Church: The Criteria Question," in *The Canon Debate*, ed. Lee M. McDonald and J. A. Sanders. Peabody, MA: Hendrickson Publishers, 2002, pp. 416–439.

McDonald, Lee M. and James A. Sanders, eds. *The Canon Debate*. Peabody, MA: Hendrickson Publishers, 2002.

McDonald, Lee M. and Stanley E. Porter. *Early Christianity and Its Sacred Literature*. Peabody, MA: Hendrickson Publishers, 2000.

Metzger, Bruce M. *The Canon of the New Testament: Its Origin, Development, and Significance*. Oxford: The Clarendon Press, 1987.

Miller, John W. *The Origins of the Bible: Rethinking Canon History*. Theological Inquiries. New York: Paulist Press, 1985.

Morrice, William. *Hidden Sayings of Jesus: Words Attributed to Jesus outside the Four Gospels*. Peabody, MA: Hendrickson Publishers, 1997.

Patzia, Arthur G. *The Making of the New Testament: Origin, Collection, Text, and Canon*. Downers Grove, IL: InterVarsity Press, 1995.

Pearson, Birger A. *Gnosticism, Judaism, and Egyptian Christianity*. Studies in Antiquity & Christianity. Minneapolis, MN: Fortress Press, 1990.

Perkins, Pheme. "Gnosticism and the Christian Bible," in *The Canon Debate*, ed. Lee M. McDonald and J. A. Sanders. Peabody, MA: Hendrickson Publishers, 2002, pp. 355–371.

Perkins, Pheme . *Gnosticism and the New Testament*. Minneapolis, MN: Fortress Press, 1993.

Petersen, William L. *Tatian's Diatessaron: Its Creation, Dissemination, Significance, and History in Scholarship*. Supplements to Vigiliae Christianae, ed. J. Den Boeft, R. Van Den Broek, A. F. J. Klijn, G. Quispel, J. C. M. Van Winden, Vol. 25. Leiden/New York/Köln: E. J. Brill, 1994.

Robbins, G. A. "Fifty Copies of the Sacred Writings," *Studia Patristica* 19 (1989), 91–98.

Robinson, James M. and Helmut Koester. *Trajectories through Early Christianity*. Philadelphia, PA: Fortress Press, 1971.

Rudolph, Kurt. *Gnosis: The Nature and History of Gnosticism*. Trans. and ed. Robert McLachlan Wilson. San Francisco, CA: Harper & Row Publishers, 1987.

Rutgers, L. V., P. W. van der Horst, H. W. Havelaar, and L. Teugels, eds. *The Use of Sacred Books in the Ancient World*. Biblical Exegesis and Theology 22. Leuven: Peeters, 1988.

Sanders, James A. *From Sacred Story to Sacred Text*. Philadelphia, PA: Fortress Press, 1987.

Sanders, James A. "Spinning the Bible," *BR* 14 (June 1998), 22–29, 44–45.

Sanders, James A. *Torah and Canon*. Philadelphia, PA: Fortress Press, 1972.

Sawyer, John F. A. *Sacred Languages and Sacred Texts*. Religion in the First Christian Centuries. London/New York: Routledge, 1999.

Schneemelcher, Wilhelm, ed. *New Testament Apocrypha*. Trans. R. M. Wilson. 2nd edn. 2 vols. Louisville, KY: Westminster John Knox Press, 1991–1992.

Schniedewind, William M. *How the Bible Became a Book*. Cambridge, England and New York: Cambridge University Press, 2004.

Seitz, Christopher R. *The Goodly Fellowship of the Prophets: The Achievement of Association in Canon Formation*. Acadia Studies in Bible and Theology. Series editors: C.A Evans and Lee M. McDonald. Grand Rapids, MI: Baker Academic, 2009.

Sheppard, Gerald T. "Canon," in *The Encyclopedia of Religion*, Mircea Eliade, Editor in Chief. New York: Macmillan Publishing Co., 1987, Vol. 3, pp. 62–69.

Silver, Daniel Jeremy. *The Story of Scripture: From Oral Tradition to the Written Word*. New York: Basic Books, Inc. Publishers, 1990.

Smith, J. Z. "Canons, Catalogues, and Classics," in *Canonization and Decanonization: Papers Presented to the International Conference of the Leiden Institute for the Study of Religion*. SHR 82, ed. A. van der Kooij and K. van der Toorn. Leiden: E. J. Brill, 1998, pp. 300–307.

Souter, Alexander. *The Text and Canon of the New Testament*. Studies in Theology. 2nd edn. Revised by C. S. C. Williams. London: Duckworth, 1913, 1954.

Stendahl, Krister. *Meanings: The Bible as Document and Guide*. Philadelphia, PA: Fortress, 1984.

Stroker, W. D. *Extracanonical Sayings of Jesus*. SBLRBS 18. Atlanta, GA: Scholars Press, 1989.

Sundberg, Albert C. Jr., *The Old Testament of the Early Church*. Cambridge, MA: Harvard University Press, 1964.

Sundberg, Albert C. Jr. "The Septuagint: The Bible of Hellenistic Judaism," in *The Canon Debate*, ed. Lee M. McDonald and James A. Sanders. Peabody, MA: Hendrickson Publishers, 2002, pp. 68–90.

Swete, H. B. *An Introduction to the Old Testament in Greek*. Revised by R. R. Ottley with Appendix by H. St. J. Thackeray. Cambridge: Cambridge University Press, 1914, reprinted by Hendrickson Publishers, 1989.

Tabberne, W. "Early Montanism and Voluntary Martyrdom," *Colloquim* 17 (1985), 33–43.

Theron, Daniel J. *Evidence of Tradition*. Grand Rapids, MI: Baker Book House, 1957, reprinted in 1980.

Ulrich, Eugene. *The Dead Sea Scrolls and the Origins of the Bible*, ed. M. Abegg, P. Flin, SDSSRL. Grand Rapids, MI: Eerdmans, 1999, pp. 51–61, 73–78.

VanderKam, James C. *From Revelation to Canon: Studies in the Hebrew Bible and Second Temple Literature.* JSJSup 62. Leiden/Boston, MA: E. J. Brill, 2000.

Walker, Benjamin. *Gnosticism: Its History and Influence.* Wellingborough: The Aquarian Press, 1989.

Wink, Walter. *Cracking the Gnostic Code: The Powers in Gnosticism.* SBLMS 46. Atlanta, GA: Scholars Press, 1993.

Wise, Michael, Martin Abegg, Jr., and Edward Cook, *The Dead Sea Scrolls: A New Translation.* San Francisco, CA: Harper Collins, 1996.

Wyrick, Jed. *The Ascension of Authorship: Attribution and Canon Formation in Jewish, Hellenistic, and Christian Traditions.* Cambridge, MA and London: Harvard University Press, 2004.

Zahn, Theodore. *Forschungen zur Geschichte des neutestamentlichen Kanons und der alltkirchlichen Literatur.* 10 vols. Leipzig: S Deichert, 1881–1929.

INDEX

Virgil 101
Vita Abercii 223
Von Campenhausen, Hans 122,
    171–2
Vulgate, the 64

War Scroll 78
Wisdom of Jesus Ben Sirach 3, 8,
    31, 59

Wisdom of Solomon 3, 8, 31, 72, 96,
    98, 104–5, 109, 114, 117,
    123, 180, 189, 232

Xerxes 66, 68

yeshivot 90